Myths of the Free Market

MYTHS OF THE FREE MARKET

Kenneth S. Friedman

Algora Publishing
New York

Library of Congress Cataloging-in-Publication Data

Friedman, Kenneth S.
 Myths of the free market / Kenneth Friedman.
   p. cm.
Includes bibliographical references and index.
 ISBN 0-87586-223-3 (softcover) — ISBN 0-87586-224-1 (hardcover)
 1. Free enterprise—Social aspects. I. Title.

  HB95.F738 2003
  330.12'2—dc21

                              2003003573

TABLE OF CONTENTS

To my wife, Janet.
Courage to never give up.
What a role model!

Refutable self-serving lies
Cause misery untold.
Dire poverty destroys the lives
Of millions in your fold!
America! America!
Your dream has gone astray.
It serves the rich and powerful
But casts the rest away!

Acknowledgements

There is a widespread belief that until we attain some pre-ordained age we are completely malleable. After this we cure like cement and change only marginally as we age. While I believe this notion may be true in a broad context, it is no more than a very rough approximation. I have been fortunate to experience formative influences well after I should have cured.

One of the most important of these was the attitude of the MIT graduate department of philosophy, which regarded students as partners in a creative endeavor, rather than passive receptacles for information. Dealing with the obligations of being a partner has contributed enormously to my personal and intellectual development. I now seek to add value to relationships, both in teaching and in the business world, by structuring them as partnerships.

As a student I benefited enormously from studying with Imre Lakatos, Sir Karl Popper, Ilya Prigogine, Abner Shimony, Huston Smith and Laszlo Tisza. It was less the subject matter they taught and more their high standards — both personal and professional — that served as role models. I strive to emulate them in my own life.

Finally, I would like to thank the American Council of Learned Societies for a fellowship in 1973 that enabled me to spend a year at the Université Libre de Bruxelles and study nonlinear thermodynamics with Ilya Prigogine. The seeds planted that year have been slow to germinate. The fruit is finally reflected in parts of this book. I hope it proves to be nourishing.

Kenneth Friedman

PREFACE

BLIND FAITH

The gap between rich and poor is now the widest in US history. This is disturbing, for if history is any guide we have unwittingly placed ourselves in grave danger.

Over the last millennium Europe has witnessed long cycles of widening and narrowing economic disparity. In each cycle, once the gap between the rich and the rest widened beyond a certain point, it presaged decline and disaster for all of society, the rich as well as the poor. Could we be seeing the first tremors of a new cycle, the outliers of the next menacing storm? In recent decades, many US citizens have come under increasing financial pressure. Since the 1970s, our number of working poor has increased sharply. Nearly all of our much-vaunted newly-created wealth has gone to the richest.

Law enforcement has been unable to cope with burgeoning drug use at all levels of society. Television and radio casually air sexually explicit programs that would have been rejected in disgust by previous generations. Sexually transmitted diseases have become pandemic. (The number of people in the U.S. infected with genital herpes now stands at 45 million and is increasing at the rate of 1 million per year.) These developments have fed a widespread perception of irresponsibility and increasing licentiousness.

Children today spend more time than ever in front of television sets or video games. They spend less with books, peers or parents. Where are they learning their values? What are the values they are learning?

The alienation of large groups of people has led to private militias and to an increase in violence that has become pervasive. With 60,000 incidents of workplace violence per year, "going postal" is part of our vocabulary. "Road rage" is another new expression and a measure of increasing violence by "normal" people. Since 1980 our prison population has increased five-fold.

These developments have exacerbated a polarization between a new evangelical Christian revival and those who are distrustful of religious dogmatism but have no solutions to the very real problems the evangelicals are addressing. Could these trends be harbingers of something more ominous, a more violent fracturing of society?

For a country that has prided itself on its resourcefulness, the inability to address such problems suggests something deeper at work. There is something, powerful but insidious, that blinds us to the causes of these problems and undermines our ability to respond. That something is a set of beliefs, comparable to religious beliefs in earlier ages, about the nature of economies and societies. These beliefs imply the impropriety of government intervention either in social contexts (libertarianism) or in economic affairs (*laissez faire*).

The faithful unquestioningly embrace the credo that the doctrine of non-intervention has generated our most venerated institutions: our democracy, the best possible political system; and our free market economy, the best possible economic system. But despite our devotion to the dogmas that libertarianism and free market economics are the foundation of all that we cherish most deeply, they have failed us and are responsible for our present malaise.

The pieties of libertarianism and free markets sound pretty, but they cannot withstand even a cursory inspection. Libertarianism does not support democracy; taken to an extreme, it entails the law of the jungle. If government never interferes, we could all get away with murder. Alternatively, if the libertarian position is not to be taken to an extreme, where should it stop? What is the difference between no government and minimal government? Attempts to justify libertarianism, even a less than extreme position, have failed.

Laissez faire, or free market economics, characterized by minimal or no government intervention, has a history that is long but undistinguished. Just as the negative effects of a high fever do not certify the health benefits of the opposite extreme, hypothermia, the dismal failure of communism, seeking complete government control of the economy, does not certify the economic benefits of the opposite extreme, total economic non-intervention.

It may seem odd, given the parabolic arc of our financial markets and the swelling chorus of paeans to free market economics, but despite the important role of the market, purer free market economies have consistently underperformed well-focused mixed economies. In the latter part of the nineteenth century the mixed economies of Meiji Japan and Bismarck's Germany clearly outperformed the free market economies of Britain and France. Our own economy grew faster when we abandoned the *laissez faire* of the 1920s and early 1930s for the proto-socialist policies of Franklin D. Roosevelt. It has become increasingly sluggish as we have moved back to a purer free market. Data of the past few decades show that our GNP and productivity growth have lagged those of our trading partners, who have mixed economies characterized by moderate government intervention.

The persistently mediocre track record of *laissez faire* casts doubt on the claim that an economy free from government interference invariably maximizes the wealth of society. In fact, there are sound reasons the pure free market must underperform well-focused mixed economies.

But despite *laissez faire*'s mediocre track record and despite powerful arguments that it cannot possibly provide what it promises, the notion of the unqualified benefit of the free market has become deeply embedded in our mythology. Apologists have exulted in claims that glorify free market mythology at the expense of reality, and also at the expense of society. Free market principles, even though they have failed in economics, have been eagerly applied to sectors ranging from politics to education, where they have contributed to societal dysfunction.

One politically popular myth, that free market economics and government non-intervention provide the basis for true democracy, flies in the face of history. The first democrats, the classical Athenians, had a word for the ideal free marketer, the *homo economicus*, working for his own economic gain but unconcerned with the community. It was not particularly complimentary, the ancestor of our word "idiot." Pericles expressed the sentiment underlying this: "We regard the citizen who takes no part in these [public] duties not as unambitious but as useless..."

We have ignored the ramifications of this as we remodeled our pantheon. We have replaced the notion of public-spirited citizens interested in the common weal, a vital part of democratic thought from ancient Athens to our founding fathers, by the invisible hand of the free market. This promises to maximize benefit for society, if only we will be idiots.

In so far as it fails to value disinterested public spirit, free market doctrine only pretends to cherish democracy. Let the people concentrate on their economic gain while their leaders rule in any manner they choose. The Peoples' Republic of China instituted free market reforms to sustain its autocratic political regime. Augusto Pinochet brutally repressed even mild political dissent while pursuing free market economic policies in Chile.

The reality of our own political power structure is that despite the primacy of our financial markets and our contemporary rituals of democracy, powerful corporations, unions and special interest groups fund political campaigns and exact repayment in the form of enormous influence on legislation. Our government is responsive primarily to these organizations, rather than to citizens. This resembles the corporatism of Mussolini's Italy more closely than any historic democracy. We are blind to the connection between corporatism and the lack of public interest in politics and in the common good.

In our enthusiasm for the dogma that any government interference is necessarily bad, we forget it was government action that ended child labor. It was government action that outlawed slavery, despite its profitability. It was government action that ended the Great Depression, after years of failure of non-intervention. It was government action that curbed the most virulent expressions of racism, that provided an education for the great majority, that created a large stable middle class. The free market did not achieve any of these goods, and there is no indication that it ever would have done so.

This is not meant to imply that everything government does is beneficial. But to start from the faith that everything government does is necessarily harmful not only disregards history; it sacrifices the ability, and even the interest, to distinguish between the beneficial and the harmful.

Just as the value of government needs to be assessed independent of dogma, the value of the free market has to be gauged in the real world. Free markets provide incentives for innovation. They enforce pragmatism at the expense of ideology. They fit production to needs and desires of consumers and they lower the price of goods. But free markets can also cause problems. Some of these stem from the pre-eminence of the short term. This endangers long-term prosperity.

Independently, free markets encourage an extreme concentration of wealth that has historically destroyed the fabric of society and led to a lower standard of living for everyone. Government intervention may be our only defense against the natural economic forces that lead to such a concentration of wealth. But the prevailing libertarian/*laissez faire* credo, even though it may be held by intelligent and well-meaning individuals, blinds us to both the danger and the potential for any response that is not generated by the free market itself. Our beliefs, despite the sincerity with which we hold them, lead us astray.

One reason we remain so tightly bound to *laissez faire* is that we lack a better economic theory. Historically, no widely accepted theory, no matter how badly it has failed, has been replaced until a better theory was found. This book suggests an alternative — nonlinear thermodynamics, the most general physical theory that applies to complex open systems. Simply, economies are complex open systems. Nonlinear thermodynamics applies to such systems. Classical physics, the model for classical economics, does not.

Nonlinear thermodynamics, for which Ilya Prigogine won the Nobel Prize in chemistry, explains phenomena in complex open systems of thermodynamics, chemistry and biology. Economies are complex open systems whose mathematical description and behavior resemble the nonlinear description and behavior of thermodynamic, chemical and biological systems. This suggests that economics may be understood from a nonlinear perspective. Such an understanding would support a very different economic paradigm.

The most important difference between *laissez faire* and nonlinear economics is that *laissez faire* assures us of a stable and benign economic equilibrium. Should an economy be temporarily displaced from equilibrium, natural economic forces will restore that wealth-maximizing equilibrium. By contrast, nonlinear economics shows that the equilibrium may be unstable. If a system is displaced sufficiently far from equilibrium, natural forces may take it even further. This process is not necessarily benign. Historically, it has led to disaster.

The instability of local equilibrium is common, and not only in chemistry and biology. In economics differences in wealth, once they reach a certain point, naturally tend to increase. In the struggle for additional wealth, pre-existing wealth has an advantage that is often decisive. The wealthy can outbid the non-wealthy for valuable information, for political influence, for the skills and technologies necessary to acquire additional wealth, dominating the most favorable technologies, products, and markets.

The rich grow richer while the poor grow poorer. This can be a dangerous destabilizing process. Throughout history it has repeatedly led to increasing violence and a decline in security and standards of living for all. Intervention may be necessary to maintain proximity to equilibrium and to prevent natural forces from destabilizing the economy.

This has ramifications for government. *Laissez faire* is prone to systematic malfunction. It has not maximized wealth. In principle it is incapable of maximizing wealth. It increases economic differences to the point that these jeopardize the stability of society and the welfare and security of everyone. There are circumstances in which government intervention may be appropriate, even vital. For this reason the doctrine of absolute non-interference, so glibly dispensed by free marketers, is pernicious. It leaves us vulnerable to the destabilization that can be wreaked by natural economic forces. Nonlinear economics would be an improvement.

In addition to incorporating a more appropriate physical model and supporting a more flexible approach to the role of government, such an alternative would fit the personal and social values that have characterized civilized societies since ancient Athens and Confucius. For there are conditions in which the components of nonlinear systems are mutually interdependent.

A nonlinear model with mutually interdependent components, while it is compatible with free markets, would support a traditional democratic view of citizens concerned with the common good. It would explain interactions among citizens with a focus on community and responsibility. It would counterbalance the centrifugal notions of libertine freedom and mutual independence that foster an each-person-out-for-himself mentality that dominates modern thought. It would provide a more viable foundation for society.

In the spirit of such a foundation, humanism provides a promising platform from which to address societal problems. Although humanism does not pretend to present an alternative to religion, it does address spiritual values and it is compatible with religious teachings while avoiding dogmatism and narrow sectarianism. It stresses the value and dignity of human life and is sensitive to quality of life. It calls attention to our relationship to each other and emphasizes our responsibility to take action not only to improve our own lives, but to enable others to do the same. It takes seriously our role as stewards of the environment.

While humanism is compatible with most religions, it is not compatible with *laissez faire.* This is because *laissez faire* implies that commitment to others, to society and to the environment is unnecessary, even pointless. So long as each person works to maximize his own immediate economic advantage, free market forces will insure the greatest benefit for society. Integrity, discipline, far-sighted action to achieve meaningful long-term goals add nothing. No wonder the popularity of *laissez faire* has corroded our traditional values.

While the consequences of this corrosion are long term, that does not make them less noxious. If we fail to stem the corrosion we face an unpleasant period of economic stagnation, social decay, and increasing violence.

To those who would regard this book as alarmist, I would respond that it is irresponsible to shout: "Stay the course!" when you see breakers on the coral reefs dead ahead. Our country has shown great resourcefulness in times of crisis. The surest way to cause grievous damage is to anaesthetize the public so that it does not notice a developing crisis until it is too late. Yet we are now blithely meandering down a path fraught with peril, heedless of the warning signs.

Evolutionary pressures have selected for a propensity to react to sudden changes in our environment. But we ignore gradual changes, including those produced by flaws in our political and economic institutions. Because of the time lag before effects become manifest, we misinterpret weaknesses as strengths. We are like a man who walks with a cane — where every day a prankster shaves one millimeter off the bottom of his cane — and so we are convinced we are growing taller. We are not growing taller, and the sooner we confront reality the less painful will be the consequences.

While this book focuses on the U.S., we have become subjects of worldwide emulation. The implications of this book do not stop at our borders, but extend to a large and growing portion of the world.

Because we are comfortable materially, it is easy to avoid examining our fundamental beliefs. This is perilous. As Goethe claimed (*Wilhelm Meister*): "We fear nothing more than reason; we ought to fear stupidity if we understood what is really frightful; but reason is too uncomfortable, it must be brushed aside; whereas stupidity is merely fatal, and that can be tolerated."

A similar sentiment is echoed by W. H. Auden:

Those who will not reason
Perish in the act;
Those who will not act
Perish for that reason.

ECONOMY

THE POVERTY OF LAISSEZ FAIRE — THE EVIDENCE

LAISSEZ FAIRE HAS NOT WORKED

"The Emperor's New Clothes" is a marvelous story. Of course, no one takes it seriously. It may be one thing, perhaps the downside of inbreeding, for a stark naked emperor to be convinced he is wearing a magnificent suit of clothes. It is quite another for the populace to go along with the fantasy. We know that people are not that gullible.

In fact, people are gullible, more than we realize. It is difficult to question widely held beliefs, particularly in uncontroversial matters where we are often blind to obvious flaws. As Nietzsche cynically observed, "Men believe in the truth of anything so long as they see that others strongly believe it is true."

For decades the most uncontroversial of disciplines, physics, accepted the Rutherford solar system model as the correct model of the atom. This envisages a central sun-like nucleus, composed of positively charged protons and electrically neutral neutrons, orbited by negatively charged planetary electrons.

Even high school physics students should be aware of the problems. For one thing, like charges repel. This electric repulsion is far more powerful than gravitational attraction. So why don't the protons fly apart? How can the nucleus be stable? Independently, a positively charged nucleus generates a radial electric field. As the negatively charged electrons orbit the nucleus and intersect this field they should continuously emit electromagnetic radiation and their orbits should gradually decay into the nucleus. How can any atom be stable?

These questions were eventually answered by a new theory, quantum mechanics. But until the advent of quantum theory the inconsistencies were hardly noticed, even by physicists.

The failure to see past widely accepted beliefs is not just a modern phenomenon. Nearly a millennium ago the great supernova of 1054 went unrecorded in Europe, though Chinese observers claimed it was brighter than Venus for weeks. The Western belief that the heavens are perfect and unchangeable blinded us to visible reality.

We have a parallel in economics. *Laissez faire* is the object of a faith that is widely accepted and uncontroversial. According to this faith a pure free market system, unencumbered by government interference, must provide the best economy. But despite our unquestioning belief and despite the appearance of prosperity so confidently exuded by soaring financial markets, there is a wide range of data (that we ignore) that calls this faith into question. It is remarkable that even economists are blind to this.

Of course, no country has a pure free market economy. Everyone knows that in all developed countries governments tax their citizens and spend 20% of GNP or more on items ranging from social programs to highways, from libraries and schools to courts and prisons, from parks to national defense. Such taxation and spending necessarily distort the pure free market.

While this observation may be valid as far as it goes, and while it may be boringly trivial to even casual students of economics, it understates how far removed we are from pure *laissez faire* and just how strange a truly pure free market economy would be.

Every country has laws that limit child labor, that protect patent rights, that prohibit profitable industries such as counterfeiting, enslavement, kidnapping, selling unethical drugs. Because such laws open the door to government interference with individuals or institutions seeking to maximize profits, they necessarily conflict with a pure free market. True believers in *laissez faire* must find them abhorrent.

Such a view — that laws against anything from slavery to drug trafficking are bad because they necessarily diminish the wealth of society — seems bizarre indeed. (Though Ludwig von Mises, a true believer consistent in his defense of pure *laissez faire*, argued against government interference with drug trafficking.)

Still, free market apologists might contend that except for such extremes, the closer we come to pure *laissez faire*, the better. But there is little evidence for even this fallback position. The U.S. has come closer to *laissez faire* than most other countries, especially since the Reagan Administration. If free market policies are the best economic policies then we should have experienced the most robust growth in the world during this period. But this has not happened. We have been outstripped by our trading partners.

Table 1: Average Annual Growth in Real GNP per Capita

Country	1980-1994	1985-1994
South Korea*	7.72%	8.17%
Thailand*	5.81%	7.74%
Taiwan*	6.20%	7.07%
Peoples' *	6.46%	5.83%
Indonesia*	3.26%	4.40%
Ireland	3.08%	4.11%
India*	3.07%	3.00%
Japan	2.88%	2.78%
Spain	1.98%	2.65%
Italy	1.62%	1.89%
Belgium	1.48%	1.88%
Austria	1.58%	1.74%
Netherlands	1.29%	1.73%
United Kingdom	1.79%	1.72%
Germany	1.56%	1.70%
Denmark	1.99%	1.61%
Norway	2.09%	1.58%
Australia	1.54%	1.47%
United States	**1.52%**	**1.32%**
Switzerland	0.84%	0.80%
France	1.31%	0.12%
Sweden	0.81%	0.06%
Canada	0.86%	-0.73%
U.S.S.R.*	-2.64%	-5.05%

(* through 1992)
(Monitoring the World Economy 1820-1992, p. 195 f. by Angus Maddison, Development Centre of the Organization for Economic Cooperation and Development.)

Countries in South and East Asia, including the Peoples' Republic of China (PRC), have achieved the fastest growth. These are not free market economies.

They are mixed economies characterized by massive and focused government intervention. They discourage private consumption and encourage savings. They single out strategic industries for protection and investment. (Government-linked corporations generate more than half of Singapore's GNP.)

Although the PRC has recently moved in the direction of a free market economy, in part to sustain its totalitarian political system, its dramatic economic growth began in 1949, well before free market elements were tolerated. Despite retaining a far greater measure of central economic planning and control than the U.S., the Chinese rate of growth has continued to outpace ours.

It is true that the developing economies of South and East Asia have benefited from strong regional growth from a low base, in contrast to the more mature economy of the U.S. But it is difficult to make this argument about Japan or Europe. Yet these mature economies have matched or exceeded our growth, despite their tolerance of higher tax rates and greater government interference in economic affairs.

Contrast our track record to that of the longest-lived socialist democracy. From 1946 to 1969, when Sweden was governed by the Social Democrats under Tage Erlander, its real GNP growth averaged nearly 3.8% (better than ours), without a down year. "Sweden's prosperity was as high as its taxation and its standards of state-sponsored health, education, and social security." (Davies, *Europe: A History*, p. 941.)

Even our own internal comparisons fail to flatter *laissez faire*. Over the past half-century we have seen lower tax rates and less government interference. We have come a long way toward free enterprise from the proto-socialist policies of Franklin D. Roosevelt. Since the Kennedy Administration we have reduced the marginal tax rate on our highest incomes from the 91% that remained in effect from the 1940s into the mid-1960s (and a brief peak of 94% during World War II) to 28% in the 1986 tax code. Yet our economic growth has slowed.

Decade	Average Real GNP Growth	GNP per Capita
1960-1969	4.18%	2.79%
1970-1979	3.18%	2.09%
1980-1989	2.75%	1.81%
1990-1994	1.95%	0.79%

(Maddison, *Monitoring the World Economy 1820-1992* p. .183, 197)

Despite our adoption of the most enlightened free market policies, our performance resembles that of a declining Great Britain in the late nineteenth century. "Britain soon lost what early lead it possessed. Industrial production, which had grown at an annual rate of 4 percent in the period 1820 to 1840 and about 3 percent between 1840 and 1870 became more sluggish; between 1875 and 1890 it grew at just over 1.5 percent annually, far less than that of the country's chief rivals... finally, British industry found itself weakened by an ever rising tide of imported foreign manufactures into the unprotected home market — the clearest sign that the country was becoming uncompetitive." (Kennedy, *The Rise and Fall of the Great Powers*, p. 228.)

Although our government policies have been increasingly *laissez faire* and increasingly friendly to corporate America, our investment, productivity and economic growth have all lagged. Similarly, as the world has moved toward purer capitalism, worldwide economic growth has slowed. From 5.5% in the 1960s, world GNP growth declined to 3.4% in the 1970s, 3.2% in the 1980s, and further in the 1990s. (Maddison, *Monitoring the World's Economy 1820-1992*, p. 227.) It is likely to decline still further in this first decade of the new millennium.

How can we look at this evidence and still maintain that *laissez faire* is the best possible economic system? Clearly it is not. Nor has it been. The "European economic miracle" of the late nineteenth century was achieved by Germany under The Iron Chancellor, Otto von Bismarck. Unlike the *laissez faire* policies pursued by England and France during that period, Bismarck's Germany adopted interventionist economic policies, guiding the development of vital industries such as steel and coal and nationalizing the railroads. Germany also provided insurance and social security for workers and free compulsory education for youth.

Whatever you might think of Bismarck's authoritarianism (whose effects were less pervasive than many suppose; while he was chancellor Germany became the first European country to institute universal male suffrage, and its universities, suffused with a measure of internal academic freedom, gained a place among the greatest in the world), the fact remains that German economic progress eclipsed that of France and England, its two major rivals. From being the weakest of the three countries, economically, technologically and militarily, it surpassed France and challenged the industrial and military might of England. Similarly, the dramatic spurt in Japanese economic growth associated with the Meiji Restoration was achieved under government regulation.

15

Contrast these economic performances to that of present-day Mexico, which has faithfully followed the guidance of the most sophisticated proponents of *laissez faire*. Mexico has vigorously pursued free market policies from privatizing state-owned industries to eliminating tariffs in the name of free trade. But it has not been a leader in economic vitality, stability of currency, or improvement in standards of living.

Mexico's privatization of state industries created new billionaires but real wages declined, the average family losing 30% of its purchasing power. The $21 billion brought into state coffers by privatization failed to prevent a currency collapse that led to the country's inability to pay interest on its debt. The forced devaluation of the peso contributed to the impoverishment of the middle class and the overthrow of a political party that had ruled for nearly a century. (Argentina, which also faithfully adhered to the commandments of orthodox free enterprise, even pegging its currency to the U.S. dollar, has experienced a similar economic and financial collapse.)

Similarly, despite aid and investment from other industrialized countries, the rapid Russian transition from communism to free market capitalism was a disaster. It more deeply impoverished the majority of its people. It reduced most of the country outside the major cities to a meager subsistence exacerbated by the collapse of communications, health care and law enforcement. This led to a decline in life expectancy. It strengthened a powerful underworld that has little allegiance to the country itself or to the quality of life of its citizens.

These examples provide a reality check that raises critical questions for *laissez faire*. If *laissez faire* is the best of all economic policies, why has it performed so poorly?

Why is our economic growth slower than that of mixed economies?

Why has our economic growth declined as we increasingly pursued purer free market policies?

Why did real per capita weekly earnings in the private non-agricultural sector fall 13% since the early 1970s, with much of our middle class able to stay afloat only as a result of a large increase in the number of two-income families? (By contrast, real wages in the mixed economies of Europe have doubled since the early 1970s.)

Why, despite an increase in the number of two-income families and also in the average workweek, has our standard of living increased more slowly than those of our major trading partners with more mixed economies?

Why have we been surpassed in real GNP per capita by a number of European countries plus Japan and Singapore (all mixed economies)?

EARLY SYMPTOMS OF ECONOMIC DECLINE

The standard explanation for our poor economic performance is that our productivity has grown too slowly. GNP per capita is determined by average productivity, the average value of goods and services produced by each person. In the long term meager productivity growth will be matched by disappointing GNP growth. Unfortunately, our productivity growth has been mediocre, despite, and perhaps because of, our adoption of purer free market policies. From an average of 3% from the end of the Civil War through the Kennedy Administration, our productivity growth is now struggling at just over 1%.

Country	Average Annual Productivity Growth: 1973-1992
Taiwan	5.3%
South Korea	5.2%
Thailand	5.1%
Peoples' Republic of China	4.1%
Ireland	4.1%
Spain	3.3%
Norway	3.2%
Indonesia	3.1%
Japan	3.1%
Belgium	2.9%
India	2.8%
France	2.7%
Germany	2.7%
Austria	2.5%
Italy	2.4%
Netherlands	2.2%
U.K.	2.2%
Switzerland	1.7%
Denmark	1.7%
Australia	1.5%
Canada	1.5%
Sweden	1.3%
United States	1.1%
USSR	-0.8%

(Ibid., p. 79, 249)

There are economists who insist that our productivity growth is better than the official numbers. But careful research has not borne out such hopeful claims. Professor Robert Gordon, a consultant for the Federal Reserve, recently completed a comprehensive study on productivity. His results show that over the past five years there has been no productivity improvement in the manufacture of non-durable goods. For durable goods (except computers), there has actually been a decline in productivity. Our entire increase in manufacturing productivity has come from the computer-manufacturing sector, which accounts for just over 1% of GNP.

But if we have adopted the most enlightened economic policies and if productivity is so important, why is our productivity growth so low? Economists have told us productivity growth depends on net business and infrastructure investment, which in turn depends on savings. So our GNP growth has been lagging because our productivity growth has been lagging. And our productivity growth has been lagging because our investment has been lagging. And our investment has been lagging because our savings rate has been lagging.

This still fails to explain our mediocre productivity growth; it just redirects the question upstream. If savings and investment are so important, why are our savings and investment rates so low? In particular, what have we done to increase our savings, investment and productivity?

Since 1980 we have tried two different approaches. The former approach, adopted by the Reagan Administration, was a return to the strict orthodoxy of laissez faire. Reagan's team lamented that we had been deceived by the liberals to worship the idol of big government. It claimed we were suffering the consequences of our idolatry in lower savings and productivity and in slower economic growth. If we wished to reap the full-flowing benefits of our economic system, we would have to return to a pure faith in the free market.

One of the tenets of this faith is that it is the wealthy who generate savings. Our lower and middle classes must spend all their income on the necessities of life and have little left over to save. Only the wealthy have the capacity to save and invest. But our oversized government has placed undue burdens on the wealthy. Government has redistributed wealth, taking from the rich and giving to the poor, who cannot save. It has also taken from the rich and given to government bureaucrats to spend on their pet projects, unencumbered by the market.

The Reagan program was designed to remedy these evils. If we were to take after-tax dollars from those who need them and so are likely to spend them, and give them to those who do not need them and so are likely to save them, we would redirect consumption into increased savings, a higher level of investment, greater productivity, and a better economy for all.

In addition, if we were to take money from government bureaucrats and return it to the wealthy, they would save it and invest it in accord with free market principles. These investments would now be regulated by the invisible hand of market prices and no longer by the perceptions of bureaucrats. Because the invisible hand automatically maximizes total wealth, at least in theory, this transfer of capital must have a positive effect on the economy as a whole. Giving more money to the wealthy would trickle down to everyone's benefit.

In keeping with this picture painted by his economic advisors, the Reagan tax cuts were geared entirely toward the rich. According to the Congressional Budget Office, Reagan's tax policies reduced the total federal tax rate (including Social Security) for the top 1% while increasing it for the bottom 90%. A 1992 study by H & R Block showed that from 1977 to 1990 the total federal tax bill for a person earning $50,000 a year increased 8%, while the tax bill for someone earning $200,000 a year decreased 28%.

Many of those supporting the Reagan tax cuts pointed to the Kennedy tax cut that reduced the top marginal rate from 91% to 70%. They claimed that this was responsible for the halcyon economy of the 1960s. Wrong! Kennedy was unable to get his proposals through Congress. The passage of his program had to wait for Lyndon Johnson, and the tax reductions did not take effect until 1964 and 1965. So what happened?

These tax cuts did mark a major watershed. But — contrary to the claims of apologists for laissez faire — it was a negative one. Real GNP growth declined from over 5% in the first half of the 1960s to 3.3% in the second half of the 1960s and 2.6% in the first half of the 1970s. The decades after these tax cuts have been marked by slower growth, higher inflation, higher unemployment, higher interest rates, and greater debt than the previous decades. After the tax cuts our productivity growth, the most important determinant of long-term economic growth, began to plummet. Long-term productivity growth declined 60% from its levels prior to the Kennedy tax cut. (The other major pre-Reagan tax cut, which reduced capital gains taxes by 30% in 1978, also marked a steep economic decline.)

Despite this history, Reagan's economic advisors, blandly confident, assured us the Reagan tax cut would stimulate the economy and bolster savings. They also assured us — at least until tax receipts plummeted — that the economic growth produced by this tax rate cut would increase federal tax receipts.

Contrary to these assurances, the Reagan tax cuts did not increase economic growth, savings, investment or tax receipts. In light of the failure of the Kennedy-Johnson tax cut, it should not be surprising that the effect of the Reagan tax cuts was just the opposite of what his economic advisors had forecast. Our savings rate, guaranteed to rise, did not even hold steady.

While our net savings had only rarely and briefly dropped below 6% of GNP from 1950 to 1980, it has been declining steadily since the early 1980s, decisively penetrating the 6% level. It has gone negative for the first time in 70 years. Even corporate investment, consistently our most positive investment sector, has failed to improve. Despite heavy borrowing and large reductions in corporate tax rates in the 1980s, corporate investment is little changed from its levels of 50 years ago when the highest corporate income tax rate exceeded 50%.

In short, the bill of goods we were sold is worthless. The Reagan Administration proclaimed that if our tax policies were tilted to favor the rich then savings and investment would rise and everyone would prosper. But contrary to the glowing promises of progress and prosperity for all, our economic growth slowed, our savings rate declined, our debt rose sharply, and all but the richest lagged.

Had we considered the effect of the Kennedy-Johnson tax cut, we might have hesitated to swallow whole hog the laissez faire revivalist message of Reagan's economic advisors. Had we looked at Western Europe, where the ratio of tax revenues to GNP is 30% higher than ours, but where savings exceed ours and productivity and standards of living are rising faster, we might have reconsidered. Had we even examined our own historical correlation between reducing marginal tax rates on the highest incomes and slower economic growth, we might have had second thoughts about sharply cutting the top marginal tax rates.

Why did we not look at the historical evidence and decide — at the very least — on a more gradual approach? Why did the attraction of free market ideology overwhelm the lessons of history? For an administration that described itself as conservative, this is astonishing, for central (if not defining) themes of conservative thought have been the precedence of history over ideology and a worry about what could go wrong with radically new policies.

From a truly conservative perspective, considering the previous failure of similar policies, the failure of Reagan's policies was no surprise. Surprising or not, that failure left us with declining savings, stagnant investment, mediocre productivity improvement, and slowing economic growth.

Our more recent attempt to deal with low productivity growth stems from the Clinton Administration of the 1990s. It reflected a different philosophy: if you can't hit the target, move the target. In the spirit of this philosophy, we introduced a new variable to the measurement of productivity and economic growth. This is the hedonic deflator, which is applied to the computer industry and adjusts the price of an item for improvements in quality.

No other major economy uses the hedonic deflator, which has been challenged as inappropriate by European economists. Our use of this measure for the past several years renders meaningless comparisons of our economic growth, productivity growth and inflation with those of other countries or our own past.

Yet the hedonic deflator is a superficially plausible measure. If the quality of an item improves, then a commensurate price increase provides the same value. What appears to be inflation — a higher price — really is not. Why, then, do other countries reject this measure?

They can make a powerful case. Suppose the hedonic deflator had been introduced in 1980. Since then, three years after the Apple II was marketed as the first personal computer, the amount of memory in personal computers has increased several million-fold. The power of microprocessors has grown ten thousand-fold. Software that comes with the computer makes it far more user friendly. Modems and the Internet dramatically widen the range of tasks computers can perform.

Today's computer is at least 500 times more valuable than the 1980 computer. The 1980 computer sold for $2,000. So our modern computer has a real value of $1 million ($2,000*500). Presently, 15 million computers are sold annually. The real value of those computers is $15 trillion ($1 million * 15 million).

Thanks to this contribution, our annual real GNP growth since 1980 would approach 10% even if the rest of the economy had not grown at all. How remarkable, when no developed country has ever managed to sustain real GNP growth of more than 5% per year and when our Federal Reserve warns that prolonged growth above 3% would stimulate inflation.

Even better, we have had 20 years of deflation. Our real GNP, including $15 trillion just from computer sales, exceeds $15 trillion. Our nominal GNP is only $10 trillion. If real GNP grows faster than nominal GNP, that must be because of deflation.

Note how misleading a picture this is of our, or any, economy. That is why other countries reasonably reject such a measure. We adopted it primarily because it makes us look better without having to take action to improve our savings rate, investment or productivity. While this may make us feel better in the short term, sub-par productivity growth in the long term has always been debilitating.

Productivity growth, investment and savings are not merely academic issues. While our economy did grow in the 1980s and 1990s, much of this growth — meager as it was — was financed by trillions of dollars obtained from borrowing and from the sale of assets. By recycling capital from our trade deficits, foreign interests have come to own an enormous amount of not only our debt (a record 44% of liquid Treasuries plus 20% of corporate debt), but also our corporate assets (10% of our total corporate stock) and our commercial real estate (one half of the commercial real estate in downtown Los Angeles, one-third in Houston and Minneapolis).

Because our trade deficits have been financed by the purchase of our bonds, real estate and capital stock, they have had little adverse short-term impact. It is the long term that is worrisome. Throughout history, and not only in the West, persistent trade deficits have been destructive. "Even when the situation was not so dramatic, if deficit became a permanent feature it spelled structural deterioration of the economy sooner or later. And this is precisely what happened in India after 1760 and in China after about 1820-1840." (Braudel, *The Wheels of Commerce*, p. 219.)

Our policies derived from our free market theology, though painless in the short run, have compromised our long-term health. As Warren Buffet put it: "We are much like a wealthy family that annually sells acreage so that it can sustain a lifestyle unwarranted by its current output. Until the plantation is gone, it's all pleasure and no pain. In the end, however, the family will have traded the life of an owner for the life of a tenant farmer." (*Fortune*, May 1988) In the same spirit, "In *Trading Places*, former Commerce Department official Clyde

Prestowitz referred to the U.S. as 'a colony in the making.'" (Philip Mattera, *Prosperity Lost*, p. 170.)

The irony is the extent to which we have positioned ourselves to be the principal agent in our downfall. In the immortal paraphrase of John Paul Jones by Walt Kelly (*Pogo*): "We have met the enemy and he is us."

LAISSEZ FAIRE — IT CAN'T POSSIBLY WORK

LAISSEZ FAIRE CANNOT MAXIMIZE WEALTH

GNP and productivity data show *laissez faire* has not maximized wealth. It is worse. *Laissez faire* cannot maximize wealth. *Laissez faire must* fail. For there are institutions that add economic value. But *laissez faire* is incompatible with these institutions. Just as classical economists are blind to the historical underperformance of *laissez faire*, they are oblivious to the demonstrable inadequacy of pure free market economics.

Consider patent protection, which functions to support successful research and development (R&D). It assures those who develop new products of an interval in which they will be free from competition and will be entitled to exact monopolistic prices. Government will intervene to prevent others from copying those products. Such an institution violates the conditions of a free market. It creates an artificial monopoly and raises the prices of those goods. Abolishing patent protection would be an economic positive in the near term, resulting in lower prices and greater consumption.

But the near-term positive of abolishing patent protection would be outweighed by a longer-term negative. Without patent protection there would be little incentive to develop new products. Others would copy those products and compete in the market, driving down prices and margins to the point that R&D could not be justified. In such an environment, no one would fund R&D and the flow of new products would soon dry up. We would be poorer in the long term. Paradoxically, despite each instance of patent protection being an economic negative, patent law itself is a positive, increasing the long-term wealth of society.

This paradox in economics parallels one in a theory of ethics, utilitarianism, that came into vogue in England at the time of Adam Smith. Utilitarianism claims that the morality of an act should be judged solely in terms of the utility of its consequences, where utility is defined as pleasure minus pain. In judging an act, one would total the pleasure it creates for each person and subtract from that total the pain it creates for each person. The act that maximizes total pleasure minus total pain is the morally appropriate act.

Utilitarianism and *laissez faire* both claim to maximize value: utility, or moral value, for the utilitarian; wealth for the free market economist. And both theories face similar questions about their notions of value. For the moral philosopher, are certain kinds of pleasure more valuable than others? For the economist, does money exhaust the notion of value?

More important to economics is a distinction within utilitarianism, between act utilitarianism and rule utilitarianism. This distinction is necessary because of a paradox, parallel to that of the value of patent protection, within act utilitarianism. Just as the repeal of patent protection would add to immediate economic value but subtract from long-term economic value, act utilitarianism maximizes the utility of every single act but cannot maximize total utility.

Suppose that by lying to your grandmother, who is about to die and so will never learn the truth, you can avoid being embarrassed. Then it is your moral duty to lie to her. For lying to her would have a positive impact on your pleasure-pain balance and no impact on that of your grandmother. Lying to her would increase total utility.

Were such a morality taken seriously, the institution of truthfulness could not develop. Whether a moral person were telling the truth or lying would depend solely on his calculation of the utilities created by the truth and by various lies.

This is an example of a self-defeating element in act utilitarianism. Honesty creates utility. But if we did not determine to tell the truth — independent of the utilities involved — there would be no moral institution of honesty. Because honesty creates utility and because it is incompatible with act utilitarianism, act utilitarianism cannot maximize utility.

This self-defeating element is avoided by a related theory, rule utilitarianism. Utility can be created by moral rules — "Be truthful." Instead of judging the moral value of each act by its own utility, we could estimate the utility created by various moral rules and retain those rules that maximize utility. We would then judge individual actions by whether they conform to the appropriate rules. This characterizes rule utilitarianism, which analyzes the value of rules as opposed to the acts themselves.

We often act on what we believe to be the best set of rules. Legal rules of evidence are occasionally responsible for the wrong verdict, finding a guilty person innocent because the court must suppress evidence. Yet we abide by these rules and do not override them, for the systematic protection of our rights is more important than any tendency of rules of evidence to cause an occasional miscarriage of justice. Similarly, we do not cheat, even when nobody is looking and the cheating would not harm anyone. We act as rule utilitarians rather than act utilitarians. From a utilitarian perspective, we do this because utility is maximized by rule utilitarianism, not by act utilitarianism.

The considerations that apply to moral theory apply equally to economics. Just as we benefit from moral rules that maximize total utility even if they diminish utility in particular cases, we benefit from institutions that maximize total wealth even if they diminish wealth in particular cases. This suggests a rule *laissez faire* that would parallel rule utilitarianism. We would adopt those economic and legal institutions that maximize wealth.

Just as act utilitarianism is self-defeating because it is incompatible with moral rules that maximize utility, act *laissez faire* is self-defeating because it is incompatible with institutions that maximize wealth. Just as rule utilitarianism remedies critical deficiencies in act utilitarianism, rule *laissez faire* would remedy critical deficiencies in act *laissez faire*.

In short, the rationale for act *laissez faire* — that it maximizes wealth — is invalid. Rule *laissez faire* (including patent protection) would generate more wealth than could act *laissez faire*. A *laissez-faire* economist truly committed to the maximization of wealth would be forced to adopt rule *laissez faire*, rather than act *laissez faire*. He would have to consider the propensity of various economic institutions to generate wealth.

But the substitution of rule *laissez faire* for act *laissez faire* — necessary for the maximization of wealth — is impossible; for "rule *laissez faire*" is an oxymoron. The enforcement of any rule is incompatible with *laissez faire*.

According to act *laissez faire*, each person naturally acts in his own best short-term economic interest. Because this is natural it does not require government enforcement. By contrast, in rule *laissez faire* each person must abide by certain rules whether or not they are in his best interest. A person must not violate copyright laws and reprint published material without paying a royalty, even if the royalty increases his cost of material or deprives him of the opportunity to sell such material profitably. Abiding by such rules is less appealing, as we know from the thriving industry of pirating intellectual material; so government would have to insure adherence to the rules. It would no longer be *laissez faire*.

Laws protecting patent and intellectual property rights are not unique. Laws against the production and sale of unethical drugs have the same effect. Without such laws entrepreneurs could establish a thriving new industry, one that would add substantially to GNP and create new wealth. It might even stimulate other industries (prison construction). Yet, in the longer term, addiction would impoverish society. Similarly, repealing those laws that insist you must have certain qualifications before you can call yourself a doctor would have the immediate effect of increasing the supply of doctors and lowering one component of medical costs. But this benefit would come at the expense of lowering the overall quality of medical care. It would be a detriment to society.

More generally, certain legal institutions may be necessary to facilitate the transition from private property to capitalism. Hernando de Soto (*The Mystery of Capital*) contends that the primary reason Third World and ex-communist countries lag the West economically is that they lack a simple coherent uniform code of law that governs property rights — how to attain them, how to transfer them, what can be done with them. Soto argues that such an institution is necessary to capitalize property, to leverage ownership into productive capital. If he is correct, and he makes a strong case, then government intervention is necessary to capitalism.

Even at the most practical level, act *laissez faire*, if practiced consistently, would negatively impact the functioning of an economy. Citing a specific example of the dysfunction of *laissez faire*'s focus on immediate gain, Robert Kuttner notes: "In Law and Economics School theory, there is even a doctrine of "efficient breach": If it is cost-effective for one party to a contract to breach it, that party should ignore the contract and pay the price. However, society pays a heavier price if norms of commitment and trust are casually breached." (*Everything for Sale*, p.64)

Clearly, a society with legal and economic institutions conducive to the development of a strong economy would create more wealth than one without such institutions. *Laissez faire* economies, because they are incompatible with wealth-creating institutions from patent protection to laws against drug trafficking, cannot create as much wealth as economies that incorporate such institutions. These institutions require the ability of government to intervene. Thus, if an economy is to maximize wealth it *cannot* be *laissez faire*. If our justification for *laissez faire* is that it maximizes the wealth of society, then our faith in *laissez faire* is misplaced.

DO WE WANT WHAT *LAISSEZ FAIRE* PROMISES?

Laissez faire has not maximized wealth. It is worse: Even in principle *laissez faire* cannot maximize wealth. It is still worse: As if these problems were not enough, there is another one. Is the maximization of wealth what we really want? This question may seem silly. Of course, we would rather be richer than poorer. But, that society has a greater total wealth doesn't mean it is we who are richer. All the wealth might belong to a single individual with the rest of us living in abject poverty. Saudi Arabia is a rich country, but half its population is illiterate and the average life expectancy there is shorter than that in Albania, China, or Turkey.

Most economists are trained to not even consider such a point. After all, they remind us, economics is a science and should be value neutral. The values of a broader dispersion of wealth and a greater average life expectancy are not part of economics. Nor should they be. (It is ironic that this sentiment represents a serious misinterpretation of Adam Smith. The patron saint of *laissez faire* was hardly value neutral. Smith, a utilitarian, wrote in *The Wealth of Nations*: "All for ourselves and nothing for other people, seems, in every age of the world, to have been the vile maxim of the masters of mankind....No society can surely be flourishing and happy, of which the far greater part of the members are poor and miserable. It is but equity, besides....")

Still, the free market system appears to fit the value neutrality espoused by contemporary economists. Any industry can be compared with any other in terms of objective arithmetic ratios: profit margin, return on investment, growth rate, economic value added. It is appropriate to invest in and develop industries with the highest ratios. This is a simple consequence of the arithmetic. In the financial community, quantitative analysts use these parameters to recommend portfolio overweighting or underweighting of various market sectors. There is no need to speculate on the moral value of the product — medical technology versus beer.

29

While the virtue of such an approach may seem obvious, increasing GNP and standards of living, the appearance of virtue is misleading. More is involved in the real world than just these arithmetic ratios. According to these ratios the most impressive industry — and by a wide margin — is the drug industry. Not Viagra and Keflex and the quinolones; not Advil and Pepto-Bismol and the over-the-counter antihistamines; but cocaine and heroin and the hallucinogens.

Although I am not privy to the details, the financial parameters of the unethical drug industry dwarf those of the nearest competitor. The CEOs of the best known of these companies, the late Pablo Escobar in Medellin and a syndicate in Cali, amassed fortunes in the billions of dollars. They must rank among the great entrepreneurs of classical economics.

In a truly free market system, unethical drugs should be the industry of choice. It is clearly the highest value-added industry. The U.N. estimates it accounts for 8% of world trade. Just the domestic market is estimated at a rapidly growing and highly profitable $150 billion per year. What a great investment! (This was also a great investment in the nineteenth century. In mid-century the defense of free enterprise in unethical drugs expressed itself in the Opium Wars. The English, stalwart defenders of free markets, free trade and maximizing profits, used military force to compel the Chinese government to acquiesce to the sale of opium to its citizens.)

Our attitudes toward this industry are inconsistent, for despite our attachment to the free market system, we have taken just the opposite tack. Even free market economists agree such drugs should be outlawed, claiming they cost the economy hundreds of billions of dollars a year. That may well be true, but such an argument seems out of place for a school of thought that has maintained, stridently, that it is *not* the job of government to optimize the economy. That should be left to the invisible hand of the free market.

The cigarette and tobacco industry (the number one cause of premature death, according to the American Medical Association) is a pale shadow of the unethical drug industry. Its financial characteristics are impressive — not surprising, considering the addictive nature of the product — though not so remarkable as those of the drug industry. There are certainly powerful arguments as to the negative effects of tobacco, comparable to those of unethical drugs, on the economy, as well as on quality and expectancy of life.

Tobacco industry executives have long known about both the addictive and the carcinogenic properties of tobacco. Despite their knowledge, they chose to not market a safer cigarette lest it damage their credibility. They deliberately misled Congress about attempts to make cigarettes even more addictive. And they targeted younger audiences. Philip Hilts quotes the assistant chief of R&D for R. J. Reynolds:

> Young people will continue to become smokers at or above the present rates during the projection period. The brands which these beginning smokers accept and use will become the dominant brands in future years. Evidence is now available to indicate that the 14- to 18-year-old group is an increasing segment of the smoking population. R J Reynolds must soon establish a new brand in this market if our position in the industry is to be maintained in the long term... (*Smokescreen*, p. 75.) [Hilts goes on to add:] Eventually, they did, with a style and ferocity unmatched in tobacco marketing history. It was Joe Camel.

Indeed, there is sound economic reason for tobacco companies to pursue such a course of action, whether openly or surreptitiously.

> This addiction, fundamental to the trade, does not develop among adults. Among those over the age of 21 who take up smoking for the first time, more than 90 percent soon drop it completely. It takes more than a year, and sometimes up to three years, to establish a nicotine addiction; adults simply don't stick with it. If it were true that the companies steer clear of children, as they say, the entire industry would collapse within a single generation. Put in market terms, the most important datum of the tobacco trade is that, among those who will be their customers for life, 89 percent have already become their customers by age 19. In fact, three-quarters had already joined the ranks of users by age 17. (*Ibid.*, p. 65.)

So it is not surprising that the tobacco companies have been disingenuous in their public pronouncements, from their pretense to a commitment to discourage young people from smoking to their misleading public response to EPA findings about dangers from second-hand smoke. Economically, they are behaving rationally. From the standpoint of free market theory, such action *must* be a benefit to society. Clearly it is not, despite the economic theory, and the behavior of the executives of these companies has been reprehensible. In some societies, less dominated by corporations purchasing political influence, it would be criminal.

In our own society, despite the damage done to both lives and the economy by tobacco, industry officials have been able to use part of their profits to purchase considerable clout in Congress, which time and again has enacted legislation favorable to the industry. Hilts notes that every item of health legislation since the 1960s has specified an exemption for cigarettes. Even after the perfidious tactics and strategies of the tobacco industry had been exposed, Congressional leaders introduced a $50 billion tax credit for the cigarette industry in the 1997 budget bill.

From the perspective of *laissez faire*, what is the difference between tobacco and unethical drugs that we should encourage and even subsidize the former but criminalize the latter? For, if the sole good is wealth, it should not matter what is the source of that wealth.

There are parallels within the ethical drug industry. Suppose a company were to discover a cure for cancer and also a drug that modestly extends the lives of patients and relieves some symptoms, provided they keep taking it. There would be powerful economic incentive to suppress the cure but to aggressively market the symptom-relieving drug. Along these lines, it is only rational — economically — that modern medicine should do most to keep chronically sick people alive. This is the most lucrative area of medical care.

The very structure of the medical industry insures the priority of profitability, even at the expense of safety and efficacy. Pharmaceutical companies have an economic incentive to minimize the money and time spent in the approval process for new drugs; so they seek to compress clinical trials into as short as possible a period, despite risks of missing longer-term effects. They apply pressure to get drugs approved for the widest range of indications, independent of efficacy.

> Professor David Reeves, chairman of the working party on antibiotic use of the British Society for Antimicrobial Chemotherapy, said that industry "has pushed quinolones very hard... Many quinolones are marginal antibiotics for treating respiratory infections. Yet the drug companies were keen to get respiratory infections as an indication, because if they were confined to urinary tract infections, you would be looking at a far smaller market." (Cannon, *Superbug: Nature's Revenge*, p. 71.)

The pressure to maximize profits also accounts for the widespread use of antibiotics at a sub-therapeutic level in livestock, the end market for nearly half our pharmaceuticals. Small doses, well below levels useful to combat infection, increase the growth of these animals and their profitability, since they are valued by the pound. But this is done at the cost of breeding drug-resistant strains of bacteria. Multiple drug resistance, unheard of decades ago, is now widespread in cattle.

Economic considerations also persuade companies to ignore products that — no matter how efficacious — have little profit potential. It has long been known that silver has broad-spectrum anti-microbial properties. The saying "Born with a silver spoon in his mouth" comes from the Middle Ages, when wealthy parents would give their children silver spoons to suck on. Of course, they knew nothing of microbes. But had they not somehow suspected that sucking on a silver spoon might have health benefits, it is unlikely that the silver spoon tradition would have developed.

Before refrigeration, some farmers used silver milk pails to prevent bacteria growth from spoiling the milk. Early settlers threw silver dollars into their water wells. Before the First World War, silver was used as an oral and injectable antibiotic. Even now, lines of Foley catheters are silver plated to reduce the risk of urinary tract infections, and silver sulphadiazine is used to prevent and treat burn-wound infections.

A colloidal silver product was recently tested at the Department of Microbiology at Brigham Young University and compared with representative antibiotics from five classes (tetracyclines, fluorinated quinolones, penicillins, cephalosporins, and macrolides) against a range of pathogens (S. gordonii, S. mutans, S. faecalis, S. pneumoniae, S. pyogenes, S. aureus, K. oxytoca, K. pneumoniae, E. coli, S. typhimurium, S. Arizona, E. cloacae, E. aerogenes, S. boydii, P. aeruginosa). The silver killed all the bacteria *in vitro* at 10 parts per million or less. Not one of the antibiotics achieved this result.

The study concluded:

> The most interesting observation was the broad spectrum that the... solution possesses.... The data suggests that...solution exhibits an equal or broader spectrum of activity than any one antibiotic tested... solution is equally effective against both gram positive and gram negative organisms....The data suggests that with the low toxicity associated with colloidal silver, in general, and the broad spectrum of antimicrobial activity of this colloidal silver preparation, this preparation may be effectively used as an alternative to antibiotics. (Revelli, Wall, Leavitt, "Antimicrobial Activity of American Silver's ASAP Solution".)

Additional testing on this solution has extended its scope as a potent antimicrobial agent. Studies at the University of California at Davis have demonstrated its ability to kill pathogenic yeasts. Tests at the Illinois Institute of Technology have shown it to kill anthrax spores (which are extremely difficult to kill, even with toxic agents). Tests in hospitals in Ghana have shown its ability to kill the *plasmodia* that cause malaria.

Most important, colloidal silver may provide a critical weapon against microbes that are resistant to antibiotics. This has become an acute medical problem.

In the 1950s, nearly all staphylococcus strains succumbed to penicillin. Presently, more than 95% of staphylococcus strains are resistant to penicillin. Fortunately, a new drug, methicillin, was found to kill staphylococcus, and in the late 1960s methicillin replaced penicillin as the treatment of choice for staphylococcus infections. But by the early 1990s, nearly 40% of staphylococcus strains isolated in large hospitals were resistant to methicillin. Vancomycin remains as a treatment of last resort for methicillin-resistant infections, but some physicians have reported staphylococcus strains that are resistant to vancomycin.

Streptococcus has evinced similarly increasing drug resistance. In the early 1970s, penicillin and erythromycin could successfully treat nearly all streptococcus infections, but we are now beset by strains that are more virulent than most older strains and also resistant to antibiotics. Recently, particularly virulent strains of streptococcus A, known as flesh-eating bacteria, have been found that are resistant to nearly all antibiotics. An antibiotic-resistant strain of streptococcus was responsible for the death of Jim Henson, creator of the Muppets.

A strain of tuberculosis, tuberculosis B, is resistant to every antibiotic in our arsenal. This is a dangerous contagious disease for which there is no effective treatment. Its spread raises the grim prospect of a deadly incurable epidemic. The effect is like a bad dream. No matter how fast we run, developing new antibiotics, the microbes are gaining on us. The threat is real that we could again find ourselves in a pre-antibiotic age. "Those who believe a plague could not happen in this century have already seen the beginning of one in the AIDS crisis, but the drug-resistant strains, which can be transmitted by casual contact in movie theaters, hospitals, and shopping-centers, are likely to be even more terrifying." (*Science*, August 1992.)

The spread of microbial resistance to antibiotics should not be surprising. Since the beginnings of life on this planet, bacteria, yeasts and fungi have been competing for turf. They have had more than a billion years both to develop their

34

own biological weapons and also to adapt to each other's arsenals by developing resistance to their biological weapons.

These biological weapons are the basis for antibiotics, so it is natural that some bacteria are resistant to antibiotics. With the widespread use of antibiotics selecting for resistant bacteria, it is to be expected that resistant strains should become dominant. The matter is made worse by the ability of bacteria to exchange plasmids, bits of extra-chromosomal genetic material that occur naturally in bacteria and may contain genes for antibiotic resistance. In this way a virulent non-resistant bacterium can pick up genes for antibiotic resistance from an otherwise harmless bacterium.

Microbes do not have a similar historical relationship with silver. Moreover, silver appears to act differently from any of the antibiotics. So it is plausible that bacteria would not develop resistance to silver. And tests at Brigham Young University in a "smart tank" containing bacteria that mutate rapidly have so far confirmed the inability of bacteria to develop resistance to silver. In light of this, it may seem surprising that the medical community has forgotten what it once regarded as a promising treatment for infectious diseases.

This is related to the economics of the industry rather than the efficacy of the product. Simply, colloidal silver is too inexpensive. It could not generate billions of dollars for drug companies. Worse, it might compete with highly profitable antibiotics in a $40 billion per year market.

This makes for strange contrasts. On one hand, there is no economic incentive for any drug company to pursue a potentially efficacious broad-spectrum anti-microbial agent that has fewer side effects than any antibiotic. On the other, there is economic incentive to spend $10,000 per physician per year on gifts and entertainment. This has influenced many doctors to prescribe new expensive drugs where older cheaper drugs would do as well. Good for the drug manufacturers, or they would have stopped the practice. But not so good for the patient. What is the difference between a gift for which there is a reasonably expected, if unspecified, payback and a bribe? How does this free market institution benefit society?

The subordination of life and health to economics is not confined to the drug producers. It characterizes our health care delivery system as well. Consider the priority of economics in health maintenance organizations (HMOs), apparently so named because they are okay only if you maintain your health. They select only the lowest risk prospects, leaving many in need of care without any medical coverage. Protocols treat laboratory results rather than patients. (It is more efficient that way, and it reduces legal liability.) Individuals with little medical training or experience commonly override doctors' recommendations on economic grounds. Doctors complain about pressure to minimize expenditures, to avoid specialists and expensive tests, even at the risk of patients' lives. Perverting the Hippocratic Oath, they are rewarded for lowering costs of care and penalized if costs exceed pre-established thresholds, independent of the needs of the patients.

One might think that the decline in quality of medical care is a necessary consequence of improving the efficiency of the system and lowering costs. But it does not appear that "...HMOs reduce the rate of increase in medical costs after an initial savings substantially based on risk selection." (Kuttner, *Everything for Sale*, p. 123)

As one would expect of a system in which the bottom line is the ultimate measure, the conflict of interest between profits and health is routinely decided in favor of profits. Profits outweigh even lives. But despite our concern about our own health and the health of those we love, HMOs have metastasized throughout the country.

Despite our spending more than any other country on health care, a recent World Health Organization (WHO) evaluation ranked the U.S. 37th in overall quality of health care. We may have different priorities from WHO, but this is hardly an impressive credential for our free market approach. Reflecting this, our life expectancy is lower than that in Australia, Austria, Belgium, Canada, Finland, France, Germany Greece, Italy, Japan, Netherlands, New Zealand, Norway, Spain, Sweden, Switzerland, and the U.K. (U.S. Census Bureau's International Data Base.) (Our life expectancy is low despite the facts that we smoke about as much as residents of other countries and that we have a lower than average consumption of alcohol and animal fats.)

What makes sense — at least on the traditional economic model — is bad for our health.

DECLINE AND DISASTER

The previous sections show that pure free markets have underperformed well-focused mixed economies, that they must underperform, and that what they offer is not what we want. It is worse yet. *Laissez faire* is leading us down a well-trodden path to decline and even disaster.

Decline

Western history has witnessed a sequence of transitions of economic (and most of the time, military and political) hegemony: in the ancient Mediterranean, from Assyria to Egypt to Persia to Greece to Rome; centuries later, from Italy to Spain to Holland and France to England to the U.S. In most of these cases, at least in the last millennium, the dominant country was supplanted not by a mortal enemy but by a country that had previously been allied or neutral, or even by a former colony. The transfer of power occurred, not as a result of an invasion or series of battles, but as a result of economic exhaustion.

Even the greatest empire, Rome, did not escape the consequences of economic exhaustion.

> But the Empire, alas, was ruined. Its exhausted finances no longer enabled it to maintain on its frontiers the compact armies which might have contained at any point the thrust of the Germans driven back by Attila, whose hordes

37

were still triumphantly advancing towards the West, overthrowing, as they came, people after people. Stilicho saved Italy only by leaving undefended all the Transalpine provinces. The result could not be long delayed. (Pirenne, *A History of Europe*, p. 27.)

In light of this history (and in light of the fact that hegemonic powers have always had the arrogance to believe their hegemony would last forever) we may wonder who will supplant us and what will be the cause of our decline to a second- or third-rate power? Historical precedent suggests that the cause of our decline is more likely to be our economic lassitude than the aggression of other countries. So what is it that determines whether a country's economy will be vibrant or stagnant, whether the country will thrive or falter? What are the early warning signs of secular economic decline?

It is characteristic of European history that the prosperity and even dominance of a country can be linked to a large middle class, reflecting a broad dispersion of wealth. One can point to seventeenth century Holland or nineteenth century England or the U.S. in the middle of the twentieth century.

During the golden age of Amsterdam, it was "'commonly said that this city is very much like Venice. For my part I believe Amsterdam to be very much superior in riches.' At the upper levels of society, this observation of a seventeenth-century English traveller could not be verified: patricians of Amsterdam, at the end of the century, had, on average, little more than half the assets of their Venetian counterparts. The Englishman, however, was more impressed by the diffused prosperity which put peasants with £10,000 in his way." (Fernandez-Armesto, *Millennium*, p. 309.)

As a burgher complained: "'Our peasants are obliged to pay such high wages to their workers and farmhands that [the latter] carry off a large share of the profits and live more comfortably than their masters.'" (Braudel, *The Perspective of the World*, p. 179-80.)

Two hundred years later, the second half of the nineteenth century was characterized by the economic, political and military hegemony of England, which enjoyed a broad dissemination of wealth. "[A]s a French correspondent writes, for 'the poor man's fortune [in the mass] in England is greater than the rich man's fortune in more than one kingdom.'" (*Ibid.*, p. 607.) In addition to — and perhaps because of — its broad dispersion of wealth, England had the highest GNP per capita in the world, and by a wide margin.

Inversely, "By the end of the (twentieth) century Britain was probably the least egalitarian of the core states — the bottom half of the population owned less than 7 per cent of all the wealth." (Ponting, *The Twentieth Century*, p. 151.) Corresponding to this, by 1994 the U.K. had a lower GNP per capita than Austria, Belgium, Denmark, France, Germany, Holland, Italy, Norway, Sweden, or Switzerland. (Maddison, *Monitoring the World's Economy 1820-1992*, p. 195, 197.)

A large and prosperous middle class has characterized our own era of world economic dominance. Even in the nineteenth century our robust economic growth was accompanied by a chronic shortage of labor. That led to a wage scale higher than Europe's and insured an increase in real wages every decade. High wages moderated our wealth disparity and contributed to the development of a middle class. (They also increased the incentive for industry to invest in productivity-improving capital equipment.)

But our middle class is now under increasing pressure. Gains in the 1980s and 1990s were limited to the wealthiest. To the extent that our middle class has been able to maintain itself, it is because of a large increase in the number of two-income households. This is unlikely to continue, as 60% of married women are employed.

Some of the pressure on our middle class is due to a development that characterized European powers in early stages of their declines: the Italian city-states of the late Renaissance, late sixteenth century Spain, eighteenth century Holland, and late nineteenth century England. These all witnessed the growth of multi-national banking and investment as a service sector producing enormous profits for those with ready access to capital. Funding foreign enterprises that would successfully compete with domestic industry resulted in an increasing concentration of wealth in the hands of a few rich investors at the expense of the working middle class.

"If one seeks the causes or the motives for Amsterdam's decline, in the last analysis one is likely to fall back on those general truths which hold for Genoa at the beginning of the seventeenth century as much as for Amsterdam in the eighteenth, and perhaps for the United States today, which is also handling paper money and credit to a dangerous degree." (Braudel, *The Perspective of the World*, p. 267) A similar, contemporary, moral is drawn by Arrighi and Silver in *Chaos and Governance in the Modern World*.

Carried in the wrong direction by our prevailing economic theory, we appear to be sailing the same course. Could it be that our misguided insistence that *laissez faire* is the only acceptable economic theory will contribute to our secular decline? George Santayana (*The Life of Reason*) observed: "Those who cannot remember the past are condemned to repeat it."

As a culture, we seem to better reflect the wisdom of Henry Ford: "History is bunk."

Disaster

If, in contrast to Henry Ford, we take history seriously, there is cause for concern: one that goes beyond our mediocre performance of recent decades. It threatens more than just our relative economic performance. Throughout the past millennium, at least in the West, a broad dispersion of wealth has been accompanied by benign periods of stability and progress. By contrast, a large and increasing disparity in wealth has been a precursor of increasing violence and instability that threatened the very foundations of society. Although it may seem odd, it is not the absolute level of wealth that mattered but rather how broadly the wealth was disseminated.

Despite differences between the economic, political and military settings of the ancient world and those of modern countries, this regularity also appeared in the days of classical Greece and Rome. When Solon ruled Athens, he acted to reduce inequality between rich and poor. He abolished certain debts, refused to allow enslavement as a penalty for the inability to pay debts, changed the tax system to benefit the middle class, and modified the electoral process to give the lower economic classes an audible political voice. This political action helped create a broad-based prosperity that fostered the Golden Age of Athens. Several generations later, Aristotle, a most careful observer, wrote in his *Politics* (Book IV): "Thus, it is manifest that the best political community is formed by citizens of the middle class, and that those states are likely to be well-administered in which the middle class is larger..."

In contrast to this, it was a wide disparity in wealth that destabilized the Roman republic. "The widening of the gap between rich and poor in central Italy as peasant farming gave way to large estates bought (and stocked with slaves) with the spoils of empire...proved fatal to the republic in the end." (Roberts, *The Penguin History of the World*, p. 231.)

Centuries later, the economic gap between the rich and the rest played a role in the decline of the Roman Empire. In the days of Diocletian and Constantine, provincial army revolts and the need to secure army loyalty led to a restructuring of provincial governments, a sharp increase in the size of the bureaucracy, and a concomitant increase in the tax burden, especially the tax on cultivated land. This tax affected the peasants and contributed to a widening income gap between the wealthy landowners and the rest of the populace, who increasingly felt they had no vested interest in Rome.

> Most of this burden had to be borne by the peasantry. But the peasants had already been paying all they could....The rich were able, through bribery and influence, to have the assessments on their holdings minimized and to avoid paying even the minimum. Therefore the period, especially in the West, saw a growth of great estates...[and] increased taxation led many of the peasants to make over their properties to the rich landlord of the neighborhood in exchange for protection from the city council's tax collectors and a guarantee of the right to live on and work the land. Thus the peasants were gradually transformed into serfs...
>
> The government thus reverted to the Oriental pattern — a despotism resting on control of an army and acting through a royal council composed of executives arbitrarily appointed by the king. The Greek experiment was abandoned...The Roman Empire in the west fell only because most of its subjects would not fight to preserve it. (Garraty and Gay (eds.) *The Columbia History of the World*, p. 236-240.)

Such a relationship has continued to characterize the West. As economic historians have subjected Europe of the Middle Ages to increasing economic scrutiny, they have discovered that a broad dispersion of wealth has consistently been associated with periods of tranquility and progress. Inversely, a large and increasing disparity of wealth has presaged violence and instability, and ultimately a collapse of the economy and society.

In the centuries following the disintegration of the Roman Empire technological innovations — the horse collar and heavy wheeled plows, as well as new crops, triennial rotation and the increasing use of water mills — improved agricultural productivity by as much as 50%. Peasants were direct beneficiaries of this greater productivity. In some regions they were able to lease lands from their lords and become, to a degree, their own masters.

As a result, the tenth through twelfth centuries was a period of relative income equality. A climate of economic and cultural vigor pervaded Europe. This period witnessed the founding of the first European universities; the development of Gothic architecture; the establishment of the outstanding school at Chartres that reintroduced ancient Greek thought (via the Arab philosophers) into Europe, and even influenced Islamic thought; the spread of the Cluny reform through the Roman Catholic Church; a revival of literature in the *romans courtois, chansons de geste, romans d'amor* and Arthurian tales; and the rebirth of historical thought and writing.

Demography saw the growth of towns, some of which had charters granting freedom to their inhabitants. One can even find traces of *sotto voce* egalitarianism in these towns. "In the tenth and eleventh centuries, when towns began their rise, they usually contained elements ranging from the martial aristocracy to simple artisans and peasants. Thereafter, the need for community solidarity when fighting a prince or lord normally stimulated ideas of common citizenship and equality before the law." (Garraty and Gay (eds.) *The Columbia Encyclopedia of World History*, p. 394.)

In economics, as well, "...the eleventh century saw the beginning of what was effectively a period of 'sustained growth' on the modern pattern, one which would not recur before the English industrial revolution." (Braudel, *The Perspective of the World*, p. 546.)

This period was progressive and open, a high tide of civilization that would recede from Europe in the ensuing centuries:

> In this expanding Europe of the twelfth century there was much curiosity and so great a thirst for knowledge that the intellectual and cultural treasure Islam had to offer... [L]earning was liberal, popular piety took many forms, the Church itself stood open. Learning was becoming more broadly based.... An open aristocracy; and an open clergy, too. Most twelfth century clerics were outward looking, accessible to their people and to their own kindred, at all levels of society...
>
> In Italy and southern France in the sixteenth century men were burned for thinking much less dangerous thoughts than a Bernard Sylvestris or William of Conches or an Alain de Lille, all members of the twelfth century circle at Chartres... The fact that toleration can be discussed at all in connection with the Middle Ages is striking enough; it underlines the magnitude of the metamorphosis which transformed the 'open' Middle Ages of the expansive twelfth century into the increasingly narrow and constricted later Middle Ages." (Friedrich Heer, *The Medieval World*, p. 3-6, 113.).

The thirteenth and fourteenth centuries, reversing the pattern of economic equality, were characterized by an accelerating disparity of income. This presaged a decline in the health and stability of society, most visible in religion. During the course of the thirteenth century it became increasingly doctrinaire, severely restricting the range of permissible thought and endangering some whose orthodoxy is now unquestioned. Even St. Francis of Assisi was fortunate to escape the Inquisition. Several of his closest followers were less fortunate.

Despite the institution of the Inquisition, the papacy declined in stature. Effects ranged from a papal legate who was forced to take refuge in the Castel Sant'Angelo (where he was bombarded with excrement) to the exile of the papacy to Avignon, from the election of three competing popes at the same time to a succession of anti-popes.

By the fourteenth century,

> Western Christendom, Byzantium and Islam, were now drawing further and further apart... to revert to what is usually considered a typically 'medieval' condition — they became closed societies, withdrawn into their separate worlds....The two most powerful estates, the nobility and clergy, cut themselves off from the masses... so did the intelligentsia...
>
> The anti-Semitism of the later Middle Ages was part of the same trend... Higher education was becoming narrower and more specialized, and the bureaucratic Church, entrenched behind the Inquisition and Canon Law and intent on theological refinement, was becoming increasingly remote from the laity and the 'people'... (*Ibid.*, p. 7-8, 89.)

This is not to deny the brilliance of thinkers of the late Middle Ages: Thomas Aquinas, Meister Eckhart, Duns Scotus, William of Ockham, Roger Bacon. But society had become closed and hostile. Aquinas's teachings were condemned by both the Church and the University of Paris. Meister Eckhart was tried, his teachings were condemned by the pope as heretical, and his writings were officially burned. William of Ockham was excommunicated. Roger Bacon died in prison.

Economies were slower to decline. Even after wealth discrepancies began widening, there was time before economies would falter. The rich continued to prosper for a century. But the economic condition of the masses deteriorated, leading to widespread malnutrition and starvation. This in turn led to violence and unrest: regicide (Edward II), protracted wars (The Hundred Years War), and rebellions (in England, the Peasants' Rebellion; in rural France, the Jacquerie and the Tuchins). It culminated in the devastation and social disintegration caused by the Black Death. The bubonic plague deeply scarred all levels of society, the rich as well as the poor.

Ironically, the succession of pandemics in the fourteenth and early fifteenth centuries was responsible for an improvement in the status of workers and a more even income distribution. These plagues decimated the working classes, with their poorer diet and sanitation, even more than the better to do. With workers in scant supply, their real wages improved. In the late fourteenth century wages began to rise, while rents and interest rates fell. Graphs in H.O. Meredith's *Economic History of England* show that the real wages of the fifteenth century were not surpassed for 400 years.

Similarly, "...a study of the purchasing power of builders' wages by Phelps Brown and Hopkins shows that the prosperity such workers enjoyed between 1400 and 1500 as a result of the redistribution of economic power by the Black Plague was not achieved again until 1870." (Douthwaite, *The Growth Illusion*, p. 47.)

The development of an incipient middle class, with moderating income inequality between the rich nobles and the workers, set the stage for the Renaissance. This marked a widespread resurgence of art, literature and music, the beginnings of modern science, a modest revival of individualism, and the birth of modern Europe. These developments benefited from a stable and peaceful society.

It may seem surprising, but this was not a particularly wealthy period. Trade and industrial production remained well below their peaks of the previous century. Historians have even talked about the depression of the Renaissance. But the Renaissance was a period of relative equality of wealth.

A new cycle of increasing income inequality began in the early sixteenth century. Imports of gold and silver from the New World contributed to an accelerating inflation that affected primarily the lower and middle classes. Due to rising costs of firewood and rents, real wages fell 50%.

As in the thirteenth and fourteenth centuries, this led to escalating violence: increased crime, pogroms, regicide (Charles I) and assassination (the French Henry IV), civil unrest (The Fronde, Huguenot rebellions, Germany's Peasants' War), and protracted wars (The Thirty Years' War, The Italian Wars, the wars of the Reformation). In the Thirty Years' War (1618-1648), Germany lost nearly one-third its population. The first half of the seventeenth century saw the first protracted decline in European population since the Black Death.

> The rich grew richer, while increasing numbers of the poor were driven very near the edge of starvation... Food riots broke out in many parts of Europe...The great dearth fell cruelly upon the poor, while the rich remained secure in their plenty... The effect of scarcity was to...contribute to growing social instability.

Famine, pestilence, and economic depression were accompanied by war. During the entire century from 1551 to 1650, peace prevailed throughout the continent only in a single year (1610) — a record unmatched since the fourteenth century. These conflicts were remarkable not only for their frequency but also their ferocity.... During the early seventeenth century, the armies of Europe reached their largest size since the Roman era.... The result was an age of revolutions in virtually all European states. (Fischer, *The Great Wave*, p. 92-7.)

The second half of the seventeenth century began a new respite for labor that was to last nearly 100 years. Between 1670 and 1730 the fraction of wealth owned by the richest 1% of households in England decreased from 49% to 39%. Similar trends, beginning soon after the midpoint of the century, appeared throughout Europe.

Once again this led to an increase in social and political stability, a decline in crime, a revival of commerce, and a flourishing of culture. The late seventeenth century well into the eighteenth was a period of exceptional creativity in areas ranging from science to music, philosophy to economics, architecture to finance. The Enlightenment provided justification for the rights of all people, not just the ruling classes. It laid the philosophical foundations for and saw the birth of modern democracy.

Yet a new cycle of widening economic disparity began in the 1730s. Between 1770 and 1812, the nominal per capita income in England fell 25% while prices doubled. In most of Europe the nobility was able to use its political influence to procure exemptions from increasingly onerous taxation, which impacted the middle class. (Things are similar today. Prior to the Kennedy tax cuts, when we had a strong economy, the average family's effective tax rate was just over 10%, while the average millionaire paid more than 80% of his income in taxes. Since then the rich have been able to reduce their tax rate by two thirds while the average family has seen its tax rate more than double. Presently the average family pays as high an effective tax rate as the richest families. Could there be a causal connection between a tax burden that falls on the middle class, increasing economic disparity, and a weakening economy?)

The pattern was similar to that which had occurred in the great waves of the thirteenth and sixteenth centuries. Instabilities of many sorts developed. One of the most dangerous was the growth of inequality. This trend appeared in both Europe and America, where wealth became more concentrated in a few hands during the period from 1750 to 1790. (Fischer, *The Great Wave*, p. 135.)

Armed bands roamed the English countryside. The Cossack Pugachev led a bloody rebellion in Russia. There were revolts in Geneva, Belgium, Holland, Poland, Ireland, and the American colonies. Assassins claimed the lives of the Swedish King Gustavus III, the Russian Czar Paul I, and the English Prime Minister Spencer Perceval. A succession of disastrous harvests in the early 1780s increased the desperation of the poor and amplified the violence, leading to the most important series of convulsions, the French Revolution. This had repercussions throughout Europe for decades.

The disparity between rich and poor peaked in the early nineteenth century. While the Napoleonic Wars were ravaging continental Europe, half of England was on poor relief.

This was followed by yet another round of sustained increases in real wages, aided by government intervention (motivated, in part, by fear of revolution). Greater economic equality again gave rise to a more stable society, the Victorian era in England and the prolonged peace on the Continent that had been negotiated at the Congress of Vienna. Despite the intentions of Metternich and Castlereagh and despite the failure of popular revolutions, the Congress of Vienna ushered in a period of persistent, if gradual, growth in civil liberties and democratic institutions.

We are now well into the most recent cycle of increasing economic disparity, which began tentatively during the Civil War, re-ignited with increased momentum during the First World War, and powered to new records in the last few decades. Our present wealth disparity — as measured by the GINI ratio, a standard measure of economic disparity — is the largest in our history (Fischer, *The Great Wave*, p. 222f.) and is continuing to increase. Our richest 1% now own more than 40% of our wealth, surpassing the previous record of 36% set in 1929. As reported in 1999 by *The New York Times*: "The gap between rich and poor has grown into an economic chasm so wide that this year the richest 2.7 million Americans, top 1 percent, will have as many after-tax dollars to spend as the bottom 100 million."

The wealth disparity cycle has been repeated often enough to generate a clear pattern. Over the past millennium a broad dispersion of wealth has been accompanied by benign periods of peace, stability and progress. Inversely, an increasingly narrow concentration of wealth has led to decline that ultimately affected all levels of society. The critical factor was not the total amount of wealth, but rather the degree to which the wealth was spread.

This pattern may explain the retarded development of Eastern Europe and Russia. In Western Europe the struggles between monarchy and nobility and the conflicts between church and state often resulted in a balance of power, neither side able to impose its will on the other. Peasants benefited from this balance. At times they were able to obtain royal or ecclesiastic guarantees of their rights. By contrast, in Eastern Europe monarchs were unable (or disinclined) to resist attacks on peasant rights by the nobility, attacks that led to the creation of a hereditary serfdom. In Russia, the tsar overpowered the nobility and the serf became property of the state. The extreme disparity between the haves and have-nots stifled progress for all.

This raises a question for a world economy. The cumulative wealth of the poorest 50% of the world's population is less than that of a handful of the richest individuals. Would sufficient economic inequalities within the world as a whole play the same role that inequalities have played within national economies?

The growing marginalization of people and countries in an apparently affluent world could provide ample grist for violence and terrorism, leading to the destabilization of even the wealthiest societies. While there has always been severe poverty, not only have economic differences grown during the course of the twentieth century, but it is now easier to be aware how badly off one is in contrast to others. With nearly a billion people chronically undernourished and with tens of millions dying each year from starvation and malnutrition-related diseases in a world that advertises conspicuous consumption, righteous indignation could catalyze violence. It is easier and cheaper to ignite such violence and incite terrorism than to prevent it. (And chemical and biological weapons are disturbingly cheap, as is human life for the desperate with deep faith in their own righteousness.) "If government does not protect the assets of the poor, it surrenders this function to the terrorists, who can then use it to win the allegiance of the excluded." (Soto, *The Other Path*, p. xxiv.)

Despite the devastating effects historically associated with too great a concentration of wealth and despite the present potential for excessive wealth disparity to wreak havoc, the tendency for wealth to concentrate is not surprising. In a struggle for additional wealth, the rich have an advantage that can rarely be overcome. Because it is natural for wealth to concentrate, problems generated by its concentration are not likely to resolve themselves. Nor are free market mechanisms likely to resolve them.

WEALTH AND TAXES

The evidence provided by wealth dispersion cycles is troubling, for in recent decades powerful forces have increased economic inequality. Technological innovations have displaced blue-collar workers. Outsourcing to low wage countries has impoverished employees who lack proprietary skills. Downsizing, one reason corporate earnings have grown faster than revenues in recent years, has bolstered profits at the expense of the middle class.

Since 1980, General Electric cut its domestic work force 40% while tripling revenue. General Electric is a representative example. In the last two decades of the millennium the 500 largest U.S. corporations saw assets and profits triple while cutting 5 million jobs. Only one of ten workers laid off by downsizing subsequently found a job paying more than 80% of his previous salary. We have compounded matters by adopting our least progressive tax code since the 1930s and by cutting government programs designed to benefit the middle class.

Due to the confluence of these economic and political forces, the top quintile of Americans has grown richer while the bottom four quintiles have become poorer. Between 1977 and 1989 the top 1% saw their incomes double. In contrast to enormous gains made at the top of the economic ladder, workers in private industry suffered a decline in average real weekly earnings.

Despite the huge increase in wealth at the upper end of the economic spectrum since the mid-1970s, the real after-tax income of our bottom 60 percent has declined, their real wealth has declined more sharply, and our poverty rate has risen. It took less than two decades to double from levels of the early 1970s. We gave back gains made in the Truman-Johnson days, and despite modest improvement in the latter half of the 1990s, one-fifth of our children are buried below the poverty level. The U.S. has a higher poverty rate than other industrialized countries, and our ratio of income of the richest quintile to the poorest quintile is far above the average of the other industrialized countries.

"Over 50 million people living in the United States in the mid-1990s had an income the same as the world average and lower than a large proportion of the population of states such as Sri Lanka, Morocco and Egypt." (Ponting, *The Twentieth Century*, p. 155.) This is partly responsible for our crime rate, with the highest level of incarceration of any industrialized state.

In such circumstances it would be prudent, as well as decent, to adopt policies to narrow the gap between the rich and the rest. A highly progressive tax code tends to enlarge the middle class while slowing the increase in affluence of the wealthy. When our top marginal tax rate was 91%, outrageous to free market sensibilities, our middle class grew and prospered, as did the country as a whole, even the rich. As our highest tax rates have been reduced, primarily on the grounds that a lower tax rate would provide incentive to be more productive, not only has our productivity lagged, but the disparity between our rich and the rest has grown.

This pattern occurred before. In the 1920s, government repeatedly reduced the progressivity of our tax code, also in the name of free enterprise. In four steps it cut the top tax bracket from 77% to 25%. Then, as now, the rich grew richer while the bottom four quintiles grew poorer. Despite the roaring stock market of the 1920s and the increased affluence of our wealthy bankers at the expense of the middle class, that era did little to establish a sound economy or a healthy society.

The history of the 1920s holds lessons that may be relevant if we wish to avoid a repetition. When natural economic forces threaten the middle class, widening the gap between the rich and the rest to dangerous levels, it may be appropriate to adopt a more progressive tax policy to protect middle America. Such a policy might counter the tendency, caused in part by natural economic forces, for income disparity to increase.

Of course, this is sacrilege. Anyone who can read lips knows taxes are bad and more taxes are worse. Wrong! There is more than just the failure of the Kennedy and Reagan tax cuts. Historically, the necessary perversity of taxation is not at all evident.

Holland, the most prosperous country in the seventeenth and early eighteenth centuries, had the highest taxes. "Observers all agree that no other state, in the seventeenth or eighteenth century, laboured under such a weight of taxation." (Braudel, *The Perspective of the World*, p. 200.) At the end of the eighteenth century, when England was becoming the dominant world economic power, its average tax rate was double that of France.

Even in the U.S., the Kennedy tax cuts marked a major decline in long-term economic growth and productivity. The 1978 capital gains tax rate cut saw a transition from strong economic growth to a recession. The 1981 capital gains rate cut also marked an economic slowdown. Inversely, the 1976 and 1986 Tax Reform Acts, which increased taxes at the top, saw the economy accelerate. Are we missing something?

That is not the only point. If we are not going to eliminate taxes altogether, any change in tax policy changes relative after-tax incomes. The more progressive the tax policy, the more it equalizes incomes. The more regressive the system (sales taxes, for which the median rate has doubled in the past 25 years; social security taxes, which have increased even more sharply), the more it increases income differences. A truly progressive tax system could mitigate the effects of natural economic forces and increase the dispersion of wealth.

But what about the conventional wisdom that lowering the top tax rates encourages our most productive people to work harder because they keep more of what they earn? What about the argument that increasing the tax bite on our wealthiest citizens decreases the capital they have to save and invest, causing a reduction in investment, lower productivity, slower economic growth, and a lower standard of living for all? What about the claim that greater economic disparity benefits everyone by generating an incentive to work harder?

The conventional wisdom sounds nice, but just the opposite may be true. Higher tax rates may increase the incentive to work harder because we would have to work harder just to maintain our after-tax income. Lester Thurow's *The Zero Sum Economy* maintains that people will work harder in the political sphere to preserve what they already have than to gain something new. Perhaps this is also true in the economic sphere.

Independently, increasing the after-tax income of those likely to spend, rather than save, increases the demand for goods. This demand generates investment opportunities, which in turn stimulate savings. The fact that investment opportunities providing a good return on investment are more important than the amount of capital that is theoretically available to invest may explain the positive correlation between a more progressive tax structure and faster economic growth.

Finally, contrary to the "incentive" argument of economic radicals of the right (including Stakhanov, Stalin's supply-side economist), history suggests excessive wealth disparity is bad for economies. Even now our trading partners have smaller disparities in wealth and income but their growth exceeds ours.

This is not intended to oppose tax simplification, though much of the complexity of our tax code has come from rich and powerful interests "purchasing" their own tax breaks. The bad will generated by, as well as the costs of, tax collection are separate issues. Still, there are ways of simplifying the tax code that provide a progressive system.

Consider a national sales tax coupled with a steeply graduated rebate, refunding much to middle and lower income families, but little or none to upper income families. Point-of-sale tax collection could be less painful and also reduce tax avoidance. It would dovetail with advice provided three centuries ago by Colbert, the finance minister of Louis XIV. Likening collecting taxes to plucking a goose, he described its aim as getting the most feathers for the least hissing.

In addition, if we aim to use tax policy to increase savings, point-of-sale collection would be effective. Because sales taxes do not tax funds that are saved and invested, this mode of taxation would encourage investment. Paying the sales tax refunds as lump sums would further encourage savings and investment.

Independently, it is reasonable to increase inheritance taxes on the wealthiest. The argument that fairness requires that individuals be allowed to keep all they earn from their hard work and talent is already questionable. Earnings capacity depends on the educational, financial and cultural infrastructure of society. Without that infrastructure, the talent and hard work might not be worth so much. Contrast Michael Jordan's earnings to Bill Russell's, Leon Russell's to Wolfgang Amadeus Mozart's, Bill Gates' to Alexander Graham Bell's.

The argument that we are solely entitled to the fruits of our labor and talent is even more tenuous if we include the hard work and talent required to be born into extreme wealth. Furthermore, a large inheritance has the same drawbacks as welfare. It has been argued, often with more validity than candor, that welfare is debilitating to its recipients. But isn't it just as debilitating to receive a large entitlement check from a trust department as a small entitlement check from the government?

Even in the case of raw talent, which we may regard as our own, to be used for personal gain, is it through some virtue of ours that we have obtained such talent? Gandhi suggested we regard our talent as a trusteeship to be used for the benefit of others as well as ourselves.

It is understandable that the wealthy should wish to retain their wealth and pass it on to their children. But it is also understandable that society should exercise its right to limit the amount of wealth to be retained or passed on. Taxation does not violate the right to private property; to the contrary. If government did not have the ability to collect revenue, it could not fund police forces and court systems. If it could not fund police forces and court systems, no one could enjoy a right to private property — for anyone could seize the property and its "owner" would have no recourse.

If government is to collect revenue, it is reasonable and moral that legislators consider the impact of different forms of revenue collection on society as a whole. It is natural that the rich would oppose anything that threatens to disproportionately reduce their wealth, that they would argue that a steeply graduated income tax or inheritance tax is unfair, or even that any inheritance tax is unfair because it is taxing money that has already been subject to income tax. But such arguments are hardly convincing. They apply equally to the much larger category of sales tax. But sales tax is regressive; so it generates no complaints about double taxation.

An alternative approach, following the tack of Reagan's economic advisors, might claim that a less progressive or more regressive tax code stimulates investment and economic growth and is better for all of society. The problem with this claim is that there is so much evidence against it — from the correlation of a more progressive tax code with faster economic growth to a millennium of evidence that excessive economic inequality is a menace to the security and standard of living of all.

Note, too, that the notion of inheritance runs counter to the spirit of free market capitalism. That spirit insists on a level playing field where the spoils go to the most productive. Such a system, according to classical economic theory, maximizes the incentive to be productive and so leads to the most efficient economy. But such a system is incompatible with inheritance, which tilts the playing field by rewarding the descendants of the rich, even if they are not productive. (Isn't it interesting that we espouse the *laissez faire* orthodoxy of flat playing fields, which serves the rich at the expense of the rest, and that where we deviate from pure orthodoxy, it is also to serve the rich at the expense of the rest?)

In light of this evidence, why would anyone wish to preclude an effectively progressive tax code? Devotees of *laissez faire* may be unaware of the historical precedents. Even more important may be their depth of faith in the principle of government non-interference. This faith, no matter how pure and well intentioned, has been a source of misdirected policies.

THE SPAWN OF "LAISSEZ FAIRE"

INSTITUTIONAL INCUBI

Our institutions shape our beliefs and are also shaped by them. It is only natural that false beliefs should spawn unhealthy institutions and that those institutions should reinforce our illusions. It should come as no surprise that institutions reflecting the spirit of *laissez faire* have contributed to our decline. We neglect the painstaking development of strong foundations in favor of the quick fix. We sacrifice our future to boost immediate satisfaction. Even where we diagnose serious problems, we show an unhealthy attraction to cosmetic repair.

This corresponds to the essence of *laissez faire* — that individuals working for their own immediate gain produce the greatest economic good for society as a whole. The institutions generated by this philosophy have their own *raison d'être* — short-term profitability. In suggesting that this is the ultimate standard for all endeavors, they subvert our understanding of value.

We are caught in a vicious circle. We have become increasingly focused on the short term in all aspects of life, reflected in statistics ranging from our debt to our divorce rate to our drug dependence. In turn, our institutions have become dedicated to the short term, eschewing the building of solid foundations in education, industry or personal lives. These institutions, in their turn, fix our attention even more exclusively on the short term. Unfortunately, our indulgences now will impoverish us later. The less we are able to change our priorities, the greater will be our ultimate impoverishment.

Short-Term vs. Long-Term Investment Horizons

It is within the financial markets that we have become most narrowly fixated on the short term. The aphorism often repeated by Robert Farrell, Merrill Lynch's eminent stock market technician, "Get rich slowly," contrasts to the expectations mirrored in the proliferation of derivative instruments geared to the short-term speculator. These instruments, which can be destabilizing to the broad market, focus the attention of the financial community on the immediate and away from the long term. The same can be said for the minute-to-minute coverage of networks such as CNBC. This suggests, mistakenly, that markets are driven by short-term news and that the essence of successful investing is rapid and appropriate reaction to changing news.

As if to underline the pointlessness of the race to be first to capitalize on each piece of news as it breaks, there is an approach to investing that lies at the opposite end of the spectrum. It provides a simple and reliable discipline — ignored by investors — that enables one to consistently outperform the market. The key to this approach is that specific sectors tend to outperform or underperform the broad market for long periods, often more than 10 years at a time. If one gets in a "right" sector early and stays there, one will do well.

The following table contrasts the long-term performance of the Pharmaceutical and Oil Service sectors. It eliminates stock selection as a performance factor by taking all the stocks listed in these sectors by *Value Line*. It eliminates market timing by calculating the appreciation of each stock from its average 1981 price to its average 1991 price:

Company	Appreciation		Company	Appreciation
Mylan	+6080%		Dresser Industries	-3%
Amgen	+3888%		Schlumberger	-5%
Alza	+3064%		Daniel Industries	-16%
Marion Merrell-Dow	+2129%		McDermott Industries	-39%
Forest Labs	+1356%		Helmerich & Payne	-46%
Syntex	+915%		Baker Hughes	51%
Merck	+871%		Halliburton	-57%
Rhone Poulenc - Rorer	+714%		Enterra	-64%

Schering Plough	+602%		Rowan Drilling	-66%
Warner Lambert	+555%		Tidewater	-66%
Pfizer	+535%		Varco	-79%
Chiron	+495%		Parker Drilling	-80%
IVAX	+476%		Kaneb Services	-83%
Bristol Myers - Squibb	+473%		Smith International	-84%
Eli Lilly	+400%		Western Co.	-84%
Genentech	+374%		Global Marine	-93%
American Home Prods	+349%		Reading and Bates	-99%
Upjohn	+291%			
Biogen	+ 86%			

Every pharmaceutical manufacturer appreciated. Every oil service stock depreciated. The worst of the pharmaceuticals nearly doubled the best of the oil service. By 1991, a 1981-dollar invested in the average pharmaceutical stock would have been worth 20 times a 1981-dollar invested in the average oil service stock.

Even though the best sectors are often contrarian, at least initially, fundamental and technical analysis and the identification of newly developing economic themes can reveal the ideal investment sectors.

Along these lines, the precious metals producers at the turn of the millennium resemble the pharmaceuticals of the early 1980s. This may seem surprising. It is surely contrarian. Investors see no similarity between the present and the 1970s, which they regard as the perfect investment climate for gold. That decade was characterized by accelerating inflation, which increased demand for gold and led to higher prices. Presently, with low inflation and with the chairman of the Federal Reserve (dutifully echoed by the gurus of Wall Street) assuring investors that inflation will remain subdued for the foreseeable future, there appears to be no reason to buy gold.

This misses the point; it is fighting the last war. It may seem trivial, but gold is a commodity whose price is determined solely by supply and demand. While inflation increases demand for gold, it is not the only factor that can do so. The primary mechanism driving gold demand today is not inflation but increased disposable income, primarily in South and East Asia. As a result of purchases of gold by investors from this region, supply and demand are not close to equilibrium. Unlike the supply-demand equilibrium of the early 1970s, worldwide off-take exceeds supply by more than 40 million ounces per year, more than half of global production.

To date, the supply shortfall has been made up by sales and loans of government gold, enabling banks, bullion banks and hedge funds to acquire a short position in excess of 300 million ounces — four years of mine supply. At some point within the next five years these sales and loans will have to be curtailed, if only because central banks will run out of gold. At that point or earlier, the imbalance will become apparent, market forces will prevail, and the excess demand will be rationed by a sharp increase in the gold price.

Of course, inflation would further increase the demand for and price of gold. But it is not necessary to have any inflation-driven demand to support higher prices. As Frank Veneroso has convincingly shown, the present supply-demand imbalance is sufficient to support a sustainable gold price in excess of $600 per ounce, even without inflation or short covering.

It is typical for financial markets to misdirect attention. Many investors will miss the appreciation in gold because they are waiting for inflation to accelerate.

CREDIT OVERLOAD

In a culture that values the near term and an economy in which credit is profitable for the financial sector, it is to be expected that credit should proliferate. But excessive credit can be a danger, not only to individuals, but to entire economies. Western economic history suggests that long-term economic cycles are coincident with, and perhaps driven by, long-term credit creation/ credit liquidation cycles.

These cycles have had an average, but highly variable, periodicity of 60 years, the last credit liquidation phase beginning in 1929. The previous one began in the early 1870s, triggered by the overbuilding of railroads and the collapse of Jay Cooke & Co., the country's largest bank. (It was even more severe in England, and English economists have called the 20 years following 1873 "The Great Depression.")

Massive credit liquidation phases have been triggered when total debt grew to the point that it overloaded the economy, causing a deflationary implosion in which debt was liquidated by a chain reaction of bankruptcies. The trauma of the resulting depression would restrain credit growth for decades until generations that had not lived through the depression repeated the excesses of their great grandparents.

A number of financial measures suggest we are once again nearing a major credit peak. Before the Great Depression ushered in by the stock market crash of 1929, the ratio of total credit to GNP peaked at a little under 2-to-1. We have now comfortably surpassed that ratio. Non-financial credit, including government debt, reached $18.3 trillion at the end of 2000, with the financial sector adding another $8.2 trillion. Our ratio of debt to GNP is approaching 3-to-1.

All areas of the economy, not just the financial sector, have participated in this orgy. In just the few years since 1995, non-financial corporations increased their debt by two thirds, to $4.5 trillion (*The Wall Street Journal*, July 5, 2000). Household borrowing increased 60%, to $6.5 trillion. The average household now has 13 credit cards. Margin debt has quadrupled in the past decade. (And there is an additional $100 trillion of financial leverage in derivatives instruments. While this is not strictly debt, it represents extreme financial leverage and can have the same impact.)

Despite the clear parallels with 1929, few economists have expressed concern about our increasing debt and the severity of the liquidity crisis it might cause. It would appear to be simple common sense that we cannot borrow indefinitely to increase our standard of living. At some point it will be necessary to start paying back. But paying back requires less spending and a decline in our standard of living. The only difference between an individual and a country is that a country with a fractional reserve banking system and most of its debt denominated in its own currency can print money and so deflect some of the deflationary impact to an inflationary one.

Because economists and politicians are not historians, they have paid little attention to these problems. Debt and derivatives have worried Congress only when they have threatened to produce immediate dislocations. The free market economist, playing Dr. Pangloss, has assured us this is and will remain the best of all possible economic worlds — at least provided government doesn't interfere. This does not reflect an awareness of the important similarities between the current cycle and previous ones. If anything, it sounds like Alfred E. Neuman: "What, me worry?"

Laissez faire has rendered a disservice by suggesting there is no need to address such issues, for the invisible hand of the free market will resolve them. These problems have been caused or exacerbated by free market policies. It is hardly likely that the policies that caused them will also resolve them.

Mutual Funds and Corporate Management

It has been widely argued that the rash of corporate takeovers and leveraged buyouts over the past two decades is bad for our economy. Because these acquisitions and buyouts have been financed with debt, they increase our total debt, already dangerously high. Also, because the debt associated with such financial leverage is often classified as "junk" and bears high interest rates, the interest burden on the company can be onerous, pressuring management to eliminate any unnecessary expenses in order to pay down debt. This typically means laying off employees who do not contribute to immediate cash flow. It means cutting R&D, which, after all, negatively impacts the bottom line — in the short term.

The problem lies in the long term. The function of R&D is to insure the long-term prosperity, or even survival, of a company by developing new products, new manufacturing processes, or new markets. Studies note that reducing R&D to preserve cash flow — mortgaging the future to pay for the present — are often early warning signs of impending decline.

Perversely, the very structure of our financial community makes it difficult for managements to maintain a healthy long-term view. Institutions manage most of our financial assets: mutual funds and trust funds for individuals, pension and profit sharing plans for corporations. Consulting firms that specialize in the selection of financial managers choose many of these money managers, especially at the corporate level. Whether or not it is admitted, one of the most important factors in this selection is historical performance. Moreover, the time frame defining such performance has been shrinking, and in some cases managed accounts are in jeopardy if they underperform benchmark indices for as little as one year.

The narrow focus on the short term is exacerbated by the tendency to link the pay of top management of mutual funds to performance. It doesn't matter why the stock goes up, whether its appreciation is a product of questionable accounting, massaging earnings to guarantee positive quarter-over-quarter results, or a product of externalizing costs, dumping toxic wastes into the public domain rather than paying the costs of treating them. It is only the bottom line, the appreciation of the portfolio, that counts.

Now suppose a fund manager has purchased a stock and a corporate raider surfaces, offering to purchase the company at a 30% premium to its current price. While the company may have outstanding long-term prospects, the compensation, and even the job, of the financial manager depends on short-term performance. He could enhance that performance by taking the 30% profit in hand and reinvesting the funds in another stock with similar long-term potential.

When it is so easy to improve one's short-term performance in hand, it is imprudent to bet one's job on long-term potential in the bush. Moreover, it has been argued that financial managers have a fiduciary responsibility to accept any offer substantially above the market. So it is no surprise that most fund managers sell out in such circumstances.

Some investment managers go further, attempting to recruit the interest of corporate raiders in companies in which they have invested. It is not that fund managers are particularly greedy. Many are salaried and do not share in profits they make for clients. But they have the same mindset that measures everything in terms of return on investment. Even the most secure and enlightened managers reinforce this mindset. CalPERS, the largest fund manager and one of the most socially conscious, in its *Domestic Proxy Voting Guidelines* and in meetings with corporate managements, pays lip service to social concerns but makes clear that it does not recognize corporate responsibility to any group other than shareholders.

It is this mindset that leads to corporate restructuring, the assumption of heavy debt, the reduction of R&D, the sale of divisions whose selling price exceeds a threshold multiple of cash flow, the termination of "redundant" employees, the adoption of golden parachutes for top management (which heightens any sense of unfairness).

More can be said. The highest-paid people in the country are the experts in corporate restructuring. These experts purchase public companies at a premium to the market with funds borrowed from broker-dealers or banks. They play the role of corporate surgeons (butchers?) and do everything possible to reduce overhead, buttress short-term profitability and cash flow, and pay down some of the debt to enhance the attractiveness of the repackaged company to investors. Once the restructuring has been completed, a new IPO (initial public offering) offers the eviscerated remains back to the public, proceeds going to pay down additional debt and reward those who structured the deal, to the tune of as much as hundreds of millions of dollars.

It is not coincidence that an MBA is worth far more than any other Masters (or Doctorate) degree, or that a short-term arbitrage mentality has diffused through the corporate psyche. Because investors "own" the company and because the jobs of the most important investors, the fund managers, depend on short-term results, the priorities of corporations increasingly reflect the priorities of their owners and the preeminence of the short term.

Aware of the potential danger to their own jobs, should their stock price decline to the point that their company becomes an acquisition target, corporate managers are sensitized to their stock price. Even in the absence of any immediate threat, they take steps to enhance short-term profitability. Because "lean and mean" sounds impressive and also encourages cutting expenses to spur immediate profitability, many upper level executives aspire to such a management style.

Despite the catchy slogan, making a company leaner and meaner doesn't necessarily make it more efficient. *The Wall Street Journal* (July 7, 1995), in a survey of large corporations that had downsized between 1989 and 1994, reported that only half of them had achieved an increase in operating profits and only one-third had experienced improved productivity (despite a general increase in both corporate profitability and productivity), but that 86% had suffered a decline in employee morale. They may have been leaner and they may have been meaner, but they were hardly more productive. For one thing, morale can affect productivity. In addition, revenues often decline in tandem with expenses.

Contrast this to the strategy of Continental Airlines. Facing the danger of their third bankruptcy in three decades, they did not follow the standard formula. They chose a pilot, not an accountant, to be CEO. Instead of reducing expenses by cutting employment, they instituted incentive pay, which raised compensation 25% over four years. Better employee morale reduced turnover 45%. On-the-job injuries and workers' compensation dropped more than 50%. Lost baggage claims and on-time service improved from near the worst in the industry to near the best. Having lost money for 10 consecutive years, the company became profitable.

Despite such evidence, announcements of layoffs are greeted with enthusiasm by the market, which quickly calculates the expected increase in profitability that should follow from reduced employee compensation. The popularity of these easy, but often ineffective, restructuring measures with corporate management stems from the widely accepted view that the market is always right. Top management's owning stock options and being rewarded by higher prices also encourages playing to the market. The perception of the market, whether or not it is accurate, drives many business decisions of corporate America.

The exaggerated significance of short-term market perception contributes to the proclivity of our corporations to select financial engineers as top managers. Companies founded by real engineers, inventors, entrepreneurs have seen control pass to a different breed. Two thirds of America's CEOs are lawyers, accountants, or advertising executives.

By contrast, two thirds of Japan's CEOs are scientists or engineers. Japanese companies are often willing to sustain losses for years to enter new sectors or gain long-term advantages in their present markets. Toyota introduced robotics into its automobile assembly plants long before such an introduction could be justified in terms of return on investment. Nissan announced that it did not expect to make a profit for five years on its *Infiniti*. It would be difficult for such a company to survive intact in this country, to resist pressure to maximize short-term profits. It would be an inviting target for corporate raiders seeking to sell the unprofitable parts of the business and milk the profit centers.

This is not to deny the propriety — in select cases — of corporate raiding and restructuring. In the 1980s Hanson Industries compiled an impressive track record by targeting companies that were undervalued because they were poorly managed. Hanson engineered unfriendly takeovers, buying these companies at a premium to the market. It then sold parts of these companies for as much as or more than it paid for the entire company — and made record profits with what was left. Such situations, however, are rare. Most takeover targets had not been badly managed, but had generated returns on equity above the corporate average before being acquired. On average, they did not perform as well under their post-acquisition management.

Were the Hansen experience common, that would question the competence of American top management, which is very highly compensated. The average American CEO makes more than 400 times the compensation of the average worker, up more than ten-fold since the early 1980s. By contrast, in Japan and Europe top management typically makes from 10 to 25 times the compensation of the average worker. We justify our generosity in compensating top management on the free market grounds that such incentive produces the highest quality management.

Again, the free market paradigm is misleading. We have talked ourselves into the dubious view that without limits, the higher the compensation, the greater the incentive, the better the quality. To the contrary, there is little to suggest that American managers, whose rewards are attached to the job title, rather than performance, are more capable than their European or Asian counterparts.

An article in *The Wall Street Journal* (March 17, 1995) reported that the CEO of Eastman Kodak received $1.7 million in bonuses, despite Kodak's profits falling short of their target. Remarkably, such treatment, lavish reward — incomprehensible to mortal sensibilities — for disappointing performance is not exceptional but has become commonplace.

In the final installment of a series of articles looking at the downsizing of U.S. corporations, *The New York Times* (March 9, 1996) wrote:

> Often cited is Robert E. Allen, chief executive officer of AT&T. Since 1986, AT&T has cut its work force by 125,000 people, but Mr. Allen's salary and bonus have increased fourfold, to $3.3 million. His salary and bonus was trimmed by $200,000 last year, but he was also awarded options worth $9.7 million.... AT&T's board says Mr. Allen is the best man to lead AT&T in the new era of deregulated telecommunication. But his critics point out that he also headed AT&T in 1990, when it bought the big computer company NCR for $7.5 billion. The NCR acquisition, AT&T eventually conceded, was all but a complete failure.

This generosity was not an aberration. In 2000 the shares of AT&T fell 70%, largely due to its mis-investment in cable. The company built up AT&T Broadband by spending $100 billion, much of it to acquire MediaOne Group and Tele-Communications Inc. But AT&T was unable to generate satisfactory returns and is now looking to sell AT&T Broadband. It may lose tens of billions of dollars. Whether its failure was with strategy or implementation, responsibility rests with the chairman of the board. Yet in 2000 his compensation was increased sharply, to $27 million.

AT&T's spin-off, Lucent Technologies, fared even worse. It made the disastrous mistake of granting credit to marginal companies so they could purchase Lucent products. In the short term, this made Lucent look good, bolstering revenues and profits. But when the marginal companies defaulted,

Lucent was left with staggering losses. The company cut 70% of its employees. It even had to sell its Hamilton Farm Golf Club, on which it had spent $45 million to provide a private golf course for its top officers. Its share value declined 99%. For his work in engineering this disaster, its CEO received a severance package of $12.5 million plus an annual pension of $870,000.

Even this is small potatoes compared with Qwest. "Qwest CEO Joe Nacchio took BellSouth to task for reportedly selling its Qwest stock. Nacchio warned BellSouth that if it continues to dump, he'll move into BellSouth's region with telecommunications services. Isn't this a little like Gary Condit chiding Bill Clinton for fondling the interns? Didn't Joe bag close to $100 million last year for dumping his Qwest shares? And isn't he scoring a similarly decadent sum this year, despite the plummeting value of Qwest?" (Al Lewis, *Denver Post*, August 12, 2001.) Qwest stock lost 60% of its value in the 18 months prior to this article (and an additional 90% since).

Then there is Liberty Digital. In the first half of 2001 the company lost $89 million. Its stock declined 95%, yet it rewarded its CEO with $140 million in stock and cash. And even this pales in comparison with the $1 billion in stock options Computer Associates had attempted to provide to its top three executives. While the bonus recently given to the CEO of Raytheon was a miserly $900,000, it came after a quarter in which the company lost $181 million and a year in which its stock price plummeted more than 70%. One could go on and on.

These examples illustrate the irrelevance of the performance of our top executives to their compensation. They are supported by surveys showing that most large corporations do not recognize, or even try to assess, differences between excellence and mediocrity in their top-level managers. This makes it is clear that the astronomic compensation offered to American CEOs is not a function of objective measures of their actual performance.

It is not even a function of their track record. A front page *Wall Street Journal* article (March 31, 1995) entitled "Failure Doesn't Always Damage the Careers of Top Executives," focused on individuals who became CEOs of major corporations despite previous failures in that, or a similar, position. A more biting article in *Financial World* (March 28, 1995) began, "Are you indecisive, stubborn? Do you have lots of friends in high places to shield you from your blunders? Then you could be the next CEO of ..."

We claim to pay CEOs so much more than our trading partners do because this pay scale attracts the best talent. But our rewarding top management independent of objective measures of their previous track record or their present performance belies this claim.

Given that extraordinary benefits are attached to the position of CEO, rather than to performance in that position, and given the overly collegial means of choosing and rewarding CEOs, there is little wonder that American corporations have failed to blow away the competition. It may be valuable to reflect how such a critical aspect of industry has evaded the discipline of the free market. It epitomizes a slogan coined by John Kenneth Galbraith: "Socialism for the rich; free enterprise for the poor."

Trade

Trade issues present an important, if controversial, interface between economics and politics. While economists agree that trade is beneficial, increasing the quantity and variety of goods available, the devil is in the details. How much trade is ideal? Here, too, *laissez faire* gets it wrong.

At the extreme of zero trade, everyone would produce everything he consumes. But it makes little sense for Alaskans to grow citrus fruits and coffee when they could buy such products in exchange for their oil, fish and minerals. No serious economists have recommended autarky.

At the other extreme, *laissez faire* recommends that the division of labor be extended to countries: each country should restrict its output to only those items it produces with the greatest relative efficiency and should trade for everything else. Economists argue: (i) because of economies of scale, each country's specializing in a narrow range of products and trading those for other products will provide the greatest quantity of goods, and/or (ii) one can maximize total production if each country will concentrate on those products it can produce with the greatest *relative* efficiency.

These arguments sound impressive — until you consider the real world. On one hand, modern technology has done much to reduce economies of scale, and the business community is reveling in its discovery of the value of smaller size and greater flexibility. On the other, it is doubtful that there are substantial inherent long-term differences in relative efficiencies.

Nor do actual patterns of trade fit this picture of specialization. Most trade takes place among developed countries, and between any two countries much occurs in items they both produce. Electric machinery and parts, vehicles, and office and data processing machines are three of our four largest categories of merchandise exports. They are also three of our four largest categories of merchandise imports.

More important, arguments for specialization, flawed as they may be, appear best against a static and sheltered background. These arguments are even less attractive in a dynamic environment, one in which industries come into existence, thrive, mature, and are made obsolete and replaced by newer technologies or tastes.

For one thing, specialization increases risk, and not just from technological obsolescence. As developing countries have discovered, painfully, specializing in any single agricultural commodity subjects one's economy to enormous and unpredictable boom-bust cycles. A more diversified economic base makes a country less susceptible to such shocks. In addition, there is often synergy among different industries. Advances in robotics have improved productivity in the auto industry. Complementing this, the auto industry has stimulated and funded advances in robotics. The relegation of industries to different countries on the basis of initial efficiency would abort cross-fertilization.

Problems with free trade would not surprise a historian. Free trade has never been universally beneficial, but has always had its winners and losers. Certain products have been profitable while others have been marginal. In Ricardo's day, England sold finished textiles and industrial goods to Portugal in return for low-margined wine. This was clearly good for England, but hardly of mutual benefit.

This explains the popularity of mercantilism. For centuries, powerful countries struggled to dominate the most profitable sectors. They even fought wars to establish and maintain their dominance. If free trade were good for everyone, it would not have been necessary to fight. The mercantilists were not stupid. This also explains why it was Ricardo, the Englishman, rather than a Portuguese, who extolled the benefit of free trade.

The one-sidedness of free trade was well appreciated by William Pitt the Younger in his remarks to Parliament about the Eden Treaty. This treaty, signed by England and France in 1786, reduced tariffs and other obstacles to trade. It was a major step in the direction of free trade between the two countries. After its signing, Pitt proclaimed the treaty was "...true revenge for the peace treaty of Versailles" that had been signed three years earlier to end the American Revolutionary War. (The French renounced the Eden Treaty in 1793.)

It is not just that free trade has historically benefited strong countries at the expense of weaker ones. Even now, free trade increases economic disparity.

It prevents less advanced countries from developing high-margined modern industry. Without protection, domestic industries that need to progress along the learning curve cannot survive competition with foreign imports.

Independently, free trade encourages corporations to reduce expenses by locating facilities in low-wage, low-tax, low-regulation countries. This redistributes income upwards from the working middle class to the rich large shareholders. In our present economic environment, characterized by excessive disparity between the rich and the rest, this may be the most dangerous aspect of free trade.

FREE TRADE VS. MERCANTILISM

A *laissez faire* system would be hard pressed to compete with an economy run according to mercantilist principles. By holding selling prices at a point such that other countries could not justify capital investment in a sector, a predatory country could eventually dominate that sector. Our strict adherence to the free market and the constraints imposed by short-term profitability have contributed to the erosion of our technological leadership and market share in industries targeted by our competitors. Many examples fit a common pattern, sketched in Adam Smith's *The Roaring 80s*:

> Japan has a network of networks. There is not only MITI, there is the Industrial Structure Council, the Telecommunications Council, and similar councils, all of which study key industries. The councils have leaders not just from business and government but from consumer groups, labor unions, the press, and universities.... The result is to socialize the risk, to take it from the individual firm and spread it, which makes it easier to have long-term goals. The long-term goal can be to have a dominant position in an industry. One example cited frequently is supercomputers.
>
> The American side of the story is a familiar one, the genius inventor and the better mousetrap. In this case the genius inventor is Seymour Cray, who left Control Data to start his own firm in the 1970s. No one else could come close to the Cray machines for speed and price, and with no Japanese supercomputers on the market, Cray sold two machines to the Japanese. But in 1981, MITI announced a program to develop a supercomputer. Cray's prospective customers in Japan seemed to disappear instantly....Two years later the Japanese had their supercomputers ready and the makers of supercomputers began an export drive by cutting prices dramatically. (p. 140-1.)

Free market economists would argue that this is perfectly acceptable. If competing countries wish to subsidize their exports to us, that is to our benefit. The more they subsidize their exports, the less we have to pay for our imports. That is good for us, not for them.

Such a response misses the point. Predatory pricing is hardly the result of a charitable desire to subsidize consumers. Rather, its aim is to price competitors out of the market, at which point the survivor can exact monopolistic prices. Monopolistic profits will outweigh the losses suffered during predatory pricing. Ultimately the consumer will pay more.

The standard reply has been that any attempt to raise prices to excessive levels would create a price umbrella, allowing new competition to enter the market. But this, too, misses the point, for it assumes an ease of entry that fails to reflect reality. CEOs of semiconductor producers have estimated it would cost at least $1 billion for a new company to enter the semiconductor industry.

Even that may understate the cost of entry into a technology intensive sector. For technology is a moving target, and by the time one has paid the entry price to develop staff, supply networks, production facilities, and marketing, the state of the art may have advanced. If one is not already at the cutting edge of technology, it is difficult to discern the direction of its movement. This increases the risk of focusing one's investment in the wrong area, targeting yesterday's most profitable sectors rather than tomorrow's.

In short, a significant technological lead — and most targeted industries are technology intensive — may be insurmountable. So even if we were to acquiesce to the assumption that free trade is the best possible system — provided everyone would adhere to it — a *laissez faire* country may be at a disadvantage if others adopt predatory policies. And others might well adopt such policies. Even if mercantilism were to lower global output, enlightened self-interest might drive a country to seek a larger share at the expense of others. Alternatively, in a world of uncertain political and economic alliances, a country may decide to retain production capability in vital sectors, even if that requires violating free market precepts.

WHY WE FALL FOR LAISSEZ FAIRE

MYTHOLOGY OF EARLY *LAISSEZ FAIRE*

If *laissez faire* has performed so poorly and constitutes such a threat, why are we so enthralled by it? For we have not always been captivated by this philosophy. It was not that long ago, during Franklin Roosevelt's presidency, that we abandoned *laissez faire* in favor of Keynesian interventionism. We did this not because of ideology but because *laissez faire* had failed so miserably.

According to free market orthodoxy, Roosevelt's abandonment of the ultimate economic truth had to be a mistake. Yet this period, characterized by aggressive government intervention, was marked by an economic resurgence. Also contrary to free market orthodoxy, as we have moved back toward a purer free market, our economic growth and productivity growth have slowed.

Why did we return so eagerly to a philosophy we had rejected because it had failed? Why have we persisted with it despite its failure?

One reason for our revival of *laissez faire* stems from our confrontation with global communism and our attempt to prove, to ourselves as well as others, the superiority of our economic system. The success of our struggle, the spontaneous collapse of the U.S.S.R., was widely advertised as proof of the invincibility of the free market.

Given the invincibility of *laissez faire* and also the perception that it has been the economic system of Western countries since the Industrial Revolution, it was but a short step to argue that free market policies have been the ultimate source of our progress of the past two centuries. (This makes for good mythology, but it is not borne out by the facts.)

Independently, the superiority claimed for *laissez faire* dovetails with personal interests. The taxes collected by government hit close to home. We can easily figure out how much more disposable income we would have if we didn't have to pay taxes. By contrast, the benefits provided by government are often indirect and we cannot measure how much they affect us. It is too easy to argue that we are net losers, we don't get fair share for our taxes, and we would be better off without government.

Professional economists have their own incentive to support *laissez faire*. Most work for large financial corporations. These corporations employ economists to increase their profitability. A *laissez faire* environment, free of government regulation, is conducive to maximizing profits. So it is to be expected that most economists should argue for *laissez faire*.

Finally, the mathematics of pure free markets is simpler than the mathematics of complex systems of constraints. Reflecting this, academicians tend to pursue models based on pure *laissez faire*. Economics departments at top universities have become pulpits for preachers of *laissez faire* and breeders of free market disciples.

There is a stale joke about the University of Chicago, one of the best-known disseminators of free market orthodoxy.

Q: How many University of Chicago economists does it take to change a light bulb?

A: None. They all sit in the dark and wait for an invisible hand to change it.

Whether or not this provides a fair caricature of the Chicago School, it is only reasonable to consider a rejoinder by the *laissez faire* economist: "It may be frustrating to sit in the dark. But if you talk to people who have tried to change the bulb, there is a consistent pattern. They have caused a short circuit and then called the electrician. Not only has he charged an arm and a leg, but in the process of fixing the short circuit he has broken the main water line. The plumber, in fixing the water line, has left huge holes in the walls. The mason, in repairing the walls, has shorted the electrical system. Sitting in the dark may be inconvenient, but trying to fix things only makes them worse. Waiting for the invisible hand of the free market to fix economic problems may be frustrating, but government interference is worse."

Such a response has become an article of faith for many who have forgotten the Great Depression and the utter impotence of free market policies to stimulate growth or employment. By the time Franklin D. Roosevelt took office, real GNP had declined 30%. Industrial production had fallen more than 50%. Iron and steel output had dropped nearly 80%. Investment had plummeted 95%. Measured unemployment had risen past 20%. And there was no sign of imminent stabilization, much less improvement.

Our faith in the beneficence of the pure free market has not been examined, nor would it stand up to scrutiny. Rather, it has gained popularity as government has grown, as the arrogance, unresponsiveness and sheer stupidity of government agencies have spawned frustration and bitterness, and as shrewd politicians have exploited this alienation. As a result of often justified emotions, many long to return to the days when government was smaller and private enterprise was able to be both private and enterprising. Since the 1980s America has been gripped by nostalgia for small government and "true" free market economics.

There may be reason to address this nostalgia in historic, as well as economic, terms. Especially in periods of change and uncertainty it is common for individuals to romanticize and long to return to the good old days — no matter how bad they were.

There are still those who yearn for the days of mediaeval chivalry, for the rustic simplicity and closeness to nature of peasant farmers. No wonder many in today's society want to see a return to the good old days of unconstrained capitalism, with government off the backs of entrepreneurs so free enterprise can "do its thing."

The problem with this longing for the past is that it has always been selective to the point of blindness. Mediaeval chivalry may have been tolerable for the extreme upper crust. The rest were reduced to lives of animals, lives blighted by chronic malnutrition and punctured by disasters, both natural (recurrent famine, the Black Death and a host of epidemics) and man-made (large and small wars, banditry and civil unrest).

> Any national calculation shows a sad story. France, by any standards a privileged country, is reckoned to have experienced 10 *general* famines during the tenth century; 26 in the eleventh, 2 in the twelfth, 4 in the fourteenth, 7 in the fifteenth, 13 in the sixteenth, 11 in the seventeenth and 16 in the eighteenth. While one cannot guarantee the accuracy of this eighteenth-century calculation, the only risk it runs is of over-optimism, because it omits the hundreds and hundreds of *local* famines...

71

The peasants lived in a state of dependence on merchants, towns and nobles, and had scarcely any reserves of their own. They had no solution in case of famine except to turn to the town where they crowded together, begging in the streets and often dying in public squares, as in Venice and Amiens in the sixteenth century." (Fernand Braudel, *The Structures of Everyday Life*, p. 74-5.)

Ignoring history, we romanticize this period just as we idealize the life of the cowboy, not realistically portrayed in Hollywood movies.

With respect to our vision of the good old days, when free market enterprise was able to "do its thing," it is necessary to retain a critical faculty and avoid romanticizing, lest we be seduced by popular mythology. For one thing, there were no such days. In our enterprising colonial days government had the power to fund public projects, regulate prices and wages, set standards, and grant monopolies. Nor did the American Revolution diminish government power. It was New York State, not private industry, that underwrote the Erie Canal. It was Alexander Hamilton who enunciated our first industrial policy. Jefferson, too, supported the public construction of roads and canals and government subdivision of new lands for small tenant farmers.

Even the good old days of the Industrial Revolution fall short of the imaginations of free marketers seeking our lost paradise. For one thing, the picture of capitalism driven by small entrepreneurs and inventors vigorously competing against each other on a flat playing field is badly distorted. It is more fiction than exaggeration. "[E]ighteenth-century manufacturers only launched their large-scale enterprises with subsidies, interest-free loans, and previously guaranteed monopolies. They were not really entrepreneurs at all..." (Braudel, *The Wheels of Commerce*, p. 193)

In addition, the golden age of capitalism was hardly a boon to most people. The Industrial Revolution achieved a dramatic acceleration of measurable economic growth, and the political system, having disenfranchised the lower and middle classes, posed little threat to the autonomy — and tyranny — of the free market. Despite such an ideal *laissez faire* environment, historians note the terrible poverty as well as the environmental degradation. Great novelists of that era, Dickens and Zola, took pains to depict the squalor and the breadth and depth of suffering.

Of course, there were some who saw only good in the new economic paradigm, but their views seem more suffused with the radiant glow of fantasy than connected to the often grim details of reality. Take, for example,

...Dr. Ure, who immortalized himself by an account of the "lively elves" who found so much sport in being useful in factories, those "magnificent edifices" that were so much more ingenious and profitable than the boasted monuments of ancient despotism. The elves had to keep lively, since they were commonly beaten when they slowed up because of fatigue. They worked harder in mines, though nobody could pretend that these were magnificent establishments; here boys and girls were chained and harnessed to coal trucks like horses, except that they were not indulged with horse collars. On their day of rest they might build up their character in Sunday schools by contributing a penny a week toward their funerals, arranged by burial clubs." (Muller, *Freedom in the Modern World*, p. 54.)

Until the mid-nineteenth century and government action to restrain the unbridled free market, most were no better off than they had been 400 years earlier. The claim: "The affluence of the rich supposes the indigence of the many," is due not to Karl Marx, but to Adam Smith (*The Theory of Moral Sentiments*).

It was the extent and depth of the misery generated by unbridled *laissez faire* that inspired the more radical social and economic proposals of the nineteenth century. This is sketched in Sir Karl Popper's critical discussion of Marx:

...his views on liberalism and democracy, more particularly, which he considered to be nothing but veils for the dictatorship of the bourgeoisie, furnished an interpretation of his time which appeared to fit only too well, corroborated as it was by sad experience... this shameless exploitation was cynically defended by hypocritical apologists who appealed to the principle of human freedom, to the right of man to determine his own fate, and to enter freely into any contract he considers favorable to his interests.

Using the slogan "equal and free competition for all", the unrestrained capitalism of this period resisted successfully all labour legislation until the year 1833, and its practical execution for many years more. The consequence was a life of desolation and misery which can hardly be imagined in our day. Especially the exploitation of women and children led to incredible suffering... Such were the conditions of the working class even in 1863, when Marx was writing *Capital*; his burning protest against these crimes, which were then tolerated, and sometimes even defended, not only by professional economists but also by churchmen... (*The Open Society and Its Enemies*, vol. 2, p. 121-2.)

Considering this picture of the free market doing its own thing, unconstrained by government interference, is this really the environment to which we long to return?

It is not that the Industrial Revolution was an unmitigated disaster. It did not invent grinding poverty, child labor, or environmental degradation, scourges that had been known for centuries. At the very least, it — and related revolutions in agriculture and science — provided the foundation for a dramatic improvement in material well-being that has benefited much of the world. It may have been necessary for this improvement. But the notion that *laissez faire* was the uniquely beneficial source of this improvement is fantasy.

We forget that the present economic status of the vast majority was attained only with the help of government interference specifically designed to restrain free enterprise. Legislation limiting or ending child labor, enforcing minimum standards in the workplace, and setting up a primitive social safety net ameliorated the worst excesses of the industrial revolution. Programs geared to broad sectors of society enabled the development of a middle class and benefited even the rich. While the most visible of these were public education, public health, and social security, other programs, vigorously opposed by free market forces, are now taken for granted as the most basic services.

> It was the gradual creation of an effective bureaucracy which brought an end to all this filth and disease, and the public servants did so against the desires of the mass of the middle and upper classes. The free market opposed sanitation. The rich opposed it. The civilized opposed it. Most of the educated opposed it. That is why it took a century to finish what could have been done in ten years. Put in contemporary terms, the market economy angrily and persistently opposed clean public water, sanitation, garbage collection and improved public health because they appeared to be unprofitable enterprises which, in addition, put limits on the individual's freedom. These are simple historic truths which have been forgotten today... (Saul, *Voltaire's Bastards*, p. 239.)

Our mythology that our economic progress of the past two centuries is due to *laissez faire* is just that — mythology. From the beginning, government tilted the playing field in favor of a chosen few. Decent standards of living associated with today's industrial societies were achieved only as a result of government interference with the free market. Until that interference, most were no better off than they had been in the fifteenth century. Yet the mythology remains intact — to the extent that we fail to recognize it as mythology.

How has this mythology survived?

At first sight, the spectacular collapse of the centrally planned economy of the U.S.S.R. appeared to decisively validate *laissez faire*. Marxist economic theory occupied the opposite end of the interference spectrum, micro-management of the economy by the central government. Marx had argued that *laissez faire* capitalism is inherently unstable and must eventually generate conditions that insure its collapse. So there was delicious irony for the free market economist in the implosion of the primary Marxist system under the weight of its own egregious economic mismanagement.

Conveniently, this apparent validation of *laissez faire* justified our self-interest. It dovetailed with two concerns, pointing in different directions. One was to maintain our dominance. The other was to encourage the rapid economic growth of our allies to serve as a bulwark against the spread of communism.

The former interest was best served by a flat playing field on which the consistent winner should be the player with the best technology and the greatest economic strength. Our trading partners would have a chance only if their governments tilted the playing field: imposing tariffs, controlling the export of capital, subsidizing fledgling manufacturers.

Such conflicting interest between dominant and secondary economic powers is not new. For centuries the dominant economic and financial power would advocate a level playing field while developing countries would impose tariffs to protect their start-up industries. "Except perhaps for Holland any European state would serve as an example, including England, where industry originally developed behind a wall of highly protective tariffs." (Braudel, *The Wheels of Commerce*, p. 332.)

We now preach *laissez faire* and flat playing fields and complain that the Japanese ignore our wisdom. Yet throughout the 1800s we ourselves adopted protectionist policies, initially to enable our domestic industries to grow without being crushed by the superior technology and financial resources of the British.

Our relationship to Britain in the nineteenth century resembled Japan's relationship to us at the end of World War II. In the 1800s, the British enjoyed an economic and technological hegemony similar to our own at the end of the Second World War. They were the ones who had everything to gain from government non-interference. It was they who preached the virtues of a flat playing field, just as we do today. We ignored them, sheltering our domestic manufacturers from British competition. We became enamored of free trade only after we achieved economic dominance.

In the seventeenth and early eighteenth centuries the Dutch were the dominant commercial power. They were the ones who had everything to gain from government non-interference. It was they who advocated a flat economic playing field. In the 1690s it was the English who ignored them, imposing heavy duties on Dutch textiles. The English became enamored of free trade only after they achieved economic dominance.

Just as the English rejected the *laissez faire* wisdom of the Dutch in the late seventeenth century and just as we rejected the same *laissez faire* wisdom of the English in the nineteenth century, it is not surprising that our trading partners should reject our identical wisdom. Nor have we been fazed by such rejection.

Our muted reaction to the protectionist policies of our allies was motivated by our latter interest, the desire to protect them — and ultimately ourselves — from the spread of communism. It was to our advantage to have our allies develop sound and growing economies, even if it was partly at our expense. Increasing prosperity would enable them to resist the lure of communism.

This self-interest encouraged us to act as though our international economic policy were a passive extension of the Marshall Plan. We turned a blind eye to the protectionist policies and government subsidies of our trading partners and a deaf ear to the complaints of our own industries that suffered as a result.

It is not that our policies were necessarily misguided. Rather, we deceived ourselves by failing to understand our own motivation. We ignored historical precedents and pretended that *laissez faire* is the only realistic alternative to communism. We assumed that our trading partners, left to their own devices, would eventually see the light and level the playing field. We elevated the claim that there are no realistic alternatives to *laissez faire* to the status of dogma.

Reality differs markedly from this dogma. There are other economic paradigms. Keynes produced a real alternative to classical economics, not just minor adjustments. He argued that the propensity to save increases as income rises. Because not all savings are reinvested, the economy can become starved for cash. This leads to a decline in demand that feeds on itself.

As industries cut production and lay off workers in response to slower sales, those workers, and others who feel threatened, curtail spending. Demand decreases further and companies, faced with growing inventories, cut production again and lay off more workers. Those workers now reduce their spending. The economy spirals downward.

Keynes argued if the economy is performing poorly it is up to government, through monetary and fiscal stimulus, to increase total demand. His recommendations appeared to be validated by our economic performance from The New Deal until the inflationary 1970s.

A very different departure from *laissez faire* was suggested by nineteenth century Austrian economist Friedrich List. Influenced by Hegel, he regarded the state as the supreme entity and one that by its very nature must be engaged in Darwinian competition with other states.

List was unimpressed with the *laissez faire* goal of maximizing total consumption. Rather, he argued, the economic strength of a country — what it can produce — must be its most important consideration. Given the overriding importance of strategic production, it would be imprudent to relinquish economic independence, even if one had to support industries that are uneconomic. Economic independence, and even dominance, could be best secured by protectionism plus heavy government investment in infrastructure and education.

Even though they have received little attention from our economists, List's views are taken seriously by our trading partners, especially those of South and East Asia. Historians, too, have been struck by their propriety. "The world was the City of London's oyster, which was all very well in peacetime, but what would be the situation if it ever came to another Great Power war?... In such circumstances, ironically, the advanced British economy might be more severely hurt than a state which was less 'mature' but also less dependent on international trade and finance." (Kennedy, *The Rise and Decline of the Great Powers*, p. 157-8.)

List would have understood Kennedy's remarks. He faulted elevating consumption and short-term profitability above other considerations because it sacrifices long-term health and security. Even today, *laissez faire* has no regard for security. Consider our privatization of U.S. Enrichment Corporation (USEC), the agency responsible for enriching the U-235 content of uranium from 0.7% in natural uranium to 4% in nuclear reactor fuel — or 95% in nuclear weapons. As a public corporation, USEC's primary mandate is to maximize profits. Suppose a terrorist organization were to offer to pay USEC a premium for weapons-grade uranium. Would a refusal by USEC be a violation of its primary mandate and its fiduciary duty to shareholders?

This question is not far fetched.

There is a serious risk of fissionable material leaking out from Russia to rogue states or terrorist groups. With fraying central control in Russia, the more of this lethal material that remains there, the higher the chance of leakage. USEC was made the sole agent for the uranium deal and given the exclusive right to import the material from Russia. The reason this unusual monopoly power was granted was that this government-owned firm, acting in the interests of national security, would ensure the most rapid import of the material. Instead, it has systematically dragged its feet, especially as it prepared for privatization. It was not in USEC's financial interest to import the Russian uranium as quickly as possible, because buying Russian fuel is more expensive than producing it in the U.S.

I learned, in the summer of 1996, that my concerns were well-founded. Russia had offered to increase its pace of delivery by 50%, only to be turned down by USEC. Instead, the organization paid Moscow a large sum not to make the additional deliveries. It also insisted the Russians keep the agreement secret — even from those of us on the decision-making committee in the White House..." (J. Stiglitz, *The Wall Street Journal*, June 2, 1996.)

The reason for this behavior is that enriching natural uranium is more profitable than de-enriching weapons-grade uranium. From the perspective of *laissez faire*, USEC's actions were appropriate. It would have been economically irrational for them to do otherwise. Yet it takes dangerously naïve faith to believe that such action, which may contribute to nuclear proliferation, is good for our country, much less the world.

THE VIRTUAL REALITY OF CLASSICAL ECONOMICS

ECONOMICS: THEORY VS. REALITY

The history of Western philosophy can be read as brilliant individuals, starting from premises that are plausible and arguing meticulously to conclusions that are preposterous: motion is impossible; absolute beauty is real but my desk is not; the most perfect being imaginable must exist; the indubitable fact that I think guarantees both the existence of God and the veracity of my perceptions; it is impossible to have empirical knowledge; it is not even possible to have evidence; nothing can exist unless it is perceived; all truth is ultimately subjective; it is logically impossible to dream.

It is easy, if not entirely fair, to poke fun at philosophy. Yet this shows how readily we can be misled by plausible assumptions and cogent argument. Where the conclusions are absurd, it is easy to realize something must have gone wrong and return to consider the assumptions and argument more carefully. This is part of the value of philosophy. But where the conclusions are politically correct, critical analysis is more difficult and we can end up embracing ridiculous views. Where the conclusions have practical consequences, there is risk of traumatic effect.

Economic thought often fits this pattern. For example, it is reasonable that labor and leisure are mutual tradeoffs. The higher the price of labor, the greater is the incentive to work rather than to enjoy leisure. And the ensuing argument, including the observation that it is always possible to offer to work for so little that one will be hired, is cogent, if not entirely convincing. But the conclusion

79

that *all* unemployment is voluntary, accepted by some economists, turns on an extraordinary extension of the normal meaning of "voluntary" and is as ludicrous as any conclusion reached by philosophers. Its implication that unemployment insurance is unnecessary, if taken seriously, risks trauma.

Economists commonly pay more attention to the structure of an economic argument than to the accuracy, or even common sense, of its conclusion. You need assumptions with certain features to take advantage of the mathematical tools of modern economics, so you tailor your assumptions to the mathematics.

The problem lies with the distance between those assumptions and reality. You would think that classical economists look under streetlights to find their keys, no matter where they drop them — for you need light, to find your keys. So you tailor your field of vision to take advantage of the light just as you tailor your assumptions to take advantage of the mathematics. Not surprisingly, there are many examples of failing to find the keys under the streetlight.

Too often, economists are so taken in by the beauty of their theoretical models that they pay insufficient attention to reality. In the spirit of diligently searching the ground under the streetlight, sophisticated models with superficially plausible assumptions may appear attractive. But it can be foolhardy to take them too seriously. The management team of Long Term Capital Management included two Nobel laureates, famous for their pioneering work in the pricing of options and derivative instruments. Still, that hedge fund lost so much money that its bailout had to be orchestrated by the Federal Reserve with the help of 14 banks and investment firms. Could there have been discrepancies between the theoretical models and the real world?

This is not an isolated example. Where economists' models conflict with historical experience, they ignore history. How different is this self-assured confidence in the efficacy of mathematical models from the caution of Alfred Marshall, the founder of mathematical economics. "I go more and more on the rules 1) Use mathematics as a shorthand language rather than as an engine of inquiry. 2) Keep to them until you have done. 3) Translate into English. 4) Then illustrate by examples that are important in real life. 5) Burn the mathematics. 6) If you can't succeed in 4, burn 3. This last I do often" (quoted in Ormerod, *Butterfly Economics*, p. 60).

The methodological poverty of modern economic modeling stems from the ability of computer models to prove virtually anything. It is often possible to work backwards from the desired results to obtain the computer models that will generate them. So there is minimal significance in the fact that there is a computer model that generates a particular set of results. Benjamin Disraeli, living today, might have remarked: "There are three kinds of lies: lies, damn lies, and computer models."

Contemporary economists, mesmerized by their theoretical models, argue for flat taxes. They do so despite the fact that in the past, lowering tax rates on the highest incomes has had negative economic consequences. In the same spirit they flaunt computer models that demonstrate the benefit of free trade to all parties, even though these models contradict common experience. These models "prove" that tariffs cause inflation and stunt economic growth. While this follows from reasonable assumptions and may be true in some virtual world, it has not been true in our history. Our low inflation industrial boom of the nineteenth century began with protectionist legislation that decimated foreign trade. Throughout the century we protected domestic industry with high tariffs. Similarly, Japanese protectionism did not cause inflation (lower than ours) or stunt their economic growth (higher than ours).

Economists systematically ignore data that fail to fit their preconceptions, especially when the data are politically incorrect. Presently it is politically correct to maintain that government regulation destroys the incentive to be efficient. Inversely, deregulation increases competition. Increased competition, in turn, must increase the incentive to innovate and provide better service at lower costs. So efficiency and service must improve and costs must fall when industries are deregulated.

The theory sounds so very impressive. But consider two of the largest industries deregulated in the past 30 years, airlines and long-distance telephone service. Airlines appeared an ideal industry to deregulate. The business is not a natural monopoly and the ease of entry is above average, insuring vigorous competition. Yet "The Bureau of Labor Statistics calculates that inflation-adjusted average fares were basically flat between 1967 and 1979 — despite sharply rising fuel prices — but rose some 50 percent in the subsequent decade." (Kuttner, *Everything for Sale*, p. 259) While fares went up under deregulation, quality of service, from legroom to food to percentage of direct flights, declined. In telecommunications long-distance rates did continue to decline after deregulation, but at a slower rate than prior to deregulation. The practical results of deregulation fell far short of the theory.

Economists' models defending free trade have fared no better. The greater the ratio of our trade to our GNP, the higher has been our unemployment. But these facts do not fit the accepted orthodoxy and the political correctness of free trade, so economists pay them no attention. It is worse. Economists' glorification of jobs created by exports is specious. It disregards the obvious fact that we lose many more jobs to imports than we create by exports. The persistent deficit in our balance of trade is an economic drag, slowing economic growth and increasing unemployment. At a time that our trade deficit was half its current level, Stone and Sandhill (*Labor Market Implications of the Growing Internationalization of the U.S. Economy*), and Duchin and Lange (*Trading Away Jobs: The Effect of the U.S. Merchandise Trade Deficit on Employment*), estimated the number of net jobs lost because of trade at between 1 and 5 million. When domestic unemployment is a serious problem, this is hardly a benefit.

(Those who blame the Smoot-Hawley Act of 1929 for restricting trade and thereby causing the Great Depression forget that the $600 million decline in our net exports accounted for only 1% of our $50 billion decline in nominal GNP, that the previous Fordney-McCumber Act [1922] increased tariffs as much as Smoot-Hawley with no negative economic effect, and that Smoot-Hawley was passed only after the stock market had begun its precipitous decline. They also forget that a change in the balance of trade for one country generates an equal and opposite change in the balance of trade for its trading partners. But our trading partners went through depressions just like ours.)

Economists "prove" if there is equal access to technology, then free trade will ultimately equalize wages of the trading partners. This has been an important component of arguments for free trade. But it leaves out critical considerations. Not only is its conclusion implausible, but we are all familiar with data that contradict it.

Our own history shows the invalidity of this free trade argument. Within the U.S. we have had free trade, equal access to technology, and more. For centuries we have had similar language and customs as well as freedom of movement from any state to any other. In spite of this, the average resident of the richest states still earns nearly twice as much as the average resident of the poorest states. For centuries the per capita income in Paris has been twice that in Brittany, despite free trade and equal access to technology.

Even if richer countries allow unrestricted access to technology, only they can provide the capital investment necessary to its profitable application. Only they can afford to build infrastructures necessary for the creation of additional wealth. So even if there is equal access to technology, free trade benefits only the rich countries. This explains why it is the rich countries that have advocated, and even insisted on, free trade, but it does not equalize wages.

You would think, and hope, that this history would make classical economists reflect on their assumptions. But in the face of a formidable array of practical counterexamples to theoretical claims supporting free trade, *laissez faire* economists have maintained faith in their theoretical models. They have argued passionately on behalf of NAFTA. They have cavalierly dismissed the worry that free trade could pose any threat to domestic labor. (Yet now that we see the effects of a worldwide labor market, even Robert Reich has acknowledged the threat posed by global pricing of labor.)

Consider, too, the impact of opening a Walmart in a Mexican community. How many mom and pop retailers and suppliers are displaced? What is the effect on them and their families? What happens to the community as a result of their inability to support themselves? Are the profits worth the dislocation and suffering, the potential destabilization of the community?

(One omission of NAFTA may provide insight into the motivation underlying that agreement. U.S. drug companies manufacture many of the same pharmaceuticals in Mexico that they make in the U.S. These pharmaceuticals sell in Mexico for a small fraction of their U.S. prices. But it is illegal, even for pharmacists, to import these cheaper but identical drugs.

This suggests that the prime purpose of NAFTA is to bolster profits by providing our corporations access to a large pool of cheap labor. The purpose has been justified by the claim that it makes us more competitive. But who is this "us"? Just who benefits from "our" greater competitiveness? In the same spirit, was our 1995 bailout of Mexican debt designed to benefit that country and its citizens, or was it designed to benefit the investors who had imprudently purchased Mexican government bonds — whose price had earlier reflected the high degree of risk?)

Simply, globalization favors the rich, as it always has. And polls show it is the rich, and only the rich, who favor globalization.

Why haven't these obvious flaws in free trade arguments and policies shaken our faith? Our continued faith in *laissez faire*, its policies and its predictions, is testimony to the power of widely accepted beliefs to withstand the clearest counterexamples.

There are yet other counterexamples to this faith. Since Alfred Marshall (and the notion, in non-mathematical form, can be traced back to Malthus and Ricardo) it has been a mainstay of classical economics that prices are stable at the marginal costs of production. Commodities should fit this picture ideally, for there are many independent producers and consumers and little opportunity to distort the price structure of an auction market. At least in theory, a price advance should encourage new production and reduce demand, forcing prices back down. A price decline should cause production cuts and stimulate new demand, forcing prices back up.

Perversely resistant to classical economic theory, most commodity prices vary regularly from below the marginal costs of production to several times those costs. Commodity (and stock and bond) prices oscillate in regular cycles with considerable amplitude and without damping. That these cycles are ubiquitous and persistent suggests they may be natural. They appear even before the Industrial Revolution. "Europe in the fifteenth, sixteenth and seventeenth centuries, although far from presenting a unified picture, was already clearly obeying a general series of rhythms, an overall order." (Braudel, *The Perspective of the World*, p. 75.)

Despite its incompatibility with fundamental principles of classical economics, the natural cyclicality of a metals market with constant demand can be simply explained (and without requiring the series of random exogenous shocks assumed by modern business cycle theorists). Suppose initial prices are "too high." High prices → (lead to) high profit projections → more investment in new projects → more new projects → increased production → greater supply → lower prices → lower profits (or losses) → production cutbacks and reduced exploration and development → decreased production → less supply → higher prices.

Because of time lags, prices can rise or decline far from their equilibrium level. New ore bodies must be discovered, reserves proven, metallurgical testing carried out and problems with refractory metallurgy solved, projects permitted, and a mine plan designed. Capital must be raised. Machinery must be ordered, built, delivered, installed and tested. An infrastructure must be developed.

These steps can take years, during which the shortage of metal drives prices far above equilibrium, encouraging the financing of many new mines. By the time the new mines begin production, so many have been financed and developed that the flood of new production depresses prices below the marginal cost of production for years. Because it is expensive to close a mine, many of these mines remain in production in spite of ongoing losses.

Silver prices peaked in 1980 at $50 per ounce. But despite a price decline of more than 90% over the next 10 years, production, much of which had been planned and financed near the peak of the cycle, increased in each of those years (except 1986), by a total of 40%. By 1990 all the new silver mines were losing money. Even the older ones did poorly. Coeur D'Alene and Sunshine Mining (which recently declared bankruptcy) were in the red every year of the 1990s, and Hecla lost money in nine of the ten years.

Silver prices have finally turned. But silver companies have been conserving cash for more than a decade by cutting back on exploration. Few new large deposits have been discovered, few new mines have been placed in production, and inventories have continued to decline, with COMEX inventories less than 10% of their peak levels of 1980.

Given the long lead-time between capital investment and increased production and also the multi-decade price cycles, it would make sense for companies to concentrate their expansion plans near the troughs of those cycles. But the financial markets are too shortsighted and financiers extrapolate trends linearly. They assume prices will remain stable or continue in the direction of the past few years. *Laissez faire* gives them no reason to do otherwise; so most plans to increase capacity are made at cycle peaks, at the worst possible time.

This is part of a broader pattern. In the late 1970s, when energy prices were high and rising, unlimited capital was available for even marginal energy projects. When energy prices declined in the 1980s, principals folded and funds invested in this sector were lost.

Now we have come half circle. It is no longer energy that excites investors. Instead, it is the technology sector that has been soaring. As a result, money has been thrown at technology stocks, from Internet companies with little prospect of ever earning a dime to semiconductor manufacturers who decided to add to capacity at the worst possible time. It is likely that most funds invested in this sector will be lost.

Yet we are told that the free market provides the most efficient allocation of capital that is possible. How can that be? How can we look at our past 25 years of badly misallocated capital investment and conclude this represents the most efficient possible use of capital? Of course, there are models that "prove" free markets allocate capital with the greatest possible efficiency. But how can we take them seriously after even a brief glimpse of our recent past?

It is easy to see why the free market is so inefficient in capital allocation. The psychology associated with cyclic performance guarantees that investors will be out of step. Investor optimism and enthusiasm are consistently the greatest at peaks of long-term cycles. Lack of interest, or even fear, is greatest at troughs. So people invest at the highest prices and disinvest at the lowest prices. (Market technicians commonly use measures of investor sentiment as a contrarian indicator, predicting market advances when investors are overly bearish and declines when investors are overly bullish.) This does not make for efficient use of capital.

Paralleling this, corporations have the greatest return on investment — both actual and projected — and the greatest ability to raise additional funds at peaks of long-term cycles. They also have the greatest incentive to build new capacity at those times, at the peak of their projected returns. So corporations, which often bear an unsettling resemblance to lemmings, also invest in the wrong sectors at the wrong times — despite assurances of the maximal efficiency of free markets.

In the late 1990s, telecommunications companies borrowed nearly half a trillion dollars to bury 39 million miles of fiber-optic cable across the U.S. In their manic phase, they built enormous excess capacity. When the mania wore off in early 2000, these companies laid off more than 100,000 workers. Several were unable to pay interest on their debt. They buried more than just fiber-optic cable.

Undaunted, unfazed by such disasters, we still sanctify the free market and accept any argument that would minimize the role of government. And so we embrace monetarism, the theory that the sole cause of inflation is a too rapidly increasing money supply. Monetarism claims that merely by regulating money supply one can maintain economic growth while holding inflation in check. The use of a simple directive — maintain money supply growth at 2-3% per year — would diminish the power of the Federal Reserve and end government's monetary meddling. For this reason monetarism has been especially popular with devotees of *laissez faire*.

But historically the connection between money supply and inflation is tenuous. Between 1820 and 1860, U.S. money supply rose five-fold, but price levels declined. Other examples go back centuries: "These episodes have been closely examined in one of the most controlled historical tests of a monistic monetarist model. The results of that test are conceded to constitute a 'contradiction of the basic hypothesis' even by a monetarist as convinced as Anna Schwartz.... Similar difficulties also appear in other attempts to correlate the movement of prices with the stock of money." (Fischer, *The Great Wave*, p. 337.)

The factors underlying the historic irrelevance of money supply to inflation are equally present today. For one thing, the velocity of money (how quickly it gets spent) is an important factor independent of the quantity of money. Its increase can cause increases in both inflation and economic growth, even if there is no change in money supply.

Independently, there are different measures of money supply growing at different rates, but few theoretical grounds to choose among them. From 1990 to 1992, annual M1 growth increased from 4% to 12% while growth in the broader measure M2 declined from 5% to 2%. Should the Federal Reserve have obeyed M1's call for monetary restraint or M2's call for monetary accommodation? From 1995 to 1998, M1 declined. M2 grew at more than 6% per year. M3 grew at more than 9% per year. Should the Fed have targeted M1, M2 or M3? Goodhart's Law, tongue in cheek, claims that no matter what measure of money supply is targeted by the Federal Reserve, that measure will prove useless as a predictor of economic growth and inflation.

In addition to this, as Lester Thurow pointed out (*Dangerous Currents*), there is irony in monetarists' insistence that we use monetary policy to control inflation. For monetarism regards money as no more than an intermediary among goods. All that counts is the relative values of different goods. Changing the value of money, the intermediary, does not change those relative values. Inflation must be innocuous, so it should not be necessary to control it.

These problems underlie the persistent failures of monetarism. Monetarists looked for a recession in 1984, double-digit inflation in 1986-7, and a recession in 1992-3. They were far off the mark in each case. Nor has monetarist policy worked. The Federal Reserve's targeting of money supply in 1979-1982 produced severe economic dislocations.

The congenital failures of monetarist predictions should not be dismissed lightly. Because it is easy to explain results that you already know, "successful" explanations of historical data are less significant than successful predictions of new events. The inability of monetarists to get the right answers when they did not know those answers beforehand is a serious flaw. In contrast to the poor predictive record of monetary aggregates, a simple, if elegant, algorithm developed by David Ranson, based solely on changes in short-term interest rates, has been remarkably accurate in predicting real GNP growth. On most accounts of causality, causal and predictive efficacy go hand in hand. That interest rates have had greater predictive power than money supply suggests a closer causal link between interest rates and economic growth than between money supply and economic growth.

But economists bury their mistakes quietly and quickly forget about them. Many observers of the economic scene, even those who are well informed, are unaware of the extent to which free market predictions and policies have failed.

These failures are only part of the problem. The most basic notions of free market economics, while they work well enough in theoretical models, hardly make sense in the real world.

Free market economists insist on a flat playing field in foreign trade. This sounds good, at least in theory. But how in the world do you measure distortions caused by culture, for example, by the proclivity of the Japanese to distinguish between foreigners and fellow Japanese, the latter often regarded as almost extended family? This ethnocentrism is responsible for a variety of features: for $3 trillion in postal savings accounts that pay less than 1% per year, enabling Japanese industry to be more competitive by borrowing at low interest rates; for the tendency to prefer domestic to foreign goods; for the pre-occupation with market share as opposed to profits; for high levels of job security provided to direct employees, independent of performance. These distort any playing field.

How do you treat the bumps caused by our own tilting of the playing field? Boeing achieved its dominance in commercial aviation thanks to a decades-old government subsidy. An Air Force order for 29 KC-135 jet tankers to provide air-to-air refueling for its fleet of B-47s and B-52s provided critical support to Boeing's venture into commercial jet aviation. (The Boeing 707 is nearly the same as the KC-135.) The excellence of American agriculture is due to the development of agricultural colleges and experimental farms, the construction of dams, government crop insurance, the Rural Electrification Association, and the Farmers' Home Administration, all funded by federal or state government.

It does not matter that we have discontinued many of these supports. Dominance, once established, tends to perpetuate itself. Inferiority, once established, also tends to perpetuate itself. "A poor country is poor because it is poor." (Ragnal Norske, *Problems of Capital Formation in Underdeveloped Countries*, p. 4.) It is impossible to measure, much less correct, the effects of historical distortions of the playing field.

As yet another example of the virtual reality of classical economics, academic economists love to talk about the efficiency of financial markets. By this they mean that the price of any financial instrument at any time appropriately reflects all the information publicly available at that time. On their assumptions that investors are fully informed and completely rational, if information that could change the price were public, the price would have changed already.

The most remarkable feature of this theory is that, if it were true, then all investing should be illegal. For if the market price reflects all publicly available information, the only way one could hope to outperform the long and broad trends would be through information that is not public. But it is illegal to trade on the basis of inside information. (Alternatively, one might regard investing as gambling, with the *cagnotte* going to brokers. But gambling is illegal in most states.)

There are other problems with the efficient market hypothesis. For one thing, closed end mutual funds often trade at a significant discount or premium to their underlying asset values. In an efficient market investors should arbitrage the difference. For example, if a fund were undervalued, one could buy the fund and sell the underlying stocks to the point that the fund would be appropriately priced. But this has not happened. The discounts or premiums in such funds have continued for months at a time.

In addition, there are investors who have decisively outpaced the broad market averages for decades. Warren Buffet, Peter Lynch and George Soros are three of the best known, but there are others. Is this merely a matter of chance, with consistent superior performance explained entirely by luck, as opposed to careful research and insight into developing trends?

To the contrary, the performance of these investors has been so consistent and so significant that the null hypothesis, that it is due to chance, is extremely unlikely. Yet Rational Expectations economists claim it is *impossible* to consistently outperform the market. Faced with the conflict between the theoretical notion of market efficiency and the reality that certain investors consistently do well, they discard reality.

Warren Buffet has expressed his opinion about the efficient market hypothesis, noting that it is easier to excel when your competitors believe there can be no advantage gained from hard work and careful research. In an interview published by *Fortune*, he quipped: "I'd be a bum on the street with a tin cup if the market were efficient." Peter Lynch, in the same vein, remarked: "Efficient market? That's a bunch of junk, crazy stuff."

In addition to the efficacy of sound fundamental research, there are technical algorithms that have worked well over decades. (While academic economists have had a difficult time generating successful trading rules, professional traders have done rather better.) Norman Fosback notes a simple regularity in *Stock Market Logic*. He contrasts a seasonal investor, who owns stock (the market average) for only the two days preceding each holiday market closing, to the non-seasonal investor who owns stock the rest of the time:

> To summarize, if two hypothetical investors, the Seasonal and the Non-Seasonal, each started with an initial capital of $10,000, they would have realized the following results (assuming no commissions) by using alternative strategies:

Strategy	Years Held	$10,000 Became
Seasonal Investor	3 1/3	$87,787
Non-Seasonal Investor	44 2/3	$ 5,855

If we combine this seasonality with favorable price tendencies over the last five trading days of every month, the results become even more dramatic: "The results of the various strategies are startlingly different. A seasonal strategy saw $10,000 grow to over $1.4 million while a $10,000 initial investment in the non-seasonal strategy shrank to a minuscule $357.... The seasonal strategy also provided a percentage return superior to the non-seasonal strategy's portfolio in 40 of the 48 years despite the fact that the seasonal strategy was only invested in the generally uptrending market about one-fourth of each year." (p. 159-163.) The probability that this is due to mere chance is vanishingly small. Random walks with small steps almost never lead to so great a divergence.

A study of point-and-figure charts by Earl Davis at Purdue University showed that trading off standard patterns was profitable from 70% to 90% of the time, depending on the patterns. (An advantage of point-and-figure charts is that they leave no room for subjective interpretation. Buy and sell signals are objectively generated.) Even in *Value Line*, which appears to use simple momentum measures to rank stocks, the higher-ranked quintiles have consistently and significantly outperformed the lower-ranked quintiles.

There are also technical algorithms that often fail but are so accurate when they do succeed that they preclude the null hypothesis that their success was just a matter of luck. The precision with which Fibonacci ratios ($\frac{1}{2}(\pm1+\sqrt{5})$ [1.618 or 0.618]) call turning points in both time and price cannot be reasonably explained as pure chance.

Finally, there are examples of violent moves in the financial markets that cannot be explained, even in retrospect, in terms of efficient markets. Consider the 1987 stock market crash in which major averages lost one-third of their value in just a few hours. What was the additional information that instantly made everything worth one-third less? What information came public on Black Monday in October 1929 that precipitated the sharp market decline that wiped out 90% of market value?

It is remarkable that a theoretical construct such as the efficient market hypothesis has survived this. True believers in a widely accepted theory, be it physics or economics, maintain their beliefs no matter how overwhelming the contrary evidence.

The very justification of *laissez faire* is problematic. The standard claim is that in the competition engendered by free markets consumers will shop to maximize the value they receive. Wares that don't provide good value will not sell and their producers will soon be out of business. Producers making what the public wants and providing it at the lowest cost will be the survivors. The most efficient producers (even if that efficiency comes from using slave labor) will have the greatest profits and will be able to expand at the expense of less efficient producers. Consumers will receive the greatest value.

It does not take a rocket scientist to find flaws. It may seem trivial, but consumers shop to maximize *perceived* value. There may be a wide gap between value and perceived value. One can add perceived value in ways that have nothing to do with real value. One can produce a product that is addictive. To an addict his favorite substance may have such perceived value that he will go without food and clothing to purchase it. That is why the unethical drug and cigarette industries are so profitable.

Alternatively, one can advertise the product, adding perceived value to a product that may have little intrinsic value. It is often the effectiveness of the advertising, rather than the quality of the product, that determines competitive destiny. "But, there are many examples of products which are technologically inferior not just surviving, but driving out of existence competitors with distinctly superior qualities. The free market chooses not the best, but the worst." (Ormerod, *Butterfly Economics*, p. 20.)

The very success of advertising poses a difficulty for the classical economist. For if consumers are completely rational then advertising, which intentionally and unabashedly targets the non-rational, should make no difference at all. Yet by appealing to sub-rational needs and associations the effectiveness of the advertising can be more important than the quality of the product. How can this be?

How does this maximize the wealth of society?

Independently, the *laissez faire* picture of many competing entrepreneurs, none large enough to dominate a market, has never been even a good approximation. It has always been advantageous to be large. There may be economies of scale, as well as greater ability to influence costs of raw materials and labor and selling prices of finished goods. Larger companies can also amass political influence and use that influence to enhance their economic status. A larger company can overpower a similar, but smaller, competitor. So even if one starts out with an economy of small entrepreneurs, that economy would naturally evolve into an oligopoly. The incentives motivating oligopolies differ from those envisioned by *laissez faire.*

In a technology oligopoly maximizing profits may be incompatible with progress. New technology can be risky. A breakthrough can change the nature of the game. Companies dominant in the old game might lose their dominance in the new game. So their incentive is to make incremental improvements to their already dominant technology, but not to change the technology itself. It is also to prevent the marketing of new technology, or to copy it and use their financial and marketing muscle to dominate that technology.

Consider economic rationality for a large drug company with successful antibiotics on the market. How should it handle the threat posed by colloidal silver? The simplest rational response would be to buy the silver company and/or its patents and to insure that the colloidal silver never reaches the market. The more efficacious the silver solution, the greater is the incentive to keep it off the market. Perversely, the better the product, the more lives it could save, the less likely it would ever get to market.

In the energy oligopoly, the incentive is to maximize selling prices, holding them just below the point that alternative energy sources would be developed. It is also to oppose alternative energy and conservation technologies or to acquire them and prevent them from reaching the market. If the energy oligopoly had a stake in the world economy its incentive might be different. But it does not, so its incentive is to drain as much as possible from the rest of the economy.

How does this benefit society?

These issues do not involve subtle or technical features of economic theory. Anyone looking at the data can see that the relationship between our trade and our unemployment is just the opposite of the dictates of free market theory. The failure of wages to equilibrate, after generations of free trade and equal access to technology, should be obvious even to non-economists who look at the numbers.

Novices can recognize the persistent cyclic patterns in both stock prices and investor sentiment, which have enabled astute stock market technical analysts to compile impressive track records. The consistency with which investment dollars have flowed into the wrong sectors at the wrong times is well known. Financial markets are palpably inefficient. Even most economists now accept the failure of monetarism. Most industries — accounting, advertising, aircraft, airlines, aluminum, autos, banks, broker-dealers, cereals, chemicals, coal, computers, consumer electronics, copper, defense, entertainment, food retailing, forest products, insurance, Internet, homebuilding, meatpacking, newspapers, oil production, oil service, pharmaceuticals, photography, restaurant chains, semiconductors, software, telecommunications, tobacco — are oligopolies, dominated by four or fewer companies.

The multiple failures of *laissez faire* are not just theoretical. The suffering caused by misguided economic policies is painfully real. We accept the suffering as a necessary consequence of the ideal economic system, primarily because *laissez faire* is so widely accepted and so uncontroversial. In this behavior we deserve Nietzsche's cynicism: "Men believe in the truth of anything so long as they see that others strongly believe it is true."

Ebullient Markets — Dangerous Economy

Mythology, taken seriously, becomes theology. It obscures reality. Our mythology of the free market has little to do with performance. *Laissez faire*, despite its reputation and despite the abject failure of the opposite extreme of communism, has performed poorly.

This conclusion may seem absurd, given the universal agreement — at least within the U.S. — on the wonders of the free market. But reality speaks for itself. Our economic and productivity growth have slowed as we have moved to a purer *laissez faire*. We have lagged our trading partners with more mixed economies. We have amassed record levels of debt and become dependent on our trading partners for capital. We have seen increasing pressure on our middle class and a growing and dangerous disparity in wealth between the richest and the rest.

We have been deluded by bullish stock and bond markets to believe that everything must be all right — for otherwise our problems would be revealed in the financial markets. This is naïve, and dangerously so. History provides an excellent example, the 1920s, which closely paralleled our last two decades.

What occurred in both periods was a decline in interest rates coupled with tax cuts for the wealthy. This produced a torrent of funds flowing into the stock market and a surge in debt. The rapid rise in stock prices led to irrational levels of investor buoyancy, to the widespread beliefs in 1929 — which we hold again today — that the market can decline only mildly and briefly and that in the long term stocks necessarily appreciate. Then, as now, this exuberance drove stocks to all-time record valuations.

Our parallel to the 1920s extends beyond our financial markets. Pervasive acquisitive materialism characterized the 1920s as well as today, as did the decline of unions. This reflected a social Calvinism that regarded wealth as a sign of grace and poverty, at the very least, as a sign of a lack of ambition and drive. The veneration of the businessman in the last two decades, even the notion of Jesus as an entrepreneur, was expressed in terms that hark back to the 1920s (Barton, *The Man Nobody Knows*). And, aided by tax cuts for the wealthy, the economic difference between rich and poor attained record levels in the late 1920s, levels only recently surpassed. Even at the top of the political ladder, President Reagan was a great admirer of President Coolidge. One of his first housekeeping actions as president was to replace a portrait of Jefferson in the East Wing of the White House with one of Coolidge.

Still, it is our excesses in the financial markets that are likely to cause the most damage, just as they did in 1929. It was widely agreed in 1929, when stock market capitalization nearly equaled GNP, that the health of our financial markets proved the strength of our economy. Economists justified the inflated stock prices and valuations of those years by claiming that we had entered a new era of technology-driven growth. Those assurances, though widely accepted, proved to be false. At its 2000 peak, stock market capitalization nearly doubled GNP. Similar assurances, offered by contemporary economists, that a new era of technology-driven growth would justify even higher valuations are no more credible.

Our previous record in stock valuations occurred in 1929, along with record enthusiasm for stocks and record financial leverage. We have now surpassed those records. Even technically, the Dow Jones Industrial Average is more overbought than at any other time in its history, trading at 250% of its 10-year moving average. (The only previous time the Dow came close to being this overbought was 1929. The NASDAQ and S&P are even more overbought.)

With respect to valuation:

(i) Using a 10-year moving average of earnings, as recommended by Graham and Dodd to smooth out short-term fluctuations, the price-earnings ratio for the S&P 500 was recently 40% above its previous record, achieved in 1929.

(ii) In the past 130 years, the S&P never sold at three times the net present value of its dividends, and only twice (1929 and the mid-1960s) did it sell at twice that net present value. Both of those times the S&P subsequently declined by more than 50% to trade at less than the net present value of its dividends. At its 2000 peak, the S&P sold at nearly five times the net present value of its dividends.

(iii) The price-to-book-value ratio for the S&P Composite is 4.7 times its average over the past 50 years. The price-to-sales ratio is 2.5 times its average over the past 50 years.

(iv) The q ratio (designed by Nobel laureate James Tobin as a measure of equilibrium in stock prices based on historical valuation) is the most overvalued in history.

To make matters worse, interest rates appear to be bottoming and may soon embark on a new secular advance. Rising interest rates would turn an important component of equity valuation negative. Record valuations within a rising interest rate environment bode ill for equity prices for the next decade.

With respect to investor enthusiasm, the number of investment clubs has risen from 7,500 to 40,000 in just the last decade. Half of our population, an all-time high, own stock. This widespread enthusiasm is reflected in the ratio of the dollar value of stocks traded to GNP. The previous peak in that ratio was 130% in 1929. It subsequently declined to 6% in 1940, and as recently as 1974 it was only 10%. Now it is over 300%.

Despite record investor enthusiasm, the market acts tired. Even though equity mutual funds had net inflows of $20 billion per month from April 2000 through September 2000, the S&P Composite declined by nearly 5%. How much money would have to flow into mutual funds to produce significant gains? What would happen if investor confidence were to wane and the flow of money into mutual funds were to decline, or even turn negative? How sharply might the market decline?

Of course, investors today believe it is different now. After all, as financial analysts are fond of reminding us: "We are richer than ever before; with more surplus cash for investment purposes than ever before."

Similarly, one of the most respected mathematical economists has written: "Stock prices are not too high.... We are living in an age of increasing prosperity and consequent increasing earning power of corporations and individuals. This is due in large measure to...inventions such as the world has never before witnessed. The rapidity with which worthwhile inventions are brought out is the result of the tremendous research laboratories of our great technology companies. Applications of these inventions to business means greatly enhanced earning power. This is a new and tremendously powerful factor... which never before existed."

This sounds impressive. The surplus cash could be the source of a new advance in the market, and new technologies could drive earnings growth at a faster rate, justifying higher price-earnings multiples and lower dividend yields. But there are no guarantees. Indeed, this is not the first time such arguments have been made.

Investors in 1929 held similar beliefs. The quote: "We are richer...," taken from *The Wall Street Journal,* was published on October 4, 1929. The passage glorifying our technological advances was written not by Alan Greenspan, but by Irving Fisher in *The New York Times* of September 5, 1929. Perhaps we should consider the wisdom of Robert Farrell: "The four most dangerous words in investing are 'It's different this time.'"

The speculative bubble in the financial markets obscures the reality that we achieved faster economic growth, greater productivity growth, higher rates of savings and investment, and a more broadly based prosperity during the mixed economy of the New Deal and the subsequent extension of those policies by Truman and Kennedy.

Despite our roaring stock market, the reality remains that our trading partners who have more mixed economies are growing faster than we. They have higher rates of savings and investment, greater productivity growth, lower levels of poverty, and greater improvement in standards of living. They have made inroads into our technological leadership.

The reality remains that more than a century ago, countries with well-focused mixed economies, Bismarck's Germany and Meiji Japan, grew faster than did the purer free enterprise economies of Britain and France. Inversely, recent transitions toward *laissez faire* by Russia and Mexico have impoverished the great majority of their citizens.

Nor is this unique. The relatively pure free market economy of the Industrial Revolution in eighteenth and early nineteenth century England did little for the quality of life of the vast majority of people. *Laissez faire* "doing its thing" produced environmental degradation and grinding poverty. For many, it was only with government intervention in the mid-to-late nineteenth century that quality of life improved beyond that of the fifteenth century.

Laissez faire has not provided a service to this country or to any other. The fact that state-planned communism is disastrous does not support the opposite extreme, pure free market economics. Neither does the fact that free market economics is amenable to strict mathematical modeling, given that the models bear so little resemblance to reality.

Free market economics has been appealing to us — just as it was previously appealing to the Dutch and the English — because it provides an advantage to the economically dominant player. This is true not only in international trade, but also in the domestic arena. Capital has inherent advantages and naturally wishes to protect and extend those advantages.

But those advantages bear the seeds of their own destruction. Without intervention to protect the middle and lower classes, a free market economy can drain money from those classes to create an extreme concentration of wealth. Historically, such a concentration of wealth has destabilized societies and adversely impacted the security and standard of living of even the wealthy. This has happened again and again. Unless we remove the blinders of classical economic theory and open our eyes to this historic pattern, it will happen yet again.

A New Economic Paradigm

An Alternative Approach

Free markets have played an important role. They have provided incentives for innovation and for low-cost production of desirable products. They have enforced pragmatism at the expense of ideology. They have facilitated exchange and provided a working definition of fair price. Attempts made to replace them, typically by government management, have come to naught.

But there is a wide gap between the practical efficacy of free markets and the claims that *laissez faire* necessarily maximizes the wealth of society and that interference is never warranted. It is these more ambitious claims that support the doctrine of government non-intervention. It is these claims that embody what John Kenneth Galbraith calls "theological *laissez faire.*"

While classical economists may summarily dismiss "theological *laissez faire*" as a grotesque caricature, theologians have a better handle on the issue. Harvey Cox, a professor of divinity at Harvard, has fleshed out theological *laissez faire* in some detail:

> The lexicon of The Wall Street Journal and the business sections of Time and Newsweek turned out to bear a striking resemblance to Genesis, the Epistle to the Romans, and Saint Augustine's City of God.... There were even sacraments to convey salvific power to the lost, a calendar of entrepreneurial saints, and what theologians call an "eschatology"...
>
> I saw that in fact there lies embedded in the business pages an entire theology, which is comparable in scope if not in profundity to that of Thomas Aquinas or Karl Barth... As I tried to follow the arguments and explanation of

the economist-theologians who justify The Market's ways to men, I spotted the same dialectics I have grown fond of in the many years I have pondered the Thomists, the Calvinists, and the various schools of modern religious thought. ("The Market as God," *The Atlantic Monthly*, March 1999, p. 18f)

In the spirit of ecumenism, it has become fashionable to cite the relevance of Zen to investing. One author claims, seriously, that day trading requires "... a certain wisdom, a Zen-like sense of ... insignificance in the face of the Market." (Millman, *The Day Trader*, p. 25.)

The diversity of failures of the free market should suffice to reject theological *laissez faire*. Flaws are plentiful. Economists without blindfolds have ably addressed its preoccupation with the short term. "[I]n an era of man-made brainpower industries, capitalism is going to need some very long-run communal investments in research and development, education, and infrastructure. Yet when capitalism's normal decision-making processes are used, capitalism never looks more than eight to ten years into the future and usually looks only three to four years ahead. The problem is simply put. Capitalism desperately needs what its own internal logic says it does not have to do." (Lester Thurow, *The Future of Capitalism*, p. 16.)

Although it has received the most attention, *laissez faire*'s propensity to imperil long-term prospects in order to satisfy the short term is not its only failing. The very structure of *laissez faire* is incompatible with wealth-maximizing institutions like patent protection. This structure renders *laissez faire* incapable in principle of achieving its own wealth-maximizing ends.

Independently, the picture of economies and financial markets painted by *laissez faire* is far removed from any school of realism. Contrary to that picture, economies are not comprised of entrepreneurs competing against each other on a flat playing field. They are oligopolies in which powerful economic interests purchase and wield significant political power. Also contrary to that picture, prices do not tend to a stable unchanging equilibrium. And economic differences do not disappear. Once they reach a certain size, feed on themselves.

The tendency of differences to feed on themselves is common and is not limited to economies. If neighboring countries have comparable military strengths there is little incentive for one to attack another. The cost of a war is too great, as is the risk of losing. But as military differences increase beyond a certain threshold the risk-reward ratio changes. It may now make sense for a stronger country to invade a weaker neighbor. By assimilating the resources of the weaker state the stronger can increase its own strength and can gobble up its neighbors one by one.

This underlies the notion of balance of power. Military equilibrium is not stable. It requires deliberate action by governments to build alliances that maintain a military balance sufficiently close to equilibrium to deter aggression.

Just as it may be appropriate to intervene to maintain a balance of military power, there may be reason to intervene to maintain a balance of economic power. Without the moderation of extreme economic disparity society has repeatedly inclined to increasing violence that triggered instability and led to a lower standard of living for all. Historically, such moderation has been achieved by massive disaster that decimated the non-wealthy and so increased their economic power. Government intervention to maintain a balance of economic power would be less painful. It would increase the long-term wealth of nations.

Laissez faire misses all of this. No wonder it has underperformed. Yet despite its palpable flaws *laissez faire* is flourishing as if there were no conceivable alternative. Why?

Widely accepted theories are truly the undead. Not even the most powerful contrary evidence can kill them. Even in physics the Rutherford model of the atom was universally accepted, despite its obvious flaws, until quantum theory. Only a better theory can dispatch an accepted theory. This is so in all sciences, including economics. To be effective, a criticism of *laissez faire* must present a realistic alternative. The ideal would be a theory that has already been successfully applied to structures as complex as economies.

Enter nonlinear thermodynamics. This theory, a recent branch of physics, is the most general theory dealing with complex systems open to exchange matter and/or energy with their environment. It explains a variety of chemical and biological behaviors.

Its significance has been enhanced by the awareness that ordinary dynamics is limited in the range of phenomena it can predict. In order to predict behavior in any science, it is necessary that the evolution of systems be insensitive to sufficiently small differences in initial conditions. Otherwise, apparently identical systems can evolve along different paths and we cannot predict how a system will evolve.

Classical dynamics fails this test. Even simple systems that are virtually identical can quickly diverge in their behavior. "Richter kept clamped to his windowsill a well-oiled double pendulum.... From time to time he would set it spinning in chaotic nonrhythms that he could emulate on a computer as well.

The dependence on initial conditions was so sensitive that the gravitational pull of a single raindrop a mile away mixed up the motion within fifty or sixty revolutions, about two minutes." (James Gleick, *Chaos*, p. 230.)

As systems become more complex, dynamic predictability, based on the positions and momenta of their component particles, breaks down completely. Near-infinite sensitivity to dynamic initial conditions precludes their use as a predictive tool.

Because of this sensitivity, dynamics cannot directly predict the behavior of complex systems. But for certain kinds of systems this extreme sensitivity to dynamic variables is balanced by decreasing sensitivity to thermodynamic variables: temperature, pressure, chemical potential. This allows for successful prediction in terms of thermodynamic variables. That is the rationale for the autonomous science of thermodynamics.

But there are limitations to even thermodynamic description. Life appears to transcend the laws of thermodynamics. The development of organisms and the evolution of species are characterized by increasing order. This cannot be explained within classical thermodynamics, for it appears to violate the second law of thermodynamics. That law identifies thermodynamic equilibrium as a state of maximum entropy (disorder). As a system approaches equilibrium its entropy increases, its internal disorder increases, its internal order dissipates. (A bathtub may start with hot water on one side and cold water on the other. After time the water will mix and it will all be lukewarm. The spatial hot-cold order will dissipate.)

Increasing internal order, apparently forbidden by the second law, has long been a source of conflict between biology and physics. Biologists, especially embryologists, faced with the palpable reality of the development of finely-tuned organs, skeletons, and nervous systems in living organisms, saw a need to circumvent the second law of thermodynamics.

This led to vitalism, theories that living systems are characterized by some unique quality, Driesch's entelechy (a mysterious whole-making factor that drives biological organisms toward some predetermined end) or Bergson's *élan original de la vie*. This enables them to evolve contrary to the second law of thermodynamics, to generate and sustain a natural internal order.

In fact, mysterious qualities like entelechy are not necessary. Nonlinear thermodynamics can explain the development of order without the need to postulate anything new. Indeed, the ability to develop and sustain a natural order is not limited to living organisms. Even though they have not generated the attention associated with order-creating biological processes, a number of chemical and thermodynamic processes are characterized by the spontaneous generation and sustenance of macroscopic order.

These processes occur in systems that are open to exchange energy with their environment, that are far from internal equilibrium, and whose evolution can be described by nonlinear differential equations with positive feedback. Simply, they occur in systems with characteristics similar to living organisms — and economies.

While such systems produce entropy in accord with the second law of thermodynamics, they can export more entropy across their open boundaries than they produce. As their remaining entropy decreases, their internal order increases. At the microscopic level, these systems are characterized by the mutual interdependence of their components and, under certain conditions, by a high degree of sensitivity to internal fluctuations and to small changes in their environment. The order that evolves is typically cyclic.

The simplest example is Bénard instability, in which a thin layer of liquid is heated from below. Up to a critical temperature gradient, the heat is dissipated by conduction. But at steeper temperature gradients, sufficiently far from the internal equilibrium of uniform temperature, a new phenomenon appears. The heat is dissipated more efficiently in hexagonal convection cells (boiling) in which large numbers of neighboring molecules no longer act independently but move in the same direction over macroscopic distances.

Nonlinear thermodynamics explains not only Bénard instability, but also the generation of structures and cycles in a variety of chemical and biological processes. It shows that these processes are compatible with the laws of physics, indeed, that they can be explained by physics.

Economies bear striking similarities to these systems. Economies, like chemical and biological structures, are open systems, often far from internal equilibrium. Their evolution can be described by nonlinear differential equations. Economies also have well-recognized positive feedback mechanisms.

Not only is their underlying mathematical description similar to that of nonlinear chemical and biological systems, but their behavior is similar. Economies, like living organisms, are characterized by stable cycles and by occasional hypersensitivity to the smallest changes in their environment.

Even though nonlinear thermodynamics has not yet been applied to economics, it could plausibly provide insight into economic structures and processes. In any case, its success in explaining the behavior of complex systems in other sciences dispels the Newtonian notion that it is always natural for the components of a system to be mutually independent. At least in thermodynamics, chemistry and biology there is a range of conditions under which a system's components naturally exhibit mutual interdependence.

In transcending the Newtonian paradigm of independent billiard balls, the success of nonlinear explanations undermines the starting point of Adam Smith, that economic behavior can be best understood in terms of individuals acting independently to secure their own immediate economic advantage. It reinforces elements of modern psychology and sociology, as well as common observation, that contradict the classical view.

In fairness to Adam Smith, survival has always been an important motivator. In the early days of the Industrial Revolution when there was no social safety net, when many died of starvation and many more from malnutrition-related illness, economic success was a critical component of survival itself. The role of economic success was understood by everyone and naturally became central to people's psyche. It is understandable that individuals engaged in such a battle for survival should focus on their immediate economic welfare.

In the days since Adam Smith, however, modern industrialized countries have woven social safety nets — in defiance of the spirit of *laissez faire*. These have distanced economic performance from survival. Consequently, the role of economic success as a motivator has declined. Concerns with other matters have come to play a greater role.

The desire to create value has led otherwise rational individuals to accept jobs that may not be in their best short-term economic interest (*Médecins sans frontières*). A sense of family has induced wives and mothers to accept less income in order to stay home and bring up their children. People have refused higher-paying jobs rather than relocating and leaving community and friends. Employees have chosen early retirement because they value leisure more than the economic benefit of continuing to work. Surveys show that a substantial majority of families would happily relinquish some income for more family time.

These behaviors illustrate the unreality of the *laissez faire* picture of independent individuals working solely for their immediate economic gain. Of course, much of this would not have been true in the days of Adam Smith. But the world has changed since then. It is only our economic paradigm that has not changed.

Ironically, devotees of *laissez faire* fail to realize how marginal is the role played by the theory's premises. The assumptions:

- individuals naturally work only for their own immediate economic gain; and
- under these conditions the invisible hand of the free market maximizes total wealth;

rarely, if ever, enter into economic calculations. They could be dropped and few but ideologues would notice. Their replacement by nonlinear thermodynamics would be a boon, freeing us from the doctrinal orthodoxy of theological *laissez faire*.

For while the nonlinear paradigm is compatible with free markets, it does not pretend that a pure free market economy will necessarily produce the best possible results. Also, because nonlinearity involves the mutual interdependence of a system's micro-components, it is open to considerations of social responsibility that have been characteristic of democratic thought since ancient Greece. (This is not meant to attribute consciousness or responsibility to a system's micro-components. It merely shows mutual independence is *not* necessarily natural, even in the world of physics.)

NONLINEAR THERMODYNAMICS AND ECONOMICS

Nonlinear thermodynamics was developed by Ilya Prigogine, for which he was awarded the Nobel Prize in chemistry in 1974. This theory, an extension of classical thermodynamics beyond its traditional limits, has important ramifications for physics, chemistry and biology — and, perhaps, economics.

The subject matter of classical thermodynamics is the quiescent behavior of systems near thermodynamic equilibrium. Thermodynamic equilibrium is characterized by homogeneity: uniform temperature, pressure and chemical potentials. Near-equilibrium states are characterized by small differences in these parameters. For many thermodynamic and chemical systems, it is possible to calculate the conditions for equilibrium and their behavior near equilibrium. The equations describing such systems are a standard part of physics curricula.

But some of the most interesting thermodynamic behavior occurs in open systems far from equilibrium. This cannot be understood in terms of classical thermodynamics. Turbulence and convection are common examples of far-from-equilibrium behavior that lie beyond classical thermodynamics. To be alive an organism, an organ, or even a cell, must be far from internal equilibrium, from homogeneity. Common processes in chemistry and biology that are characterized by stable cycles take place in open systems far from equilibrium.

These systems and the behaviors peculiar to them are the subject matter of nonlinear thermodynamics. They are characterized by a principle of self-organization. As they evolve they generate new and stable internal orders that can sustain themselves even in the face of changes in their environments.

The simplest and purely thermodynamic example is Bénard instability, in which neighboring molecules "cooperate," moving in the same direction at the same time over considerable distances to dissipate heat in macroscopic hexagonal convection cells. At a greater level of complexity nonlinear thermodynamics explains oxidation and reduction cycles in chemistry. At still greater levels of complexity, large molecules form templates for their own reproduction. Manfred Eigen and Peter Schuster incorporated this into an explanation of the evolution of life, an explanation far more plausible than small molecules coming together in random interactions to form macro-molecules. In Eigen and Schuster's view, there is a positive feedback reaction in which molecules form templates for the production of other molecules. Nucleotides produce proteins, which in turn produce more nucleotides. (*Naturwissenschaften*, 1978, p. 341f.)

A system will generate nonlinear behavior only if:

(i) It is open, able to exchange matter and/or energy with its environment.

(ii) Its evolution can be described by non-linear differential equations.

(iii) The equations describing its evolution allow for positive feedback.

(iv) It is sufficiently far from internal equilibrium.

Under these conditions microscopic fluctuations within the system may not be suppressed, but may be amplified to the point that they bring a new macroscopic order to the system, an order that is typically cyclic.

Economies satisfy these conditions:

(i) They are open and exchange matter and energy with their environment (e.g. trade).

(ii) Their evolution can be described by nonlinear differential equations.

(iii) They commonly exhibit positive feedback. Higher inflation → higher inflation expectations → a propensity to spend faster, before prices rise further → a higher velocity of money → still higher inflation...

(iv) They are often removed from internal equilibrium. With respect to the distribution of wealth, the more wealth concentrates in fewer hands, the further removed is the economy from internal equilibrium.

The same sorts of equations that describe the evolution of chemical and biological systems can also describe the evolution of economic systems. But the nonlinear characteristics of economies do not stop there. Even though economies are vastly different entities from chemical systems or biological organisms, their behaviors draw attention to similarities between economics and chemistry or biology.

These behaviors cannot be explained in classical economics, but they correspond to common patterns of nonlinear thermodynamics. One characteristic of these patterns is their cyclicality. As early as 1947, Dewey and Dakin (*Cycles: The Science of Prediction*) called attention to the predictive value of the regularity of business and financial cycles. (Also see W. Mitchell, *Business Cycles* [1927].) Several prestigious groups and journals study these cycles, whose periods range from the controversial 60-year Kondratieff cycle to Kitchin cycles of 3-4 years.

The outstanding technical work of Ian Notley (Yelton Fiscal) is based on the superposition of price-generated cycles of different periods, ranging from more than 30 years to approximately two months. Ravi Batra (*The Great Depression of 1990*) has applied the historical cycle theory of Prabhat Sarkar to economics and has argued for coincident 30-year cycles in inflation, money supply and government regulation.

Cycles figure prominently in the work of Joseph Schumpeter. (Unfortunately, it appears that few economists, even among disciples of Schumpeter, are familiar with nonlinear mechanisms that generate cyclic behavior or with the thermodynamic, chemical or biological counterparts to economic cycles.) There are also longer-term cycles. European history has been characterized by an inflation cycle of between two and three centuries (Fischer, *The Great Wave*).

In addition to cyclicality, the occasional extreme sensitivity of nonlinear systems to minute changes in their environment, overreacting by orders of magnitude to insignificant stimuli, is characteristic of financial markets, despite conflicting with classical economic theory. There are many examples of sharp price moves in response to minor events, or to no apparent event at all.

Through most of 1985 and 1986, inventories of non-ferrous metals were declining. Even as they fell to historic lows, prices remained low, suggesting to industry that there was no need to add to in-house inventory. When prices finally began to rise, even in the absence of significant news, managers who had been sedated by stable prices to the point of letting internal inventories run

107

down desperately tried to rebuild stocks. Prices soared, nickel up five-fold in less than a year and other non-ferrous metals more than doubling in that same period. The stock market crash of 1987, in which broad averages lost one third of their value in hours, despite the absence of significant news, is another example in which a large change, rather than being self-limiting, fed on itself.

This sensitivity is an effect of a positive feedback loop between prices and perception. Rising commodity prices cause a perception of scarcity, which leads to more buying and still higher prices. Falling stock prices cause a perception that something must be wrong, scaring away buyers and prompting the cautious to sell. Concentrated buying leads to more buying. Concentrated selling leads to panic. Just as the crossing of a critical threshold leads to qualitatively different behavior on the part of thermodynamic, chemical or biological systems, it can lead to qualitatively different financial or economic behavior.

Contrast the nonlinear approach to that of classical economics. On the standard equilibrium account such sensitivity is impossible. Any price change must be self-limiting. In the absence of new information any rise in prices must bring in at least as much selling (those who would sell at the higher price but not the lower one) and no additional buying (as people who refuse to buy at a lower price surely won't buy at a higher price). This can exert a downward, but not an upward, force on prices. A decline in price must produce just the opposite effect. Natural economic forces tend to restore any equilibrium.

According to most texts, this is a necessary truth. The necessarily non-negative slope and continuity of the supply curve and the necessarily non-positive slope and continuity of the demand curve entail prices *must* be stable around their equilibrium. Wrong!

Classical equilibrium theory is not true by necessity. It is not true at all. The problem lies with the seemingly innocuous extension of local stability to global stability. Given that IBM closed at $100, an investor, liking the company's prospects, might be willing to buy the stock at $99. He might or might not be willing to buy the stock below $99.

If IBM opens the next day at $98, he may buy it. If, however, it opens at $50, he may be spooked into reconsidering his "buy" decision. He may believe something must be seriously wrong, even though he has no idea what it is. If everything were all right, he may reason, there wouldn't have been so much selling and so little buying from other investors to drive the price so low. Thus, that this investor may have been willing to buy at $99 does *not* entail he would be willing to buy below $99. (This is the rationale for "buy-stop" and "sell-stop" orders, to buy a stock once it advances beyond a given price or to sell a stock once it declines below a given price.)

This is what happened in the oil price crash of 1985 and the stock market crash of 1987. Potential buyers disappeared when — and because — prices plunged. These may seem to be isolated occurrences. In fact, this type of behavior is more common than many suppose, and it plays an important role in financial markets.

The rapidity of the rise in stock prices can cause investor mania and become a primary motivation for new buying. These new investors, previously afraid to buy at lower prices, are now afraid of being left behind, of missing easy and automatic appreciation. (How many individuals who would not touch a stock or mutual fund in the early 1980s invested heavily in the late 1990s, after stocks, mutual funds, and market averages had appreciated more than ten-fold?) In market panics, the severity of the price decline scares investors — who would not sell earlier at higher prices — into dumping their positions. Margin debt introduces a feedback mechanism that amplifies the decline: the lower stock prices go, the more margin calls go out, the more margin debt must be liquidated, the more stock must be sold, the lower stock prices go.

The same feedback mechanisms that cause euphoria and crashes contribute to normal market cyclicality. Momentum investing is common even in normal times, and from investors who are unaware that they are momentum investors. The longer a stock performs well, the greater is the confidence of investors that it will continue to perform well. The price advance itself generates new buying as investors, concerned about risk at a lower price, become increasingly comfortable as, and because, the price moves up. Momentum buying, feeding on itself, carries the price beyond a reasonable level and sets up the next decline. The decline is a mirror image of the previous advance, in which momentum investors sell the stock primarily because it is declining. In their haste to get out, they sell it at a price below a reasonable level, setting up the next advance.

There is also long-term positive feedback between financial markets and the economy. In a secular bull market, investors' wealth increases as their stocks appreciate. Their additional wealth increases their comfort in spending more. The wealth effect stimulates the economy and leads to higher corporate profits. Higher profits support higher stock valuations, which further increase investors' wealth, leading to even more spending. In a secular bear market just the opposite occurs. This feedback increases the amplitude of long-term economic and financial cycles. So much for a self-correcting market!

There are similar feedback mechanisms within industry. The ethical drug sector has consistently provided an above-average return on equity and above-average growth combined with below-average risk. According to classical economics, such an industry should attract sufficient capital to foster enough competition to reduce its return on equity to the average. Yet these superior returns have persisted for more than half a century, the result of another positive feedback cycle. Researchers, marketers, etc. are attracted to the top industry, which can choose the best of them. Their contributions allow this industry to continue to outpace others.

These examples illustrate a major difference between a nonlinear worldview and that of classical economics. In nonlinear systems cycles and non-uniformities are natural, requiring no special explanation. By contrast, classical economics regards a uniform unchanging steady state as natural. Cycles and non-uniformities are deviant and require special explanation. It is a weakness of the classical view that even ingenious attempts to explain standard nonlinear behavior appear forced.

Traditional economic theory has been handicapped by the need for assumptions that are mathematically tractable within its paradigm. The nonlinear paradigm has an important advantage in this respect. The conditions necessary to nonlinearity — open systems, far from internal equilibrium, whose evolution can be described by nonlinear differential equations in which there is positive feedback — are more realistic than those necessary to classical economics.

What are the ramifications of an economic theory based on nonlinear thermodynamics, as opposed to one based on *laissez faire*? An immediate effect is to free us from the *laissez faire* conception of people as interested only in their own immediate economic welfare. This conception conflicts not only with our own experience, but also with traditional views. Aristotle regarded people as by nature political animals who understand that they do not live in a vacuum, but that their own well-being and security depend on the well-being of their community. In contrast to *laissez faire*, in a world characterized by nonlinearity independent action will be natural under certain conditions while mutual cooperation will be natural under other conditions. This lies closer to the view of the classical Greeks, and also to common sense.

At a more practical level, *laissez faire* sees natural economic forces as purely benign, leading to and maintaining a stable wealth-maximizing equilibrium. Any interference with those forces can only diminish total wealth. By contrast, nonlinear steady states may be unstable and natural forces may lead systems away from equilibrium. There is no assurance that this process is benign. To the contrary, there is historical evidence that it can lead to disaster. It may be appropriate to intervene to mitigate the effects of these forces.

This is not intended to imply that a nonlinear approach is incompatible with free markets. It is incompatible with theological *laissez faire*, with the doctrine that any interference whatsoever with the free market must diminish economic performance. But it fits with the unfettered operation of the market within a broad range.

(It may be reasonable to extend a nonlinear approach beyond economics. The flow of history resembles nonlinear systems in its cyclicality. Historians from Arthur Schlesinger to Jose Ortega y Gassett, from Arnold Toynbee to George Modelski, have argued for the importance of cycles in history. William Strauss and Neil Howe (*Generations, The Fourth Turning*) claim that generations at similar phases of different historical cycles have the same worldviews and the same collective personalities.

Independently, there are times that the direction of history can be highly sensitive to minor events, a typical feature of nonlinear systems. How would the world be different if the field of battle at Waterloo had been dry? What if Marx had had the money to leave England for the U.S.?

Perhaps there are similar sensitivities in individual lives. "There is a tide in the lives of men, which, taken at the flood, leads on to fortune; omitted, all the voyage of their life is bound in shallows..." (Shakespeare, *Julius Caesar*). While history cannot be described in terms of differential equations, nonlinear thermodynamics at least suggests analogous mechanisms for historical patterns of structure and change.)

The most important implications of nonlinearity for the present U.S. economy are based on the feature that once a nonlinear system crosses a critical level, called a bifurcation point, there are new solutions to the differential equations describing its evolution. These solutions entail new and different behavior. Rules that had previously predicted behavior no longer apply. Forces that had previously been applied with success to change the behavior of the system no longer work. A system that had been controlled by these forces may spiral out of control.

Presently, evidence supports the conjecture that in our record stock market valuation and our record debt, both surpassing the previous records made in 1929, we have crossed important bifurcation points. The positive feedback loops characterizing the unwinding of this state express themselves in vicious circles leading to a downward economic spiral:

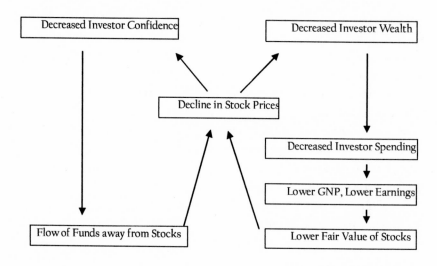

This sort of cycle is not just a twentieth-century phenomenon. The bursting of speculative bubbles in 1837, 1857, 1873, and 1893, bubbles incubated by the new technology of railroads, led to stock market declines of 50% or more. All of these declines touched off economic contractions. There is no reason to think things are different today. The annual rate of change in the S&P Composite is the single most accurate of the Commerce Department's leading indicators. This suggests that the wealth effect may have a consistent effect on spending and GNP.

If the bursting of our technology-financial bubble were to cause similar behavior, how severe could this downward spiral be? At its high in 1929, stock market capitalization reached 80% of GNP. From 1929 to 1932 the stock market lost nearly 90% of its value. The capital loss was 70% of GNP. The concomitant contraction in real GNP was 30%. At its 2000 peak, stock market capitalization was 180% of GNP. A 60% decline in market value would correspond to a capital loss of 108% of GNP, almost 50% higher than the loss following the 1929 peak. If the ratios remain the same, this would suggest a nearly 50% decline in our real GNP.

Is a 60% stock market decline likely? Unfortunately, it could easily be greater. The only historical parallel with a stock market as overvalued as our current market was 1929, which resulted in a 90% decline. Even our 1973 bear market, in which stocks were not so overvalued and in which the financial bubble was far smaller, saw a decline of 60%. Independently, a drop in the average price-to-sales ratio or the price-to-dividend ratio to their average values over the past 50 years would result in at least a 60% market decline.

Is it likely that we will have the same ratio between the loss of financial wealth and the loss of GNP? Some measures suggest the ratio could be larger. In 1929, only the wealthiest owned stocks. Many of these individuals did not change their spending habits as a result of the stock losses. Now, half of us own stocks. It is plausible that a sharp market decline would affect more people and result in a more widespread curtailment of spending. In addition, our personal financial leverage is greater than it was in 1929, suggesting that a financial loss would have a greater impact.

There are some positives as well; though it is not likely that they could save the day. The Federal Reserve has the ability to increase money supply and lower short-term interest rates, which should stimulate the economy. In 2001, the Federal Reserve eased aggressively, lowering short-term interest rates 11 times, to a multi-decade low. Ominously, that is the first time since the Great Depression that repeatedly lowering the discount rate did not give the economy an immediate boost, and also the first time that such action left the stock market lower than it was when the Fed began easing.

This suggests that something is different now. If, in fact, we have crossed a bifurcation point as we had in 1929, if the economy is sufficiently out of balance, then one might expect Federal Reserve actions to be ineffective. And with the discount rate below 2%, the Fed is dangerously low on ammunition. (In addition, excessive monetary stimulus could endanger our currency. Worries about a collapse of the dollar could restrain monetary stimulus.)

A factor more likely to cushion our economy may be that in an economic contraction we would import less. Our balance of trade would improve, slowing our economic decline, albeit at the expense of our trading partners. But this would be a relatively small effect.

All in all, it would be foolish to assume that some ineffable and infallible invisible hand will protect our economy from a severe contraction. It would be imprudent to neglect the very real possibility of economic catastrophe.

Unfortunately, the effects of such a catastrophe could extend beyond the economy. It is possible that we have crossed yet another bifurcation point, a transition that could make matters even worse. For we now have a record economic inequality between the rich and the rest. Historically, extreme levels of economic inequality have uniformly led to an unraveling of the social fabric.

For the first time in history we may be aware of this pattern. Hopefully, we will act wisely on the basis of such awareness. If we fail to do so, I fear it is likely that we shall experience yet another round of increasing violence, widespread decline in the quality of life for all, and a potential breakdown of our political and social systems.

Appendix

Nonlinear Economics

Nonlinear processes can be described by sets of differential equations. The solutions to these equations describe behavior that is typically cyclic. The purpose of this appendix is to illustrate the nature of these equations and their solutions. The discussion is simplified in that quantitative assumptions have been chosen to make the mathematics easier. Despite the simplification, the examples illustrate nonlinear themes and their relevance to economics. (The mathematics underlying these examples and the physical chemistry paralleling them are lucidly discussed in Ilya Prigogine's *From Being to Becoming*, chapters 4-6.)

In the first example, consider the evolution of two variables: inflation (I) and unemployment (U). If there is no unemployment, workers will have leverage with respect to their wages. Wages and inflation will chase each other, causing inflation to accelerate. Assume, as suggested by scale invariance, the rate of increase of inflation is proportional to the rate of inflation.

(1) $dI/dt = k_1 I \ (k_1 > 0)$

If there is unemployment, there will be less upward pressure on wages and also less demand, so there will be less inflation pressure. The higher the unemployment, the smaller the acceleration in inflation, and for sufficiently high unemployment, inflation will decelerate. Assume the relation is linear.

(2) $dI/dt = k_1 I(1 - k_2 U) = k_1 I - k_1 k_2 IU$

Now, consider unemployment. If there is no inflation, fiscal and monetary stimulus should reduce unemployment. Assume the decrease in unemployment is proportional to the level of unemployment.

(3) $dU/dt = -k_3U$ $(k_3 > 0)$

If there is inflation economic stimulus will be restrained by the fear of accelerating inflation. The higher the inflation, the more restrained will be the monetary and fiscal policy and the less will be the reduction in unemployment. Again assume the relationship is linear.

(4) $dU/dt = -k_3U(1 - k_4I) = -k_3U + k_3 k_4IU$

To simplify the mathematics, assume $k_1k_2 = k_3k_4 = k_5$.

(2') $dI/dt = k_1I - k_5IU$

(4') $dU/dt = k_5UI - k_3U$

Equations (2') and (4') are the equations generated by the Lotka-Volterra model, used in ecological modeling. The most common use of this model is the predator/prey relationship, in which I represents the number of prey and U represents the number of predators.

Left to itself, the prey population increases at a given rate, k_1 (equation 1). But the prey population also decreases by some fraction, k_1k_2, of the number of predator-prey encounters (equation 2). Predators, left to themselves, lack adequate nutrition and their population declines at the rate k_3 (equation 3). Thanks, however, to the nutrition provided by the prey, the predator population increases by some fraction, k_3k_4, of the number of predator-prey encounters (equation 4).

The steady-state solution to equations (2') and (4'), in which both inflation and unemployment are permanently fixed at their initial values, is

(5) $I_0 = k_3/k_5$; $U_0 = k_1/k_5$

Greater insight comes from considering what happens if inflation and unemployment are displaced from their steady state values. Set

(6) $I(t) = I_0 + Ie^{\omega t}$; $U(t) = U_0 + Ue^{\omega t}$

where (6a) $|I/I_0| \ll 1$; $|U/U_0| \ll 1$

Insert equation (6) into equations (2') and (4'), neglecting higher order terms in I and U. This generates the dispersion equation:

(7) $\omega^2 + k_1k_3 = 0$

In the inflation-unemployment example both k_1 and k_3 are positive, yielding stable orbits that describe ellipses around the steady state point (I_0, U_0).

(8) $I(t) = I_0 + Ie^{i(\sqrt{k_1k_3})t}$; $U(t) = U_0 + Ue^{i(\sqrt{k_1k_3})t}$

Higher inflation (I↑) → monetary and fiscal restraint → slower growth → higher unemployment (U↑) → less demand → lower inflation (I↓) → monetary and fiscal stimulus → faster growth → lower unemployment (U↓) → greater demand → higher inflation (I↑)...

Despite the failure of this example to capture the full range of nonlinear behavior and despite its oversimplified assumptions, it captures the rotational, cyclic, aspect of the Phillips curve, an aspect that often goes unnoticed. (Where each year represents a point on the I–U curve, the line connecting consecutive points is characterized by a persistent clockwise rotation.) This provides a glimpse of one mechanism that generates economic cyclicality.

Slightly more complex assumptions yield a broader range of nonlinear behavior.

In a second example, consider the velocity of money (V) and the rate of inflation (I). If there is no inflation, assume the velocity of money will asymptotically approach some limit, V_0. Assume the rate of change in V is proportional to the difference between the actual velocity of money and its ultimate zero-inflation limit, V_0.

(9) $dV/dt = k(V_0 - V)$

If there is inflation, then inflationary psychology (Ψ) will lead people to spend more quickly and to borrow more and save less. The velocity of money will increase. This provides a positive feedback mechanism. Higher inflation → greater inflationary psychology → a higher velocity of money → still higher inflation. Choose a measure of inflationary psychology such that the relationship between inflation and inflationary psychology is linear ($\Psi \propto I$). Assume the relationship between this measure of inflationary psychology and the velocity of money is quadratic ($\Psi \propto V^2$).

(10) $dV/dt = k(V_0 - V) + k_1\Psi = k(V_0 - V) + k_1V^2I = k_1 (A + V^2I - BV - V/k_1)$
where $A = kV_0/k_1$ and $B = (k - 1)/k_1$.

Now consider the change in inflation. If there is minimal inflation initially, monetary accommodation will cause inflation to increase. Assume the higher the velocity of money, the greater the sensitivity of the system and the greater the change in inflation. Assume the relationship is linear.

(11) $dI/dt = k_2V$

To the extent that there is noticeable inflation, restrictive monetary policies will increase interest rates and dampen the rate of inflation. Assume the degree of tightening (T) is proportional to both the rate of inflation and the velocity of money ($T = k_5VI$). Also assume that the (negative) change in inflation is proportional both to the degree of tightening and the velocity of money: ($dI/dt = -k_6TV = -k_5k_6V^2I$).

(12) $dI/dt = k_2V - k_3V^2I = k_3 (CV - V^2I)$

where $k_3 = k_5 k_6$ and $C = k_2/k_3$.

To simplify the mathematics, assume $k_1 = k_3 = 1$, and $B = C$.

(10') $\quad dV/dt = A + V^2I - BV - V$

(12') $\quad dI/dt = BV - V^2I$

Equations (10') and (12') embody a model developed by Prigogine and Nicolis, called the *Brusselator*. This model has been successful in explaining a wide range of cyclic behaviors in chemistry and biology.

From equations (10') and (12') the steady state is

(13) $V_0 = A; I_0 = B/A$

We get the time-dependent solutions for $V(t)$ and $I(t)$ by treating these equations like the Lotka-Volterra equations, (2') and (4'). The dispersion equation is:

(14) $\omega^2 + (A^2 - B + 1)\omega + A^2 = 0$

Provided $B > 1 + A^2$, the real parts of ω are positive. This generates true instability and a limit cycle. The steady state is not stable. If the system is displaced even the smallest distance from the steady state, it moves further away from that steady state. It eventually rotates around it in a closed curve at an angle to the Cartesian coordinates that — significantly — is independent of its initial displacement. A system that has been barely displaced from its steady state will, in time, behave exactly like a system that started far from the steady state.

Qualitatively, increasing inflation leads to greater monetary restraint. This raises interest rates enough to reduce spending and lower the velocity of money. But it takes time for inflation to subside. Inflation has its own momentum, and prices continue to rise even in the face of a slowing economy and increasing inventories. When inventories rise past a certain level, they exert downward pressure on prices. Inflation eventually subsides. Then, after inflation and the velocity of money have been declining for some time, with inflationary psychology drained from the system, a new round of monetary accommodation lowers interest rates. Economic growth and the velocity of money increase. But with an overhang of inventory still to be worked off, sellers are in no hurry to raise prices. So there is a time lag before this increased velocity of money translates into higher price levels. Eventually, a new inflation cycle begins.

This explains why inflation is a lagging indicator. It also shows that exogenous shocks to the economy are not necessary to generate business cycles. The smallest internal fluctuation, which need not be generated by any external event, gives rise to the same cycles as if one had started with the random exogenous shocks postulated by modern business cycle theorists.

Adding just one more element of complexity opens the door to a wider variety of nonlinear phenomena. Suppose we include a diffusion term (corresponding to the trickle-down effect in economics) in the Brusselator.

(15) $dV/dt = A + V^2I - BV - V + D_V \partial^2 V/\partial r^2$

(16) $dI/dt = BV - V^2I + D_I \partial^2 I/\partial r^2$

where D_V and D_I are constants for the rates of diffusion of V and I.

Now the system can act in new ways. As the value of B increases beyond particular constants, called bifurcation points, new solutions appear to equations (15) and (16), triggering a variety of new behaviors. Among the solutions to these equations one can find (i) non-uniform steady states, spatially periodic, in which different points have different, but unchanging, values of V and I; (ii) limit cycles, discussed in the previous example (obtained whenever $D_V = D_I = 0$); and (iii) economic waves propagating across the system without damping. In none of these cases does the system tend to any uniform stable state.

Note how radically different is this picture of the behavior of nonlinear systems from the classical picture of quiescent uniform steady states. Even in thermodynamics, chemistry and biology non-uniformity and cyclic change are natural behaviors underlying persistent structures. A quiescent uniform steady state is unstable at the micro-level and cannot persist. Any fluctuation away from that steady state will be amplified and will lead the system further away. And the system will not return to that steady state. Even for simple systems in the natural sciences it is impossible to remain in an unchanging steady state.

Consider how different is this picture of natural behavior from the standard picture of stable quiescent equilibrium that prevailed in the days of Adam Smith. Imagine how economic theory might have developed had the nonlinear paradigm been available in those days. Given the progress we have made in understanding open systems in the natural sciences — and economies are open systems — would it not be appropriate to re-examine economic theory in the light of this progress?

For it is plausible that there are aspects of economies whose evolution can be described by differential equations similar to those above. This makes it plausible that there is economic behavior that parallels the nonlinear chemical and biological behavior investigated by Prigogine and his colleagues. It calls attention to the possibility that successful endeavors to explain the economic counterparts to this chemical behavior will draw attention to "new" economic phenomena, phenomena that have hitherto gone unnoticed because they do not fit the traditional paradigm.

POLITY

VALUES, SCIENCE, REASON

"Nothing is more dangerous than an idea, when it is the only one we have" (Émile A. Chartier). Despite its manifest shortcomings even within economics, the non-interference philosophy of the free market has done much to shape our attitudes in areas ranging from politics to education. If we are not blinded by the false mystique of *laissez faire*, we may be open to alternative perspectives. Acknowledging the possibility of valuable worldviews and priorities beyond those of the free market, we may look at society through the eyes of other disciplines. For we have made significant progress in the social sciences as well as the natural sciences.

Even in value theory, regarded by many as the academic discipline least likely to break new ground, we have advanced. This progress can serve as a general guide to addressing difficult open-ended issues.

Consider the right to life case, which has rested on the following argument:

(i)   Every person has the right to life.

(ii)   The fetus is a person.

(iii)   Therefore, the fetus has the right to life.

(iv)   The fetus requires the mother's womb to exercise that right to life.

(v)   Therefore, the fetus has the right to the mother's womb.

(vi)   Although the mother may have the right to her own body, the right to life outweighs the right to decide what happens to one's body.

(vii)   It is always wrong to invert these moral priorities, to take the mother's right to decide what happens to her body as more important than the fetus's right to life.

(viii) Therefore, abortion is always wrong, independent of circumstances.

This argument is widely accepted as logically valid. If the premises [(i), (ii), (iv), (vi), (vii)] are true, then the conclusion must be true. The debate has focused on the truth of the second premise. Is (or at what point is) the fetus a human being, a person morally entitled to be treated on the basis of his own interests? At one end of the spectrum it has been argued that the egg is a person as soon as it is fertilized. At the other end it has been claimed that whatever it is, it is not human until it leaves for medical school.

Contrary to claims of the religious right, it is not at all obvious that the zygote, the fertilized egg, is a person. The zygote does not have a brain. It never did. It does not have a heart. It never did. It is not sentient. It never was. Even under a microscope, we would not recognize it as human. It is so different from anything we have ever regarded as a person that it is surely reasonable to question whether it is a person with moral rights.

This is not to deny the close relationship between a zygote and a person. Biology texts routinely tell us that under favorable conditions the zygote will develop into a person. But this in itself implies the zygote is not yet a person. A child, not yet an adult, develops into an adult. A bunch of raw recruits, not yet a well-trained military force, develops into a military force. The caterpillar, not yet a butterfly, develops into a butterfly. A fertile egg, not yet a chicken, develops into a chicken.

If the zygote is not yet a person but the just-born baby is, at what point does the fetus become a person? Science does not answer this question. The development of the fetus is a continuum from the fertilization of the egg to birth. This continuum is punctuated by discrete changes: the first electrical discharge from the brain, the first heartbeat, quickening. No one of these events is so much more important than the others that it defines the point of personhood.

A religious approach may appear simpler, turning on the question: "When does the soul enter the body?" But scripture does not discuss when this occurs, or even whether ensoulment is instantaneous or gradual.

Independent of scripture, when the fetus becomes a human being has a moral component. Where does the major moral difference lie among:

(a) entering a fertility clinic and spilling unfertilized egg cells on the floor;

(b) entering the same clinic and spilling fertilized egg cells on the floor; and

(c)   entering a nursery and killing babies?

Were the egg a person as soon as it is fertilized, the important difference would lie between (a) and (b). Were it to become a person at a later point, the difference would lie between (b) and (c). That the major moral difference lies between (b) and (c) suggests, at least from a moral perspective, that personhood is not simultaneous with conception. Our laws reflect this view.

Note that it is not just a question of life. We show no compunction about using antibiotics to kill bacteria, insecticides to kill mosquitoes or cockroaches, radiation or chemotherapy to kill cancer cells. Most of us eat meat. We kill a flower by plucking it. Imagine the carnage that goes on in a perfume factory. None of this strikes us as morally wrong.

The claim that all life has value, simply in virtue of being alive, is unconvincing. Persons, or at the very least, sentient beings, are the source of moral value. Even then it does not follow from strictures against unnecessary killing that a greater quantity of sentient life is automatically good. Those who would not kill a mosquito may spay or neuter cats and dogs. Contraception is not necessarily immoral.

People have struggled fruitlessly over abortion issues for decades. But recent work by philosophers, Judith J. Thomson in particular, has cast the anti-abortion argument in a new light. Thomson argues that a person may have a right to an abortion even if the fetus is a human being from the time of conception.

She suggests you imagine yourself involuntarily plugged into the kidney machine of a violinist who needs the use of your kidneys to survive. To unplug yourself would kill the violinist. Do you have the moral right to unplug yourself, independent of how you came to be plugged in, and also independent of any inconvenience, pain or risk associated with remaining plugged in? Surely, the violinist has the right to life, even if he plays badly. And his right to life supersedes your right to decide what happens to your body. Surely, it would be kind, perhaps beyond the call of duty, to remain plugged in. But what about the claim that you do not have the moral right to unplug yourself? "I imagine you would regard this as outrageous, which suggests that something really is wrong with that plausible sounding argument I mentioned a moment ago." ("A Defense of Abortion," *Philosophy and Public Affairs*, v. 1, n. 1 [1971].)

The facts that a person has the right to something (life) and requires something else (the use of your kidneys or his mother's womb) to secure that right do not guarantee his right to that something else. You surely have the right to your car. But suppose someone has stolen it and the only way you can get it back is by overtaking and apprehending the thief. And suppose my car is the only available car. Your right to your car plus the fact that you need my car to secure that right does not automatically give you the right to my car. In the same manner, that the fetus has the right to life but requires its mother's womb to secure that right does not automatically give the fetus the right to its mother's womb — so the mother may have the moral right to unplug herself from the fetus, even if the fetus is a human being. For, even though the fetus has the right to life, that does not guarantee him the right to his mother's womb.

This important (and surprising), albeit negative, contribution has not resolved the abortion issue. But it has brought a new level of understanding to the issue. The standard argument against abortion does not work. Abortion may still be morally wrong, but it must be shown to be wrong for other reasons, and the circumstances and intentions underlying an abortion may play a role in its morality.

This reflects progress in an issue far from the realm of science. It has advanced our understanding of an important moral question and shown that more is involved than we had previously thought. At the same time, our theoretical understanding of the moral considerations involved in abortion is not the only issue, or even the primary one. Nor is it just a religious issue.

The sanctity of human life is not confined to the Bible, nor is it confined to religious thought. It occupies a central place in secular foundations of morality, from utilitarianism to Kant's deontology. It is morally wrong, on all accounts, to treat human life lightly. Yet the prevalence of abortions is only one symptom of a broader failure to value persons. Ironically, many pro-life positions, in their aggressive insensitivity to the plight of the mother, fail to come to terms with the basic moral issues and exacerbate the problem.

The abortion debate itself, which encourages self-righteous anger on both sides of the issue, is not well focused. How do we teach the dignity of life? How do we encourage people to take responsibility for their lives so that they will avoid unwanted pregnancies in the first place? These are practical problems whose solution requires compassion for individuals. Without that compassion, we lack the very moral sensitivity we find wanting in others.

Still, our moral understanding can inform our moral sensitivity, and we can progress in moral understanding in the same way we advance scientific understanding. Science can serve as a model for other fields, including values. We have scientific beliefs and we act on them. We even teach them to our children. At the same time, we know our beliefs have changed dramatically over the centuries, and they may change again. We are fallible, and the possibility that we are wrong even now mandates openness on our part and a willingness to change should the evidence dictate. Hopefully, we also teach that openness.

But — hopefully — we teach more than mere openness and tolerance. Clearly, science has made considerable progress. Moreover, this progress is not random, but has been generated by the interplay of creativity and rational criticism. We have standards, even though we may not be able to state them explicitly. Although almost anything may be tried, not just anything goes.

To be acceptable, a newly proposed theory must explain the evidence explained by the extant theory. It must be expressible in a simple and elegant form that is compatible with other accepted theories. It must add to our understanding, ideally by explaining new phenomena.

Nor is science a special discipline with its own rules. Scientific reasoning conforms to general standards of evidence and rationality. The mechanism by which evidence supports a theory, independent of its subject matter, is just the low probability there would be such evidence if the theory were not true. The discovery of that evidence increases the likelihood the theory is true, whether or not it is a theory of science.

Within science, the geological theory of continental drift receives some confirmation from the fact that the east coast of the Americas fits (roughly) into the west coast of Europe and Africa. If the continents were once part of the same land mass and had drifted apart, one would expect such a fit. But the fit would be unlikely to occur by mere chance. As detail of the fit increases, it becomes increasingly less likely that it would have occurred by chance, and the confirmation of the continental drift hypothesis increases. So the discovery of additional features — the fit of the (Permian) Cape Mountains of South Africa with the (Permian) Sierras of Buenos Aires, the (Precambrian) Hebrides with the (Precambrian) Labrador formation, the gneiss plateau in Africa with the similar Brazilian pampas — adds to the confirmation of the theory. The discovery of close genetic similarities between flora and fauna on both sides of the Atlantic adds still further confirmation.

In the same way, the nineteenth century discovery of Akkadian tablets in Brazil — "Barzil" is the Ugaritic word for iron — supports the non-scientific historical theory that Phoenicians landed in South America at least two thousand years ago. These tablets contained idiomatic expressions unfamiliar to nineteenth century scholars, and so were pronounced fraudulent by Ernest Renan, an eminent Biblical scholar of the time. Given that nineteenth century scholars were unaware of Ugaritic idiom, it is virtually impossible that such tablets had been forged. They would not have contained idiomatic expressions unless they had been inscribed by the Phoenicians.

There are differences between the sciences and non-scientific disciplines, mostly related to the well-developed structural characteristics of scientific theories, especially in the natural sciences. But good reasoning is good reasoning in all disciplines. It is not the case that there is one standard for science and a different one for other intellectual disciplines. It is appropriate to apply the same standards of reasoning to questions of values as those accepted in science and history, law and mathematics.

These standards, while they imply toleration for new scientific, historical or moral theories, also make it clear that there are objective criteria by which all understanding is to be judged. Not all scientific theories are equal or mutually incommensurable. Not all historical explanations are equal or mutually incommensurable. Not all value judgments are equal or mutually incommensurable. In all disciplines there are widely accepted standards of rationality that can be applied to argue for the superiority of certain theories or explanations or values.

In light of these standards, what are appropriate values in today's world?

HUMANISM

THE PROPRIETY OF HUMANISM

Although controversial, humanism is an appropriate guide to values. Admittedly, humanism has a questionable reputation — as atheistic, anti-religious, anti-individualist, and even amoral. For many, the term "humanist" is an insult. But humanism has been unfairly maligned and careful consideration will show its value. Indeed, the tactics used to besmirch humanism have been used in other contexts as well. It is wise to be aware of these tactics and to reject them.

It is common to play a game with labels, for they can have emotive power even if they have been drained of their cognitive value. Politicians, in particular, find such tactics useful, for labeling can be effective with an audience that desires to reduce a difficult world to simple terms. The desire is understandable. But reality is too complex, and the process leaves the audience open to manipulation.

Even familiar categories such as liberal and conservative cannot be applied across the board. For there are many dimensions — defense, economics, education, the environment, equal opportunity, morality, the prison system... It is rare that a person is liberal (or conservative) on all issues. And these notions change over time. In the days of Adam Smith, *laissez faire* represented a liberal economic position. Today it is a highly conservative position.

Even more difficult for a simplistic position, it is impossible to consistently be a liberal (or conservative) on all issues. There is a valuable conservative tradition that regards the appreciation of great literature as an essential part of education and would recommend the formal study of "Great Books." Yet these wreak havoc on conservative morality.

> The silliest way to defend the Western Canon is to insist that it incarnates all of the seven deadly virtues that make up our supposed range of normative values and democratic principles. That is palpably untrue. The *Iliad* teaches the surpassing glory of armed victory, while Dante rejoices in the eternal torments he visits upon his very personal enemies. Tolstoy's private version of Christianity throws aside nearly everything that anyone among us retains, and Dostoevsky preaches anti-Semitism, obscurantism, and the necessity of human bondage. Shakespeare's politics, insofar as we can pin them down, do not appear to be very different from those of his Coriolanus, and Milton's ideas of free speech and free press do not preclude the imposition of all manner of societal restraints. Spenser rejoices in the massacre of Irish rebels, while the egomania of Wordsworth exalts his own poetic mind over any other source of splendor. The West's greatest writers are subversive of all values, both ours and their own..." (Bloom, *The Western Canon*, p. 29.)

Given the different dimensions in which one can be conservative or liberal, and given that one can be both liberal and conservative on the same issues at the same time (despite the ranting of some politicians, the two concepts are not mutually exclusive), the reduction of "liberal" to a blanket term of scandal may appear surprising. This is especially so given that our country fared better under the liberal economic policies of the New Deal and its successors than under the more right-wing economic policies of the past two decades (or those of the 1920s). Throughout the entire spectrum of society, not just its upper crust, people increased their wealth and led better lives. We have forgotten this track record of economic liberalism. In our new use of "liberal" as a pejorative, the most derogatory epithet in either political party, we have also forgotten the positive things previous thinkers had to say about liberalism.

> Liberalism — it is well to recall this today — is the supreme form of generosity; it is the right which the majority concedes to minorities and hence it is the noblest cry that has ever resounded in this planet. It announces the determination to share existence with the enemy; more than that, with an enemy which is weak. It was incredible that the human species should have arrived at so noble an attitude, so paradoxical, so refined, so acrobatic, so anti-natural. Hence it is not to be wondered at that this same humanity should soon appear anxious to get rid of it. (Ortega y Gassett, *The Revolt of the Masses*).

(This is not to deny that some liberal thinkers have advocated stupid and pernicious policies. So have some conservative thinkers. It is instead to deny the propriety of treating their positions as expressing the core of liberalism – or conservatism. It would be more intellectually honest, and more accurate, to simply describe, as Spiro Agnew had done, those liberal patronizing academicians who saw themselves as the new elite as "effete pointy-headed intellectual snobs.")

Even though our redefinition of "liberal" has failed to improve the quality of government, it has simplified political discussion. Rather than having to analyze a candidate or political platform, we have only to decide whether he, she or it can be labeled "liberal." This game has zero content. It is a dangerous game because it appears to have content.

Merely calling one's government a "Peoples' Republic" does not give citizens a greater voice in government; nor does it lessen its exploitation of citizens. Yet, it would appear that, if a republic is responsive to the needs of its people, then a Peoples' Republic must be even more responsive. It is not. Arbitrary definitions or labels cannot change reality. They just delude people as to the nature of reality. (Lincoln once asked how many legs a horse would have if you called its tail a leg. He reminded his audience that "four" is the correct answer. Calling a tail a leg doesn't make it a leg.)

Playing with words distracts from substantive issues. Is government responsive to the needs of all citizens, as opposed to just those of big business or big labor or special interest groups? What modifications to its institutions (or personnel) would make it more responsive to citizens? Do government policies sacrifice the long-term health of the polity to the short term? All governments redistribute income by collecting taxes and providing services. Is our income redistribution fair? Does it achieve an appropriate purpose? By focusing on labels we avoid the real issues.

Humanism is endangered by these word games, threatened with being redefined by the religious right and reduced to a label of opprobrium. This would be a shame, for it is one of the finest traditions of Western civilization.

Before characterizing humanism, consider the alternatives. Deism? But which Deus? Is Allah the same as Adonai the same as Jesus Christ the same as the Holy Spirit? Within Christianity, is the Unitarian God the same as the Greek Orthodox God the same as the Roman Catholic God the same as the God of the Church of the Latter Day Saints? Within Islam is the God of the Sunnis the same as the God of the Shi'ites the same as the God of the Sufis? What about the Baha'i? Is the Buddhist notion of *dharma* the same?

Is this important? Unfortunately, it is. The exclusive nature of Western religions has long fostered contentious animosity. Time and again the violent fruits of this animosity have stained Western history. Violent religious strife has an unpleasant history that extends back to the Old Testament narrative of the Israelites' conflict with the tribes of Canaan. The religious zeal of the fourth crusade expressed itself in sacking Christian Constantinople and enthroning a harlot on the patriarch's seat of St. Sophia's church. The Reformation and Counter-Reformation spawned some of the bloodiest wars on record. Within Islam Sunnis and Shi'ites have been persecuting each other for centuries. Both have persecuted the Baha'i (whom they regard as non-Muslim, despite the fact that the religious matrix of Baha'i is clearly Islam).

Many of the early European settlers in the New World were Christians fleeing religious persecution by other Christians. The Common Protestantism that developed in the early nineteenth century was both anti-Catholic and anti-Semitic. Anti-Catholic societies, the Know Nothings, fomented riots and burned Catholic churches and convents. In 1838, Lilburn Boggs, the Governor of Missouri, issued the order: "The Mormons must be treated as enemies, and must be exterminated or driven from the State if necessary, for the public peace." As late as 1893 the mayor of Toledo, Ohio called out the National Guard to protect local Protestants from a rumored Catholic murder plot.

Despite our supposed progress toward a more civilized world, religious intolerance has not yet been eliminated, as painfully witnessed by the conflicts in Northern Ireland, the Middle East, and the former Yugoslavia. Even in the U.S. deep animosities still lie close to the surface, especially among fundamentalists, for whom denomination is important. In 1983 the leadership of the World Congress of Fundamentalists expressed its feelings toward ecumenism by describing the Roman Catholic Church as "the mother of harlots and abominations of the earth." One of the few elements Louis Farrakhan and Pat Robertson have in common is their anti-Semitism.

Our long history of bitter religious strife shows how easily denominational orthodoxy can lead to conflict and violence, for people have proffered different and conflicting notions of God and God's laws. How do we decide which of these to accept? Through divine revelation? But few have experienced divine revelation, and those who claim revelation provide accounts that often differ from one another. (Also, how does one prove a revelation was divine?)

Should we decide which notion of God and God's laws to accept through the literal interpretation of scripture? But which scripture? The Old Testament, the New Testament, the Book of Mormon, the Qur'an, the Vedic Scriptures, the sutras of Shakyamuni? Suppose there were agreement on a particular scripture, say, the Bible. But which version of the Bible should it be? In the early nineteenth century public schools required the Protestant King James Bible, rather than the Douay Bible, a translation of the Latin Vulgate. Roman Catholics protested in vain.

Suppose, further, there were agreement on a particular version of a particular scripture. But how should that scripture be interpreted? The claim that the King James Version of the Bible is literally true still fails to fix a particular interpretation. Does Joshua commanding the sun to stand still imply a geocentric universe? Does the passage in Genesis: "And the Lord God formed man of the dust of the ground, and breathed into his nostrils the breath of life, and man became a living soul," imply that a fetus becomes a living person when it first breathes? Does Abraham having had two wives and Jacob having had four support polygamy? Does the institution of slavery in the Bible mean we should likewise condone slavery? (Martin Luther appeared to suggest this in his *Admonition to Peace: A Reply to the Twelve Articles of the Peasants in Swabia.* "Did not Abraham and other patriarchs and prophets have slaves?... For a slave can be a Christian, and have Christian liberty, in the same way that a prisoner or a sick man is a Christian, and yet not free.")

Thus, substituting Deism for humanism would fail to solve the problem. We would still have to specify which Deus, which scripture, which version, and which interpretation. At each step the same sort of disagreement would recur. And at each step an answer would vindicate an ever-decreasing minority of "true believers" at everyone else's expense.

"STRICT CONSTRUCTIONIST" AS A LABEL

The problem with labels, positive or negative, is that they are used to obscure or distort reality, to sell a position based on an emotionally appealing misrepresentation. A striking contemporary example, "strict constructionist," is a pleasant-sounding euphemism that has been used to disguise views many find unpalatable.

Initially a term of conservative reaction against the liberal civil rights activism of the Earl Warren (President Eisenhower) Supreme Court and implying that a strict interpretation of the U.S. Constitution is incompatible with judicial activism, "strict constructionist" justices and courts have been far more activist than the Warren Court. It is just that theirs has been a right-wing judicial activism. It has not been how judges interpret the Constitutional propriety of judicial activism. Rather, it has been how right wing they are. But "strict constructionist" sounds better.

Contrary to the picture of an excessively liberal Supreme Court painted by the far right, the Supreme Court was designed to be a conservative institution and has generally filled that role. The appointment of long-time judges tends to select wealthy conservative individuals. Lifetime appointment insulates justices from political controversy and may make them unsympathetic to new social and political trends.

The Supreme Court ruled that slavery was protected by the Constitution and that the Missouri Compromise was invalid because Congress did not have the right to prohibit slavery. It struck down the federal income tax; it repeatedly applied the Sherman Antitrust Act to unions but refused to apply it to corporations; it struck down child labor laws and state laws limiting the work week, as well as minimum wage laws; it struck down laws that prohibited racial discrimination by private individuals and upheld state laws requiring segregation; it upheld state laws permitting the forced sterilization of the "congenitally unfit"; and until Roosevelt threatened to expand the court with his own nominees it struck down all the major New Deal programs. Hardly liberal!

Despite this history and the often deeply conservative tenor of our highest court, our far right insists a major problem with our government has been our excessively liberal, coddling, Supreme Court. They have fought to replace liberal activism with "strict constructionism," which appears to imply fidelity to the principles of our founding fathers. The appearance is misleading. The rulings of our present Supreme Court, with a majority of "strict constructionist" justices, belie any such fidelity.

Since the days of our independence both conservatives and liberals have accepted the principle of "a wall of separation between church and state" (a phrase coined by Thomas Jefferson). The present Court, ruling in favor of a law granting tax exemptions to individuals who send their children to parochial schools, has compromised that principle.

At the same time, by overturning earlier rulings and withholding the protection of religious freedom from an Indian using peyote in a religious rite of the non-Christian Native American Church, it has undermined the Bill of Rights. In his opinion for the majority Justice Scalia wrote: "It may fairly be said that leaving accommodation to the political process will place at a relative disadvantage those religious practices that are not widely engaged in; but that [is an] unavoidable consequence of democratic government..."

But isn't that just the point of a Constitutional guarantee of freedom of religion? In a democracy there is no need to protect religious practices widely engaged in and regarded as politically correct. The purpose of the First Amendment is to provide protection for "religious practices that are not widely engaged in." This is just the protection Scalia withholds.

How different is Scalia's vision from James Madison's observation: "Who does not see that the same authority which can establish Christianity, in exclusion of all other Religions, may establish with the same ease any particular sect of Christianity, in exclusion of other sects?"

It is difficult to see how Scalia's view reflects the intent of our founding fathers. "A leading conservative scholar...called Scalia's opinion a 'paradigmatic example of judicial overreaching...[in which] use of precedent borders on fiction.'" (Kairys, *With Liberty and Justice for Some*, p. 106.)

"Strict constructionists" introduced a new notion, intent, into deliberations. Government is exonerated in violating a person's civil liberties unless malicious intent can be proved. Not only is this notion absent from the Constitution. It is destructive to the spirit of the Bill of Rights. That spirit maintains government must follow certain rules. Those rules are inviolable, independent of intent. The burden of proving malicious intent would effectively nullify the protection that is the purpose of the Bill of Rights.

Due process is one of the most important subjects addressed in the Bill of Rights. Five of the ten amendments speak to this issue. One of the heinous practices the Bill was designed to prevent was using torture or coercion to extract a confession from a defendant and using that confession to convict him. Yet in *Arizona vs. Fulminante*, the Supreme Court ruled a conviction could stand despite a coerced confession being part of the evidence. The "strict constructionists" ruled this was a "harmless error."

In other areas the Court ruled that "socially inappropriate" speech in schools may be censored. (Where is this in the Constitution?) At the same time, in overturning a Minnesota conviction of teenagers who had burned a cross in the yard of an African-American family, the Court made its decision in terms of a new set of standards, not found in the Constitution or the writings of our founding fathers. It rejected decades of tradition and precedent.

It is easy to understand why people would want to use the expression "strict constructionist." It paints a more pleasant political picture than "radically right wing," and it is easier for one who is labeled a strict constructionist than one who is labeled radically right wing to get confirmed as a justice. Still, it is one thing to question whether there are circumstances in which judicial activism, from either the left or the right, is appropriate. It is quite another to misrepresent right wing judicial activism as "strict constructionism."

THE FOCUS OF HUMANISM

During the Renaissance the term "humanist" referred to teachers of what Cicero had called "*studia humanitatis*": grammar, rhetoric, and poetry. These teachers, having started from this base, proceeded to concerns about a civilized way of life, taking up moral and political philosophy. This provides the link to the broader notion of humanism, to the concern for the dignity of man (an expression coined by Pico della Mirandola, a fifteenth-century Italian humanist).

Augustin Renaudet provides a concise sketch of this broader notion: "The name of humanism can be applied to an ethic based on human nobility... What is essential remains the individual's efforts to develop in himself or herself, through strict and methodical discipline, all human faculties, so as to lose nothing of what enlarges and enhances the human being." (Braudel, *The History of Civilizations*, p. 340)

Braudel goes on to add: "In a certain sense, too, humanism is always against something: against exclusive submission to God; against a wholly materialist conception of the world; against any doctrine neglecting or seeming to neglect humanity; against any system that would reduce human responsibility.... Humanism is...an embattled march towards the progressive emancipation of humanity, with constant attention to the ways in which it can modify and improve human destiny." (p. 340-1) This doesn't seem so terrible. Responsibility and discipline are desirable goals, as is the emancipation of humanity.

More can be said about humanism in terms of its etymology: "It comes from *humanitas*: which since the time of Varro and Cicero at least, possessed a nobler and severer sense in addition to its early vulgar sense of humane behavior... It meant the process of educating man into his true form, the real and genuine human nature... Above man as a member of the horde, and man as a supposedly independent personality, stands man as an ideal: and that ideal was the pattern towards which Greek educators as well as Greek poets, artists, and philosophers always looked. (Jaeger, *Paideia*, v. 1 p.xxiii-xxiv.)

Perhaps the most succinct characterization of humanism comes from Buddhism, in which many sects regard Shakyamuni Buddha as God. Nichiren, a perceptive thirteenth-century student of Buddhist teachings, saw a different significance: "The real meaning of the Lord Shakyamuni's appearance in this world lay in his behavior as a human being." (*The Major Writings of Nichiren Daishonin*, v. 3) Walt Whitman expressed a similar sentiment, most directly in his notebook draft (section 49):

> Mostly this we have of God;
> we have man.

Humanism encompasses an optimism that people are capable of improving their lives, even without help from the supernatural. But it does not deny the beauty and value in religious sentiment, and it is compatible with most religions.

Contrary to claims of those who routinely denigrate humanism, the best-known humanists were deeply religious. Erasmus was unquestionably a devout Catholic priest, despite his criticism of abuses of the Church. He edited the works of St. Jerome, and he included a theme of humanism — and the Reformation — in the forward to his translation of the New Testament into Greek: "Would that these [the Gospels and the Epistles of St. Paul] were translated into every language...and understood not only by Scots and Irishmen but by Turks and Saracens." His illustrious twelfth-century predecessor, John of Salisbury, had been exiled from England by Henry II because of his support of Thomas á Becket.

The Italian humanists of the Renaissance argued for freedom and tolerance, for the study of morals, politics and economics as opposed to metaphysics and theology, for the value of social utility rather than monasticism and asceticism. They valued a simple Biblical piety as opposed to the scholasticism of the late Middle Ages. Yet none had an anti-religious or anti-Christian bias.

Religion has enriched our lives. In the East, as well as the West, it has inspired great literature, architecture, art, and music. The belief that people have souls has had a civilizing effect and has mitigated harsh and inhumane treatment. In the sixteenth century the Spanish Church sharply criticized the brutal enslavement of the Amerindians by the entrepreneurial Conquistadors.

In modern society religion is a valuable counterweight to the sterility of materialism. It has enabled people to understand their lives in a more profound context and to relate to others in more meaningful ways. It has reminded them of their spirituality, that they are more than animals. It has encouraged many to develop compassion and empathy and to muster the courage to act on those sentiments. The profound compassion illuminating the life of Mother Teresa presents an ideal that moves us all.

But while religious sentiment has led many to act out of concern for others, it is not necessary to subscribe to any set of religious beliefs to cherish such ideals and act accordingly. To act on such ideals is part of the humanist tradition and may have prompted John Dewey's claim that humanism is the highest expression of religious faith.

In addition, religion has a darker side, which humanism seeks to avoid. Western religions have claimed to be the sole repository of the most important and unquestionable truths. In defending orthodoxy, correct belief, they have denigrated intellectual integrity because it can corrupt faith and open a door to heresy. In Western religious traditions doubt, the antithesis of faith, is anathema. But without a capacity and willingness to entertain doubt and meaningful self-reflection, religious belief can degenerate into dogmatism. For this reason religious orthodoxy can be an impediment to tolerance and understanding. This impediment is reinforced by a transcendent source of beliefs, which generates appeals to authority and is unable to resolve differences among different authorities.

Religiously, we live in gated communities. Rather than encouraging people to widen their embrace of others, religions have introduced yet another dimension of insider versus outsider. This incubates collective egoism and xenophobia and has been one of the most fertile breeding grounds in history for prejudice, discrimination, and ultimately, violence.

Some religions, in their characterization of God's omnipotence, have denied free will and encouraged people to seek the source of and solution to their sufferings outside themselves. This can be an obstacle to self-improvement, for it discourages people from taking responsibility for their lives. The very notion of a transcendent God has fostered a hierarchical class of priests as intermediaries, demeaning the status of ordinary people.

In the extreme, the judgmental nature of Western religions denies any value in people. It is not just that we are imperfect. It is how we stack up against God, the embodiment of perfection. Our shortcomings generate a revulsion, most harshly vented by Jonathan Edwards: "The God that holds you over the pit of hell, much as one holds a spider, or some loathsome insect, over the fire, abhors you, and is dreadfully provoked, his wrath towards you burns like fire, he looks upon you as worthy of nothing else, but to be cast into the fire; he is of purer eyes than to bear to have you in his sight; you are ten thousand times so abominable in his eyes, as the most hateful and venomous serpent in ours..."

Jonathan Edwards was not unique. This has been a recurrent theme in Christianity. It permeates the writings of St. Augustine and St. Jerome and plays a role in Protestant traditions. Martin Luther wrote: "Further, there is in man a positive inclination to evil, a disgust for the good, a hatred of light and wisdom, a delight in error and darkness, a flight from and abomination of good works, a race toward evil." The denigration of even the well-meaning individual, the focus on imperfections glaringly revealed in the harsh light of contrast to God, also characterizes the writings of John Calvin. "No work of a pious man ever existed which, if it were examined before the strict judgment of God, did not prove to be damnable."

In contrast to this sentiment, humanism focuses on the value in persons. It seeks to enable people to overcome their weaknesses and realize their potential, rather than instructing them in the *Truth*. Issues of right versus wrong get replaced by issues of win — challenging and overcoming problems, extending horizons, nurturing wisdom, developing appreciation and compassion — versus lose. This encourages a virtue-based, as opposed to a rule-based, morality.

A framework for such a focus is provided by the notion of interconnectedness. We are not monads. Our actions affect everything around us, and we in turn are affected by our surroundings. While individualism may be a strand in our values, so, too, is responsibility. We forge our own destinies, but not in a vacuum. We are all part of the same interactive network.

This notion has found expression in venues as diverse as the poetry of John Donne, post-Jungian depth psychology, and the Gaia environmental movement. It is implicit in Buckminster Fuller's notion of spaceship earth and in David Bohm's holomovement theory. It plays a metaphysical role in the Buddhist doctrine of dependent origination, and also in the Hindu and Jain traditions. It lies at the heart of *ahimsa*, the doctrine of not causing pain to any living being because we are all interrelated.

Einstein captured the essence of this view: "[The human being] experiences himself, his thoughts and feelings as something separated from the rest — a kind of optical delusion of our consciousness. This delusion is a kind of prison for us, restricting us to our personal desires and to affection for a few persons nearest us. Our task must be to free ourselves from this prison by widening our circle of compassion to embrace all living creatures and the whole of nature in its beauty."

On a more fashionable note, this is a theme of learning organizations. "At the heart of a learning organization is a shift of mind — from seeing ourselves as separate from the world to connected to the world." (Senge, *The Fifth Discipline*, p. 12.)

Perhaps this notion of a web of mutually dependent life was expressed most eloquently in the moving speech attributed to Dwamish Chief Seathl (Seattle), responding to the government's proposal to relocate Northwest Indian tribes onto reservations:

> How can you buy or sell the sky, the warmth of the land? This idea is strange to us. If we do not own the freshness of the air and the sparkle of the water; how can you buy them?... This we know: All things are connected. Whatever befalls the earth befalls the sons of the earth. Man did not weave the web of life; he is merely a strand in it. Whatever he does to the web, he does to himself... One thing we know. Our God is the same God. This earth is precious to Him. Even the white man cannot be exempt from the common destiny. We may be brothers, after all.

This calls us to understand our actions from a broader perspective, rather than restricting ourselves to immediate consequences. In just the last half century we have destroyed a significant portion (with some estimates as high as 50%) of our planet's tropical rainforest. These forests enrich soil, reduce erosion, and provide habitats for many species of animals. They also regenerate our atmosphere by absorbing carbon dioxide and producing oxygen. (Boreal forests, which are also under attack, are even more efficient, absorbing nearly two tons of carbon dioxide per acre per year.) The destruction of forest to provide timber or beef to mature economies or cropland to developing countries has negative consequences for the entire ecosystem, even if they are not immediate economic consequences.

How can we deal reasonably with such issues that affect all life on the planet, that are inherently multi-national, but that also provide profits for the few who immediately benefit from the byproducts of forest destruction? Closer to home, how can we deal with similar considerations related to greenhouse gas emissions and global warming?

The spirit of humanism is to resist the temptation to narrow focus, but to act with broader vision. In explaining why we should care about such questions, why we should value a broad perspective, diverse traditions have suggested an independent moral component of the universe.

For Plato, immutable moral truths are more real than the physical world. For Kant, synthetic *a priori* moral truths rank with truths of mathematics and causality in their universality and necessity. The notion of karma (Sanskrit for "action") stresses the power of moral causality across lifetimes. It may be appropriate to understand the great prophets of the Old Testament as advocates of moral causality, rather than canny analysts of geopolitical developments.

Is it possible that a society that permits such a gap in wealth that fur coats for rich children are sold in the same neighborhoods where other children are sleeping in the street is morally impaired?

Such a view of a moral, even spiritual, universe is not an expression of soft-headed musing. Einstein, hardly fuzzy-minded, observed: "Everyone who is seriously involved in the pursuit of science becomes convinced that a spirit is manifest in the laws of the universe — a spirit vastly superior to that of man, and one in the face of which we with our modest powers must feel humble."

Humanism, inherently ecumenical, embodies the substance of a moral and spiritual universe without religious dogma. Theoretical truths about the nature of God, the relation between God and man, or even what language(s) God speaks are unimportant.

It is easy to look back at the classic heresies and wonder what all the fuss — and bloodshed — was about. It is also easy to wonder whether an image of God so concerned about the specific beliefs of individuals and so willing to punish people for having the wrong beliefs is not demeaning of God. By contrast, what matters is the actions we take to fulfill our own potential as people, to help others fulfill their potential, to exercise our responsibilities to the environment, our community, family, friends and neighbors.

INDIVIDUALS *VS.* CLASSES

Humanism has been accused of representing collectivist morality, denying the importance of the individual. Contrary to these allegations, humanist authors have not elevated any collective body to a source of value, but have focused on persons. How can people lead more meaningful, more spiritual, more responsible lives?

Humanism is a philosophy of individualism, seeing the source of value in persons (Kant, Mill, Jefferson). It differs sharply from collectivism, which maintains that individuals have value only as citizens of a special nation, representatives of a favored class or race, or participants in predetermined movements of history (Plato, Hegel, Marx).

It is easy to take for granted the humanist view that value resides in persons, rather than collectives. We value ourselves, our families, and our friends as individuals, as *who* we are. But as people are removed from our immediacy, we tend to think of them as members of a collective — what they do or what class they belong to. These two opposing views, the individual valued as a person in his own right and the individual valued for his function in society, have both played roles in history. Both shape society today.

The roots of individualism lie deep. Pericles' classic account of democracy dates from the golden age of Greece. He commented approvingly that while not just anyone could propose national policy, anyone could judge such policy. Participation in the political life of the city-state was a duty of all citizens, not just the rich and powerful. Thucydides, the historian of the Peloponnesian War, believed that actions of individuals are instrumental in determining the course of history.

In religion the doctrine that everyone has a God-given soul values each person as an individual. As early as the twelfth century, artistic depictions of judgment day showed individuals being judged on the basis of their acts. The radical views of the Reformation, that everyone should interpret Scripture for himself and that a person's salvation depends only on his faith, add impetus to the importance of the individual. Biography and realistic portraits depict actual persons as opposed to class-based stereotypes. The classical ideal of education, as opposed to training, values the individual as an end, not just a means to collective accomplishments.

Today we casually assume individualism is the only tenable view. Yet opposing views have been dominant in most of Western civilization. As old as Pericles is Plato's proposal for a rigid, hierarchical society and his view of justice as a state in which people perform only their class-based roles. For a thousand years after the fall of the Roman Empire the notion of individuality was suppressed.

Even the Enlightenment, which we celebrate for its egalitarian sentiments, was but a step in the right direction. Its spirit was far removed from today's ideals of democracy and individualism. Rousseau's general will of the people, while appearing to endorse personal freedom, substitutes "general will" for "wills" and "the people" for "people." It leaves little room for civil liberties. His advocacy of faith in and obedience to a civil religion, under pain of death, lies closer to a dictatorship of the proletariat than to democracy. Nor did individualism and democracy fare better at the hands of the social science spawned by the Enlightenment. Saint Simon and Comte advocated autocratic government run by elite experts.

The victory of the Enlightenment, modest as it was, was short lived. The Romantic movement of the nineteenth century, while it produced outstanding literature, art and music, was largely a negative reaction to the failure of the Enlightenment to meet the overly optimistic expectations of Reason. There was an unbridgeable gap between the ideals of Voltaire and Condorcet and the realities of Robespierre and Napoleon.

Widespread suppression in the wake of the Napoleonic conquests ignited an anti-French nationalism that rallied around hereditary nobility and traditional religion. It provoked a wave of reactionary philosophy in diametric opposition to the philosophy of the Enlightenment with its glorification of reason and the individual and its notion of the brotherhood of all people. The Romantics stressed the ascendancy of Culture at the expense of Civilization. This had many dimensions: the priority of community over individuality, of the pastoral and rustic over the urban and cosmopolitan, of custom over contract, and of sentiment over reason. At its extreme, the glorification of the community at the expense of the individual found expression in the adulation of an atavistic, tribal religiosity and in the state worship of Hegel. Very much a collectivist, he argued for the absolute primacy of the state over the individual:

"One must worship the state as a terrestrial divinity..."

"All the worth that the human being possesses — all spiritual reality — he possesses only through the state."

In keeping with this he characterized true freedom as the complete subjugation of one's will and conscience to the state. In his view of history, the world spirit makes deterministic progress by itself, immune to influence by individuals. This metaphysical determinism — in which individuals have no role to play — was later transferred to an economic matrix by Marx.

This philosophy, in which the value of an individual is extrinsic, rather than intrinsic, exhausted by class, function or nationality, reflects history. European countries, with roots in the Middle Ages, were ruled by monarchs and nobility, independent of character or competence. Simply as a function of birth, nobles were more valuable than commoners and deserved a social perch from which to look down on the masses.

"In some districts, where they built walled villages to separate themselves from the peasantry, the zaścianki, or 'nobles-behind-the-wall' constituted the whole population. They preserved their way of life with fierce determination, addressing each other as Pan or Pani, 'Lord and Lady', and the peasants as Ty, 'Thou.' They regarded all nobles as brothers, and everyone else as inferiors... They always rode into town, if only on a nag; and they wore carmine capes and weapons, if only symbolic wooden swords. Their houses may have been hovels; but they had to have a porch on which to display the family shield... As late as the 1950s, sociologists found collective farmers in Mazovia who shunned their 'peasant' neighbours, dressed differently, spoke differently, and observed complex betrothal customs to prevent intermarriage." (Davies, *Europe: A History*, p. 585-6.)

American democratic sensibilities, untarnished by the medieval experience, have found such attitudes alternately amusing and offensive. Mark Twain's *A Connecticut Yankee in King Arthur's Court* mocks class-bound societies with savage wit. Such barbed humor is justified. For class-bound consciousness is damaging to both individuals and societies.

For one thing, the exaggerated importance of class dulls the incentive to excel. If one's destiny is predetermined by anything — by God's will, according to early Protestant theologians, or by karma in some interpretations of Hindu or Buddhist doctrine, or by disabilities or class or sex or race — there is little point in struggling to change. Any effort to improve must be wasted.

Even well-meaning attempts to compensate for prior discrimination (as opposed to leveling the playing field) by lowering standards for selected classes have caused damage. Performance tends to reflect expectations and match standards. Lowering standards for selected groups has diminished their performance. It has also generated the view that the "beneficiaries" of lower standards are inherently less capable — for otherwise, they would not need a separate set of standards. It has led some to question the credentials of those who have excelled by the most stringent measures. Were they just beneficiaries of reverse discrimination?

An attitude of realistic individualism may be preferable, even for the historically disadvantaged. "It is not necessarily a conspiracy of silence that the historical record is so thin in detailing women painters and writers of the early Renaissance or black nuclear physicists and Hispanic political leaders of the early twentieth century. Sometimes the record is thin because the accomplishments were too. I expect many people will reflexively find these observations racist. But I am not asserting that, say, people of African descent cannot compete equally — only that their ancestral culture did not give them the tools and opportunity to do so. To me the real racism lies in the condescending assumption that we must equate all cultures to assuage African Americans, or any other minorities, instead of challenging them to compete with, and equal, the best in the culture where they live now." (William Henry III, *In Defense of Elitism*, p. 14.)

As Shelby Steele observed ("The New Sovereignty," *Harper's Magazine*, 1992): "In a liberal democracy, collective entitlements based upon race, gender, ethnicity, or some other group grievance are always undemocratic expedients. Integration, on the other hand, is the most difficult and inexpedient expansion of the democratic ideal; for, in opting for integration, a citizen denies his or her impulse to use our most arbitrary characteristics — race, ethnicity, gender, sexual preference — as a basis for identity, as a key to status, or for claims to entitlement."

While even well-meaning attempts to impose class-related standards have foundered, benign motivation itself has been rare. Most attempts to base action on class distinctions have reflected a darker visage. Genocide is the extermination of large numbers of people just because they belong to a particular class. Even though purported differences among classes have been exaggerated or totally fabricated, they have been used to justify the creation of under-classes, to deprive individuals of basic rights, and to treat people as though they were subhuman.

The Nazis called the theories of relativity "Jewish physics." They claimed to readily identify "Jewish music," clearly inferior to "Aryan music." Is there really such a thing as Jewish music? Is there a greater similarity among Bernstein, Bloch, Castelnuovo-Tedesco, Copland, Dukas, Gershwin, Glass, Mahler, Mendelssohn, Milhaud, Offenbach, Schoenberg, Johann Strauss (whose father was Jewish) and Weill than among Berlioz, Bruckner, Chopin, Field, Grieg, Nielsen, Paganini, Schumann, Sibelius, Smetana, and Tchaikowsky — each of whom is a different nationality? Is Robert Duncanson, a distinguished member of the Hudson River School of painting and the first African-American artist to gain international fame, an oreo? Or is there something subtly African-American in his work that persistently eludes art historians and critics?

This is not to deny that styles can be associated with nationalities: the German *Heldentenor*, French Impressionism, African-American blues, Neapolitan love songs, Jamaican reggae. But these are generalities, not constraints. George Gershwin composed exquisite blues. Jose Greco, the most famous Spanish dancer, had an Italian father and grew up in New York City. Even in the easy cases, class-based generalizations have been unreliable.

Despite this and despite the disasters caused by social policies based on class considerations, they still appeal. Many are always eager to jump on the next proof of the inferiority of a class of people, typically people who had been previously looked down upon and oppressed by the society.

Now that racism is regarded with abhorrence, we forget how deceptively easy it has been for such benighted doctrine to become mainstream wisdom, especially when we can cite "science." In the mid-1800s the eminent zoologist, Louis Agassiz, claimed that the brain casings of blacks were smaller than those of whites. He argued that too much education for blacks would cause their brains to expand beyond cranial capacity and that the resulting pressure would cause serious brain damage. (Paul Broca made similar claims with respect to women — their smaller brains necessarily restricted their intellectual capacity.) In the late 1800s, "In London, the Royal Historical Society sponsored a series of experiments on its Fellows showing that the brain-pans of those with Celtic names were inferior to those of Anglo-Saxon origin." (Davies, *Europe A History* p. 817.)

The Anthropological Society of London rejected Darwin's theories, refusing to believe that blacks are the same species as whites. They insisted that blacks must be the result of a separate and inferior creation. In the same spirit, "...the 1903 edition of the *Encyclopedia Britannica* contained the following entry under 'Negro': 'weight of brain, as indicating cranial capacity, 25 ounces (highest gorilla 20, average European 45); ...thick epidermis...emitting a peculiar rancid odor, compared...to that of a buck sheep.'" (Clive Ponting, *The Twentieth Century*, p. 23-4.)

Even today it takes little to revive such views, but with increased sophistication and more modern "science." The IQ controversy that has raged in recent decades provides an example. Popular scholarly books note that African-Americans have lower IQs than whites, with average scores lagging by 15 points. They claim this proves African-Americans are genetically less intelligent than whites — so remedial programs aimed at the African-American community are doomed to fail.

Several authors have implicitly suggested eugenics to maintain the intelligence of the community. In some cases this recommendation is explicit. Roger Pearson, an ex-editor of *The Mankind Quarterly*, often cited in Murray and Herrnstein's *The Bell Curve*, has written: "If a nation with a more advanced, more specialized, or in any way superior set of genes mingles with, instead of exterminating, an inferior tribe, then it commits racial suicide." (Miller, "Professors of Hate," *Rolling Stone*, October 1994.)

Pointed, yet reasoned, rebuttals might have been enough to dismiss this theory of genetic inferiority, had it not said what so many wanted to hear. It has been noted that several generations ago IQ tests validated popular beliefs of the time by proving that Jews are less intelligent than northern Europeans. The same tests now validate currently popular beliefs by showing that Jews are more intelligent. Somehow, proponents of IQ have not seen anything odd in this. Nor have they seen anything odd in tests showing 15-point differences in IQ between Catholics and Protestants in Northern Ireland and between Sephardim and Ashkenazim in Israel.

Questions have been raised, not only about the statistical weakness of the results (with R^2 for data in *The Bell Curve* typically less than 0.1), but with IQ itself. For one thing, it is questionable whether intelligence is one-dimensional and can be represented by a single number. Language, mathematics, art, music, spatial relations, athletics, humor, abilities to remember verbal or visual detail, to "read" people, to mimic, to improvise, to discern subtle differences or similarities, or to see deeper significance involve skills that may be mutually independent. Individuals may have different aptitude profiles. Multi-dimensional profiles cannot be captured in single numbers.

With the idea that measures of mutually independent dimensions of intelligence may contain more information than a single number, Robert Sternberg at Yale University has designed multi-dimensional intelligence tests. These have greater predictive reliability than IQ in job performance — and show no race-based differences.

Perhaps the weakest link in arguments that IQ tests measure differences in native intelligence is our lack of an adequate theory as to what intelligence is. IQ did not grow out of any attempt to understand intelligence. Rather, it developed from the pragmatic approach of Alfred Binet in the early 1900s. Binet, a psychologist who had noted that children's mental abilities develop at different rates, was asked by the French government to design a test to predict how different students would perform in the French education system. He, and many successors, tried a variety of questions, keeping those that correlated most highly with predictive success.

Psychometricians are too happy to look at the correlation between academic performance and results on IQ tests — which is there by design, as questions that did not correlate were dropped — and to conclude it is intelligence that accounts for both high IQ scores and academic success. This is unsound methodology. The correlation between IQ and academic success, no matter how strong, cannot support the claim that both can be explained by some unidentified third factor, intelligence, whatever that may be.

Consider the difficulties, both in school and on standardized tests, of people who are dyslexic or have attention deficit disorder. Many of these individuals are brilliant. Because we have independently decided that their difficulties are not related to intelligence, we have designed alternative tests that are not biased by these problems. Is it possible that there are other, subtler, factors that adversely affect large numbers of people? Such a question is not intelligible to many psychometricians, for intelligence is defined as the result of the IQ test, and as long as these results correlate with academic success there is no need to change the test.

Aside from problems related to the understanding of intelligence, the view that the underperformance by blacks on IQ tests can be explained genetically is implausible and is widely rejected by geneticists. The human race has presumably descended from the same ancestors, and it is doubtful that there have been enough generations to produce a genetic divergence sufficient to yield significantly different intelligence among races. In fact, different races are remarkably similar genetically. There is far less genetic variation within our entire species than within a single population of East African chimpanzees.

Even more difficult for proponents of race-based intelligence, different phenotypic characteristics (for example, pigmentation and serology [blood types]) generate different racial classifications. So, which phenotypes should we use to define and categorize races? If we believe that underlying genetic structures are the most important factors, using phenotypic morphology to infer underlying genetic structure can lead to the wrong results. For these reasons, geneticists as well as anthropologists have argued that race is not a useful biological classification.

(In general, the argument that if we cannot readily find an environmental explanation to account for a difference in test scores, then that difference must be genetic — is problematic. Nevertheless, it remains popular and was recently used to suggest that differences between mathematics scores of males and females on the Scholastic Aptitude Tests could be due to a sex-linked "math gene.")

It is not just the broad genetic and evolutionary evidence that militates against large race-based differences in intelligence. There is convincing, if non-technical, evidence supporting the claim that there are important non-genetic components of IQ. The fact that measured IQ scores throughout the world increased by 15 points during the course of the twentieth century can hardly be taken as validating a dramatic genetic improvement. Independently, it has been claimed that listening to Mozart's Sonata in D for two pianos, K.448, improves IQ test scores. For children, it has been claimed that the study of music resulted in an average IQ improvement of 34 points. It is utterly implausible that auditory stimulus should have so immediate a genetic impact. That such modest changes in environment can produce so large an improvement on IQ tests belies the claims of Herrnstein and Murray (*The Bell Curve*), that 60% of IQ — or of Arthur Jensen, that 75% of IQ — is hard wired.

This is not to deny the persistent outperformance, or underperformance, of different groups. It is rather to claim that on the basis of our present knowledge of biology, genetics accounts for none of this. The burden of explaining this rests entirely on institutional structures and cultural values. This may have positive ramifications. For we can seek to identify healthy institutions and positive cultural values and foster their development.

Despite these considerations, claims of racial inferiority remain popular. It may be that people, especially those who have been demeaned and downtrodden themselves, need someone even lower to look down at. Feelings of superiority may fill some deep-seated psychological need. Even if this were the case, it is unlikely that such fulfillment would compensate for the damage threatened by this sort of belief. Humanism, centered on respect for the individual, provides a framework for the moral irrelevance of class-based distinctions.

HUMANISM AND GOVERNMENT

A HUMANISTIC RATIONALE FOR GOVERNMENT

Despite its primary concern with the individual, humanism differs from *laissez faire* and libertarianism in that it is not implacably opposed to government. Rather than regarding government regulations as necessarily counterproductive, an unhealthy intrusion of incompetent politically motivated micromanagement, a humanist view encompasses the awareness that many of these regulations were adopted to protect individuals from the law of the jungle, from flagrant exploitation by unscrupulous profit maximizers. Rather than regarding government as essentially depraved, a humanist appraisal of government follows from its fundamental respect for the individual.

The Kantian dictum of treating persons as ends in themselves does not extend to institutions. Whereas persons are always to be treated as ends rather than merely means, institutions are no more than a means to enable people to improve their quality of life. To the extent that an institution has the opposite effect, it should be changed or eliminated. This applies to government; and the imperative to change or eliminate institutions which no longer served the desired end was regarded as a sacred civic duty by our founding fathers.

Seeing the primary source of value as the individual and seeking to change governments that suppress that value does not make humanism opposed to government, not even to interventionist government. But from a humanist perspective government has no intrinsic value. Its value lies in what it can add to the lives of its citizens. The ideal is a synergy between society and individuals,

151

society providing an environment conducive to individuals' developing their potential, individuals appreciating that environment and helping to sustain and improve it. In the spirit of this symbiosis, and unlike *laissez faire* and libertarianism, humanism is willing to entertain a positive role for government.

The notion that government can play a positive role is accepted in much of the world. But it is controversial at best in the U.S. Here the suggestion that government can add value borders on heresy. The term "bureaucrat," positive Europe and Asia, is a demeaning slur in the U.S.

Our cynicism with respect to government is understandable. Its egregious waste is undeniable. Consider, "Waste and Mismanagement - the $436 hammer. Bought by the U.S. Navy, this ordinary hardware-store hammer cost $7 **plus**: $41 to order; $93 to determine that it worked; $102 for something called manufacturing overhead; $37 to insure the availability of spare parts; $90 to pay a contractor's general administrative costs; $56 to pay a finder's fee; and $7 for the capital cost of money. The total: $436." (Figgie and Swanson, *Bankruptcy 1995*, p. 47.)

The sinister side of the misuse of power, spying on citizens or using government agencies to harass politically unpopular groups, has received its own publicity. Injudicious use of political power has inspired bumper stickers that read: "I love my country, but fear my government."

Some of this is culture. We are predisposed to fixate on the negatives of government. There are similar instances of waste and misuse of power in Europe and Japan. But revelations of such misconduct do not create the furor that would rage here. Many Europeans reacted to Watergate with bemused cynicism, acknowledging that this sort of thing goes on all the time and wondering why we were making such a fuss. Reciprocally, Americans marvel that European and Japanese pedestrians will wait at an intersection for a "walk" sign, even when there is no traffic.

These attitudes run deep. Most histories are political histories of elites. The cultural artifacts of civilizations in the East as well as the West were built by ruling aristocracies, the primary patrons of the arts. The association of culture with aristocracy and government typifies these civilizations. "Culture is simply the aristocratic ideal of a nation, increasingly intellectualized." (Jaeger, *Paideia*, v. l, p.4.)

By contrast, we are more congenial to plutocracy than aristocracy, like the Texan at the art gallery who, when asked by a gushing connoisseur, "What could be more wonderful than the ability to create magnificent works of art?" growled:

"The ability to buy them." Our collective attitude toward aristocracy is best distilled in the pointed jibe of Theodosius Dobzhansky: "I for one do not lament the passing of social organizations that used the many as a manured soil in which to grow a few graceful flowers of refined culture." (*Mankind Evolving*, p. 325.) Even our most accomplished aristocrat, Jefferson, endorsed anti-aristocratic sentiments.

Despite our antipathy to aristocratic culture, our country has produced outstanding artists, authors and composers, acceptable to even aristocratic sensibilities. Whitman, Poe and Dickinson are among the great poets of the past two centuries. Melville, James, and Faulkner are among the major novelists.

In music and philosophy, moreover, we have achieved a uniquely American contribution, one of the common people. Blues and country western have their roots in the lives and music of ordinary people, often living at the margins of society. In philosophy, self-reliance and the value of the common person and common labor characterize our homebred religions and are central themes in the writings of the Transcendentalists. These themes stress the irrelevance, at best, of social status. The poetry of Whitman delights in the ordinary, in both its form and its substance:

> If you want me again, look for me under your soles.
> You will hardly know who I am or what I mean,
> But I shall be good health to you nevertheless
> And filter and fibre your blood... ("Song of Myself")

Just as our suspicion of aristocracy is compatible with outstanding cultural achievements, our wariness of political power is compatible with effective democratic institutions. The U.S. Constitution and Bill of Rights is a remarkable essay in limiting the power of our own elected government. As such, it represents an important legacy and tool for the protection of civil liberties. It reflects a feature that pervades American political history: our values maximize the scope of individual freedom, even at the expense of constraining our elected representatives.

Within the context of our historic suspicion of government, consider the sentiment voiced by Sir Karl Popper in *The Open Society and Its Enemies*: "I am inclined to think that rulers have rarely been above the average, either morally or intellectually, and often below it. And I think that it is reasonable to adopt, in politics, the principle of preparing for the worst, as well as we can.... How can we so organize political institutions that bad or incompetent rulers can be prevented from doing too much damage?... Democracy... provides the institutional framework for the reform of political institutions. It makes possible the reform of institutions without using violence, and thereby the use of reason in the designing of new institutions and the adjusting of old ones." (v. 1, p. 121-2.)

Based on this view, even a deep-seated skepticism about the quality of politicians need not emasculate democratic government. Our proclivity to protect individuals against untrustworthy governors has not paralyzed our polity. Our government functions despite the common knowledge that while some laws and programs have been well conceived, others have been dismal failures.

For the most part we have been realists, recognizing that government has achieved both good and bad and refusing to throw out the baby with the bathwater. Part of that realism is the understanding that whether laws will have lasting effect is determined less by how they are instituted and more by how successfully they address real needs.

Even major changes forcibly imposed on people have had little lasting influence. The French Revolution shattered the old aristocracy and changed who became the exploiters and who the exploited. But it did little to change the exploitation itself, and it was to be generations before the structural changes imposed in 1789 by the Estates General/National Assembly had an effect on the lives of the common people. *"Plus ça change, plus c'est la même chose"* was a theme of Tocqueville's *The Old Regime and the French Revolution*. The same has been said about the Russian Revolution, comparing Stalin with the tsars.

Yet government intervention, even before the French Revolution, when it addressed needs felt by ordinary people, had lasting and positive effect. In the fourteenth century Venice built cargo vessels with state funds in her Arsenal and made them available to private enterprise. The Venetian government also strictly regulated the guilds, insisting on high standards of quality that contributed to the long-term reputation — and prices — of Venetian goods.

In the same vein, despite the failure of the French Revolution to achieve the ideal society of the *philosophes*, legislation of that period produced lasting benefits. The Napoleonic Code of Law, still the basis of legal systems in continental Europe and Latin America, simplified legal structure and made it possible for any citizen to know what were his (theoretical) rights, even against his own government. Similarly, the replacement of archaic currencies and weights and measures by new decimal-based standards had practical value and was retained throughout continental Europe after the defeat of Napoleon.

Modern governments support infrastructures in which individuals benefit indirectly from a sound and healthy community. They develop programs to foster a middle class, including social security and state-funded education. They even support basic research — fortunately, for it is often of dubious value for the private sector to spend on basic research. Not only is there uncertainty as to whether that research will generate value, but even if it does, there is no assurance that the company itself will benefit. Yet rates of return on basic research have been calculated as high as 50%. It was government, the Department of Defense, not the free market, that developed the technology underlying the Internet (originally called the "Arpanet," after DARPA). Generations earlier, during World War II, it was government, again the Department of Defense, that developed the foundational technology for computers.

Despite our faith in the free market, it is our government that fostered many of the most important technology breakthroughs of the last century. Even now, government accounts for nearly half our R&D spending.

Other areas of beneficial government intervention include legal protection against flagrant misuse of physical or economic power, protection for the environment and for workers, minimum safety standards in food, drugs and other sensitive consumables, and a social safety net that upon occasion has mitigated large-scale disaster. They also include the protection of rights we have long taken for granted.

Unfortunately, *laissez faire* has so exacerbated our mistrust of government that we are barely able to acknowledge even these accomplishments. Worse, this paradigm has undermined government's ability to perform its legitimate roles. For, it entails that public spirit is not part of rationality, which begins and ends with individual economic goals. We may complain that politicians are corrupt. Yet corruption is only rational, according to *laissez faire*, for we are all trying to maximize our immediate economic benefit. And that, we are told, is best for society as a whole.

It is in reaction to this perceived rationality of acting only in our immediate economic self-interest that we have tried to make our laws maximally specific, eliminating flexibility in order to minimize opportunity for corruption. It may seem odd, but this is a cause of mediocrity in government. Placing the tightest constraints on government employees makes such positions less attractive to

155

capable persons who want to exercise responsible judgment. Even for competent bureaucrats, the personal risk-reward ratio is so skewed to inflexibly following standard procedure that their most prudent course of action may be incompatible with what is best for the community.

> Sometimes government cannot act even in the face of immediate peril. In the early morning hours of April 13, 1992, in the heart of Chicago's downtown Loop, the Chicago River broke through the masonry of an old railroad tunnel built in the last century. Several hundred million gallons of water from the river were diverted from Lake Michigan into the basements of downtown office buildings, knocking out boilers, short-circuiting countless electrical switches, ruining computers, and turning files into wet pulp. Total losses were over $1 billion. Several weeks before the accident, the leak in the tunnel had come to the attention of John LaPlante, Chicago's transportation commissioner, a public servant with thirty years of exemplary service. He knew that the river was immediately overhead and that a break could be disastrous. He ordered his engineers to shore it up. As a provident administrator, he also asked how much it would cost. The initial guess was about $10,000. His subordinates then went to a reputable contractor, who quoted $75,000. Although the amount was a drop in the bucket of his huge budget, the discrepancy, seven times the original estimate, gave Commissioner LaPlante pause. He knew exactly what to do. He put it out for competitive bids. Two weeks later, before the process had even begun, the ceiling collapsed. (Howard, *The Death of Common Sense*, p. 59-60.)

This approach to public service runs counter to democratic tradition, which regards individuals as competent and honest, even public spirited, at least until proven otherwise. Our early codifications of law were brief by modern standards. They did not try to spell out the appropriate action for every eventuality, but rather indicated the spirit of the law. It was assumed, as a matter of course, that the public servant understood this. He could be trusted to go to the store to buy a hammer, and he would be held accountable for his performance.

Perversely, in seeking to insure good government by eliminating all flexibility, we have compromised government's ability to deal with unforeseen circumstances and to grapple with issues that threaten the spirit, if not the letter, of the law. We have also raised the cost of government enormously. Philip Howard notes that several years ago the Department of Defense spent $2.1 billion on travel and an additional $2.2 billion on paperwork to insure compliance with written policies.

All of this reflects the spirit of *laissez faire*. Unfortunately, this spirit — which regards public servants as officious and bumbling and politicians as rogues looking out for only themselves — can too easily generate self-fulfilling prophecies. Our previous *laissez faire*-fest, in the 1920s, elected Coolidge and Harding, among our least capable presidents.

A broader horizon suggests that *laissez faire* and rogue politicians may be anomalous. For most of our history the free market was not the universal standard and we had a better opinion of our political leaders. Is this only appearance? Were we just more naïve then? Or might there be some relationship between expectations and performance, even in public service?

It is hard to believe it has been just a perceptual change from idealistic naïveté to realistic cynicism. We were not that naïve in the days of Washington, Jefferson, Lincoln, or Roosevelt. People often perform to expectations, even in government. As national needs increase and as political leaders rise to the challenge of meeting them, the reputation of politics improves and government attracts individuals of greater capability and higher personal standards. This increases respect for and expectations of government, which leads to further improvement. It is plausible that such expectations are partly responsible for the higher standard of public service in much of Europe than in the U.S.

Presently, with expectations that politicians lack minimal standards of integrity and that civil servants lack minimal standards of competence, we assume capable people with high personal standards do not enter politics or government. Government is then left to the mediocre and to those for whom personal or sectarian religious agendas are a higher priority than civic duty.

Attempting to improve government by narrowly circumscribing the range of action of government employees preserves a situation in which the desire for a low-responsibility sinecure outweighs civic responsibility. This is ironic. Our actions, based on our disparagement of government, have created that which we disparage. Simple common sense — regarding public servants as public-spirited and capable, empowering them to uphold the intent of laws, and holding them responsible for their actions — would be more viable.

Common sense would also be aware of the accomplishments of government. It would not be bound by the dogmas that government is necessarily evil and that less government is automatically better. It would be open to the possibility that only an interventionist government could resolve some of our most serious problems.

CURBING EXCESSIVE POWER

Unfortunately, common sense runs afoul of deep-seated faith. In our current frame of mind the very notion that interventionist government could play a positive role is unworthy of serious consideration. It runs counter to received wisdom about politics and economics — that government is bad and the free market is good. This wisdom supposedly reflects the spirit of Jefferson and is *the* American tradition. To question it is to slander freedom, liberty and rights.

How far off the mark is this received wisdom! Government can be and has been beneficial. The free market, left to its own devices, can inflict grievous injury. Advocates of strong central government can find broad support in our history. Our founding fathers who framed the Constitution rejected the Articles of Confederation because it provided for a weak and ineffective central government. The philosophical struggle of the Civil War pitted Abraham Lincoln's vision of a strong central government against Jefferson Davis's ideal of a loose confederation of independent states. The suggestions that the Articles of Confederation, as opposed to the Constitution, and that Jefferson Davis, as opposed to Abraham Lincoln, represent *the* American political ideal are outrageous. They should not be accepted uncritically.

It may seem strange, given how much we idolize Thomas Jefferson as the champion of small government, but it is plausible that even Jefferson would support a larger role for government in today's society. Jefferson was motivated by his vision of a country of independent farmers — not wage earners — who were economically self-sufficient (and so immune to economic coercion) and who were committed to the common good. In the absence of other sources of coercion he regarded a strong central government as the primary threat to the independence of those citizens. Jefferson was concerned to limit that power. In his writings and in legislation he opposed efforts to strengthen central government. Yet the spirit of Jefferson's animus was directed not just against government, but against any power that threatened citizens' independence.

Jefferson's concern is appropriate today. It is natural for power — economic, political, military — to concentrate. Having more power than your opponent enables you to overwhelm him and appropriate his power base, increasing your own strength. Because it is natural for power to concentrate, it requires a focused effort to insure an ongoing moderation of power.

Although the nature of power has not changed, today's economic and political landscapes bear little resemblance to those of Jefferson's day. Few independent farmers are left. We have become a technology and service society in which economic and political power are concentrated in multi-national mega-corporations. Unlike the community of self-sufficient farmers Jefferson had envisioned, most citizens are wage earners and are subject to economic intimidation, primarily from private industry. As a result, the locus of his concern, excessive power, now lies outside government.

For the very reasons we worry about government acquiring too much power, we should be equally concerned about non-governmental institutions — corporations, unions, special interest groups — acquiring too much power. Perhaps we should be even more concerned. Differences between government and non-governmental institutions in both structure and responsibility suggest corporate power may pose a greater threat than government.

Our government was structured by individuals acutely sensitive to the danger of unbridled power. It is divided into independent legislative, executive and judicial branches so that each might restrain overweening ambition and excessive power in either of the other two branches. "Ambition must be made to counteract ambition." (Madison, Hamilton, Jay, *The Federalist*, no. 47.) It is legally bound to honor a wide range of individual rights.

By contrast, corporations are controlled by a tiny fraction of society and lack significant structural restraints. If a corporation should go so far as to commit a felony, its owners and management are normally shielded from prosecution. It is remarkable that the same people who are so concerned about the power of government stoutly defend the autonomy of corporations. This shows the extent to which deeply held beliefs can blind the faithful. The content of our beliefs may have changed since the Middle Ages. The depth of our faith has not.

Jefferson, himself, despite his persistent concern to guard against the erosion of civil liberties, was not one of the faithful. He had no patience with the encroachments of organized capital, despite its having far less power than it does today. "I hope we shall take warning from the example of England and crush in its birth the aristocracy of our moneyed corporations which dare already challenge our government to a trial of strength, and bid defiance to the laws of our country."

Jefferson even argued for an amendment to the Constitution that would strictly limit the power of corporations. More than a century later Abraham

Lincoln wrote: "Corporations have been enthroned and an era of corruption in high places will follow, and the money power of the country will endeavor to prolong its reign by working upon the prejudices of the people until all wealth is aggregated in a few hands and the Republic is destroyed. I feel at this moment more anxiety than ever before, even in the midst of war."

A Jeffersonian sensitivity to the danger of excessive power, whether in the hands of government or private entities, suggests an extension of the balance of powers beyond government. It would endeavor to insure that no institution, government or private, could acquire enough power to dominate society. Government could play a role in maintaining this balance of powers.

Consider the conflict between capital and labor. Their mutual opposition is healthy — provided there is a reasonable balance of power between them. The tendency of capital to concentrate is a major premise of Marx's argument as to the inevitability of class revolution. But capital concentration can be beneficial. As a result of a small manufacturer being acquired by a larger company, its product may become better marketed and more widely available. A larger company can devote more capital to improving technology, which can lead to higher quality, lower prices, safer working conditions and less pollution. It can devote more resources to anticipating changes in technology, tastes and the economic environment.

Some concentration of capital is necessary for commerce. Indeed, modern society could not exist without concentrated capital. The problem lies in too great a concentration of capital and too great a concentration of power in the hands of capital — or labor.

It is the political arena that must mediate the balance of power. Within this arena labor has sought restraints on employer flexibility, a high level of job security and benefits, and a secure social safety net. It has sought to moderate the power of capital by a steeply progressive tax code so that income differences at the pre-tax level are reduced at the after-tax level.

Capital, by contrast, has sought a free hand to reduce costs by eliminating unions, by exporting jobs to low-wage regions, by replacing labor with technology. It has sought to minimize the social safety net because the weaker and less reliable the safety net, the greater the incentive to work, the greater the supply of labor, the less the cost of labor, and the greater the profits. And it has sought to maximize its economic advantage by a flat or regressive tax code, in which a pre-tax income difference is translated into at least as great an after-tax advantage.

By and large, labor requires the intervention of government to achieve its ends, while capital requires its abstention. Not that this consideration should decide the issue. Contrary to accepted political wisdom, government intervention is not automatically good or bad in itself. It can be either a blessing or a curse, depending on its aims, scale, flexibility, and means of implementation. The appropriate role of government is not well decided by ideological reflex. It may depend on the state of the local and global economies as well as local culture.

Presently, natural economic forces have placed labor at a severe disadvantage to capital. The globalization of industry facilitates the transfer of jobs to low-wage economies. While global trade is not new, the ability to hire a global workforce has made available a vast supply of labor. The displacement of workers by lower cost foreign labor (or technology) translates increased domestic unemployment and lower wages into higher profits for large international corporations. The widespread elimination of middle management also increases corporate profits at the expense of the middle class. It may be impossible to resolve the problems caused by this wage displacement without government intervention.

Is it possible to resolve them at all? Is government capable of cushioning the dislocation and impoverishment caused by such powerful global economic forces? Probably. Our trading partners are exposed to the same macro-economic forces that impoverish our working middle class. Yet they have less poverty and a smaller disparity of income. Their productivity and standards of living are rising faster than ours. Their progress suggests it is irresponsible to blame the decline of our middle class solely on irresistible economic trends.

Our political actions can make a difference. They have made a difference. Roosevelt's New Deal and the extension of those policies by Truman and Kennedy fostered increasing economic equality from the 1930s into the 1970s. (There were one-third as many people below the poverty line in 1980 as there were in 1950.) But subsequent policies have led to a sharply increasing disparity of income.

Perversely, recent actions of our government, rather than redressing the excessive imbalance between the rich and the rest, have aggravated it. Dismantling programs designed to assist the working middle class while changing the tax structure to benefit the wealthy has further tilted the scales against the middle class. In general, the unbundling of government services, from social security to medical insurance to education, eliminates cross subsidies. Ostensibly a means to increase efficiency by making each program self-funding, it is in reality a means to enable the wealthy to avoid subsidizing the lower classes. This increases economic disparity, but does so under the guise of making government more fiscally responsible.

(Ironically, many middle class workers have voted for candidates who would eliminate programs that benefit them. It is a tribute to the power — and danger — of sophisticated political advertising that many, intending to vote against government handouts to others who are undeserving, have in effect voted for their own impoverishment.)

We have acted in other ways to aid capital to the detriment of those who work for a living. The Federal Reserve is a private corporation, owned by major banks. It sets monetary policy for the country and has consistently set policies that favor the banking industry and entrenched capital. Its high real interest rates have transferred wealth from generally poor borrowers to rich lenders.

> By creating an economic environment in which inflation-adjusted interest rates have been stubbornly high, central bankers in the developed world have presided over a huge transfer of income from both households and ordinary businesses to banks and other financial institutions. They have turned the world of industrial capitalism into a world of finance capitalism. And the financially shortchanged workers have been transformed into a strange new twenty-first century class of indentured capitalists — rooting for the interests of capital because work itself no longer pays the bills....
>
> The Federal Reserve's anti-inflation hysteria is, pure and simple, special interest politics, practiced by an institution almost totally free of effective oversight. As a class, bankers are creditors who have a strong interest making sure that the money that they lend out...is paid back in money that does not lose value through time. The central bank is most concerned to limit inflation because inflation depreciates the value of the assets held by the commercial banks. (Wolman and Colamosca, *The Judas Economy*, p. 142-3, 149.)

In contrast to its recent behavior, it would be appropriate for government to make the tax code effectively progressive, to invest in human capital through programs that provide middle-class training and increase employment, and to moderate the flow of employment to low wage countries. It may be impossible to reverse the direction of major worldwide economic forces. But it may be possible to soften their impact. Moreover, if imbalances are minor, they may be corrected by small doses of intervention, but if they become excessive, more dramatic intervention will be needed.

The most intractable obstacle to achieving such reforms is that the interests of our country are not the same as the interests of powerful corporations, which have the political muscle to block reform. Given their enormous power, it is virtually impossible to pass legislation contrary to their interests. It is easy — and dangerous — to underestimate the effect of economic power purchasing political influence to enhance that economic power. This may be the most dysfunctional aspect of our economic/political system. The positive feedback mechanism: (economic power → political influence → more economic power → more political influence) can lead to an intolerable concentration of political and economic power.

The doctrine of the perfection of the free market supports this vicious circle. This doctrine serves as a justification for policies that support the rich at the expense of the rest. It has been furthered by large corporations and by right-wing foundations seeking an alternative philosophy to Social Darwinism – the claim that to hinder the rich, the fittest in the struggle for economic survival, is to violate the laws of natural selection. Social Darwinism has been discredited as unsupported (and unsupportable) by scientific evidence, and these groups have sought an alternative philosophy that supports the rich.

The extension of *laissez faire* as the ultimate paradigm applicable not only to the economy, but to all areas of society, seeks to apply free market considerations to judicial and political as well as economic thought. The policies it recommends, which model everything on market transactions, play into the hands of those seeking to increase their already excessive concentration of wealth and political power. These policies undermine the spirit of our founding fathers, who sought to establish a republic, not a plutocracy.

It is unfortunate that our founding fathers, so keenly aware of the need for a balance of powers, lacked the prescience to extend this notion from the political arena to economics. For the same considerations that militate against an excessive concentration of political power militate equally against an excessive concentration of economic power. This concentration of power endangers our democracy as well as our economy.

In the face of this, it is appropriate and in the spirit of our founding fathers that we take responsibility for our economic and political system. Being enthralled by *laissez faire* makes it more difficult to do this. We are unperturbed by the increasing concentration of economic and political power because of our faith that the invisible hand of the free market will maintain a stable and most comfortable equilibrium. So long as we don't interfere, this will remain the best of all possible worlds. Isn't it pretty to think so? But given the multiple failures of *laissez faire* it would be foolhardy to think so too seriously.

Unless we act to maintain the independence of our political system, natural forces will lead us away from equilibrium, to an increasing concentration of political and economic power in the hands of a few rich oligarchs, and ultimately to the disaster historically associated with excessive economic inequality. Unfortunately, our bias against any intervention plays into the hands of the rich and powerful who seek to increase their wealth at the expense of society. In this context *laissez faire* and libertarianism are a disservice.

While true believers in *laissez faire* may casually dismiss the need for an independent activist government and may claim that government intervention — at least at the domestic level — is never necessary, such a claim is implausible. Free market economists may believe natural economic forces would have eventually created a middle class or that they would have ended the Great Depression. But there is little evidence to support such faith.

Moreover, an environment of widespread and intense economic suffering is unlikely to give free market and democratic forces an unlimited period of time to alleviate massive suffering. The New Deal programs were passed, not so much out of charitable sentiment, but out of fear that social unrest wrought of economic despair might imperil society. While we do not presently face this danger, we do face increasing economic imbalances that our system is incapable of correcting.

Independently, the notion that free market forces might somehow induce corporations to curb pollution is as believable as "The Emperor's New Clothes." Thanks to generations of grandfathered exemptions and lax enforcement, Texas oil refineries spew out five times the pollutants of the average California refinery, where environmental standards are universal and enforced. The Texas refiners have little incentive to reduce pollution. Rather than purchasing pollution-reducing capital equipment or paying a premium for cleaner feedstock, it is a better investment to finance political campaigns and use political influence to gut threatening environmental legislation.

Given the choice between profits and the health of society, industry has consistently acted to maximize profits. In the early 1980s the oil industry bitterly fought efforts to phase out leaded gasoline. They relied, in part, on a study showing such a phase-out would cost $100 million. But other studies showed that just the medical costs of continuing to use leaded gasoline would be far greater. Despite these studies, regarded by most as balanced and accurate, the oil industry continued to oppose a phase-out. The refiners would have to spend the $100 million, but they would get no credit for the saved $1 billion per year or for the saved lives. Economically, their priorities were rational, notwithstanding the adverse health effects.

In spite of increasing public concern about environmental degradation, these priorities have not changed. We are presently seeing a re-run of the leaded gasoline battle in industry's attempt to block tougher standards for fine particle pollution, estimated to kill tens of thousands of people each year. In the choice between profits and lives, the priority is still profits.

This priority has not changed because it is built into the system. It is characteristic of the competition inherent in *laissez faire* that every company seeks economic advantage over its competitors. As a rule, no company willingly places itself at a potential disadvantage, no matter what the consequences for society at large.

Unfortunately, what is good for profits may be bad for many people. Houston recently displaced Los Angeles as the smog capital of the country. Its pollution produced in the course of violating environmental standards kills hundreds of people per year. It aggravates the illnesses of thousands of others. It sullies the quality of life for millions.

A humanist view of government might assess the damage done to those living in Houston as too high a price to pay for the additional profits obtained from disregarding environmental standards. It might be less inclined to value profits over lives. It might be more inclined to enact and enforce ground rules that protect citizens.

It might be less attentive to industry lobbyists anxious to protect profits. These lobbyists typically argue that government regulations hamstring industry, placing us at a disadvantage to our trading partners. This political imposition of environmental costs, they insist, endangers our economy.

Their claim is doubtful. Most of our trading partners have environmental regulations similar to our own. They cannot externalize their environmental costs any more than we can. The playing field is reasonably level. Moreover, the very threat of strict government regulations, of standards requiring anything from alternative, cleaner, fuels to more fuel-efficient cars, has spurred advances in technology. These have ranged from reformulated gasoline – which refiners had claimed was technologically impossible – to more efficient and less polluting automobiles, which Detroit had claimed was possible only at the cost of dramatic reductions in the weight and safety of the vehicles.

Detroit's self-serving pessimism was as excessive as that of the refiners. Modern cars not only get double the gas mileage, but they emit less than 10% of the pollution of pre-1970 cars. They are, on average, 20% lighter. But they are also safer, with fatalities per passenger mile down by nearly 50%.

It is revealing that these results showing the benefit of government regulation are so detrimental to the spirit of the pure free market that some *laissez faire* apologists have argued that government environmental, safety and mileage regulations have actually made cars les safe. Such arguments, which adjust the number of fatalities – they must, because the actual number has declined sharply since the regulations – border on travesty. They show the extent to which deep faith in the efficacy of the free markets and the dysfunction of any government regulation can lead true believers to the most awkward contortions to save the theory.

In the same spirit, that mandated standards are at best unwieldy and at worst disastrous, the chemical industry lamented that OSHA standards limiting exposure to vinyl chloride, a hazardous carcinogenic gas used in the production of polyvinyl chloride (PVC) would cause the demise of the domestic PVC industry. Yet the cost of compliance was only 7% of industry estimates, and the industry is healthy today.

Industries have often issued dire predictions that tough mandated pollution standards would cause massive bankruptcies. These predictions, just as far-fetched as those of the opposite extreme – environmentalists' forecasts of impending Armageddon – are partly attempts to blackmail government into leaving industry alone, into leaving everything to the free market. On the lobbyists' account, standard free market forces, in which every good is subject to an auction, would provide the most efficient means of remediating any environmental problems.

Their claim would benefit the industries they serve, but it is implausible. Leaving environmental decisions to the highest bidder may aid industrial polluters by lowering the cost of environmental "compliance." This would aid the bottom lines of the polluters and the bidders. But it would serve neither the general public nor the environment.

Of course, the very notion of bidding to pollute (as opposed to mandating environmental standards and allowing the market to meet those standards in the most cost-effective way) seems absurd. It is easy to dismiss such an idea of auctioning the environment as ludicrous and unrealistic. But it is palpably real.

It is widely documented that the best-funded candidates usually win. It is also clear that getting elected is the highest priority of candidates. So industry lobbies, which play an important role in the funding of political campaigns, are treated with special care. Our form of government, in which well-targeted campaign contributions, directed by lobbies, often result in legislative or executive dispensations, is tantamount to such an auction. Money buys influence, and sometimes much more.

This is plutocracy, not democracy. Most of us know this, but we are unable to do much about it. What would it take to restore real democracy, a government in which people vote and money does not? Simple answers have been offered, but most do not work.

Rejecting Liberalism

Freedom, Rights, and Libertarianism

Humanism is a valuable tradition. It has spoken with eloquence for liberty, tolerance and human rights. It provides an attractive foundation for government, a foundation that stems from fundamental respect for the individual. This foundation supports a reasonable and flexible view of government, one that fits with democratic traditions.

Libertarianism is different. It denies the humanist view that the purpose of government is to enable citizens to improve their lives, but instead claims government should do as little as possible, period. Despite its incompatibility with humanism, libertarianism is popular today.

This is understandable. Libertarianism is just a generalization of *laissez faire*, from the doctrine that government should not interfere in the economy to the claim that government should not interfere in anything. Given the popularity of *laissez faire*, it is understandable that libertarianism should be politically correct. Still, given the flaws inherent in *laissez faire*, we may wonder if libertarianism might be similarly flawed.

In light of the contributions governments have made, we may also wonder why libertarians are so eager to summarily rule out any government interference. Given these contributions, we might think that libertarians must have powerful arguments to justify their desire to eliminate, or at least minimize, government. But the proposed justifications of libertarianism do not work. *Laissez faire* cannot support libertarianism, given how poorly it performs in its own field. Even the

169

standard libertarian appeal to liberties, rights and freedoms raises more questions than it answers.

Libertarians typically justify their beliefs in terms of civil liberties and human rights. They claim government interference is wrong because it jeopardizes these. Of course, liberty and human rights are unobjectionable. Since the Enlightenment the notion that each person has inalienable rights to life, liberty, conscience, and the pursuit of happiness has become a tenet of nearly all societies. We fought our Revolutionary War to defend our liberties and rights. Surely, no one would find fault with these institutions.

Still, it is possible to be a champion of civil liberties and human rights and also a staunch opponent of libertarianism. Despite the roles liberty and rights play in our political system, we have given them little thought. Libertarians assume that the nature of these concepts is self-evident. Wrong! Careful analysis is needed if liberty and rights are going to be the basis of a political doctrine. For despite our knowledge that they are good, even the simplest questions about them do not have easy answers.

What are rights? Our founding fathers talked about civil liberties, but also about inalienable rights. Are these the same? The Bill of Rights addresses civil liberties, rather than rights, in that its primary concern is to limit government action, not to facilitate intervention to provide rights. Is this a meaningful distinction?

What is the source of rights? (People have argued about this for centuries.) Do all living beings have rights? Do living beings that have feelings have additional rights? Do sentient beings that are intelligent have yet additional rights? Do governments have rights? If so, what bestows rights on a government? Is it possible to give away rights or barter rights? Are certain rights inalienable while others are negotiable? What makes a right inalienable?

What is it to violate a right? Presumably, a civilian retains his right to life even after being drafted. Suppose an enemy sniper shoots and kills him. Has that sniper violated his right to life? Does it matter whether the shooting takes place on the battlefield or in a hospital? Consider a person confined to a wheelchair. Does the lack of a ramp to a public building violate his right to enter that building? Or does he still have that right — nobody may eject him — even though he may be physically incapable of exercising it? Similarly, does a person's right to see imply an obligation of society to provide him with glasses?

If you drive while intoxicated, is it wrong to violate your right to drive on public roads? Or have you relinquished that right? What is it to involuntarily relinquish a right? In the same spirit, what happens to the inalienable right to liberty of a convicted felon?

People speak of infringing on rights. Is that the same as violating rights? If you have the right to drive on public roads, is requiring you to take tests evaluating your eyesight, driving ability, and knowledge of the rules of the road infringing on that right? Is collecting a toll or requiring a license infringing on that right? If you have a right to bear arms, is requiring a license infringing on that right?

Not only is the nature of rights far from evident, but rights commonly conflict with one another. These conflicts pose practical, as well as theoretical, problems.

It is widely agreed that all people have the right to the benefits afforded by new medical technologies. But it is also claimed (in the 1948 U.N. Declaration of Human Rights) that individuals have the right to profit from scientific devices they invent. Where resources are limited, these rights may be mutually incompatible. Do you have the right to consume mass quantities, if doing so condemns others to starvation?

Some religious communities bar women from education. Yet women, as much as men, have a right to an education. At the same time, communities have a right to practice religions of their choice. What determines the rights of a religious community? Rights of individuals, religious groups, and the state have often come into sharp conflict. How do you adjudicate such conflict? (Did the Indian government have the right to ban the Hindu practice of suttee?)

Libertarians claim that government necessarily endangers our rights. To the contrary! Without a code of law and a government capable of enforcing that law, there can be no meaningful rights. (What is the significance of the right to anything if you have no recourse against someone bigger and stronger taking it away?) Even contractual rights presuppose government and a legal framework within which contracts are defined and enforced. Given that rights require at least the potential for government intervention, the libertarian notion that government is bad because it interferes with our rights is strange, indeed.

Rights to receive material benefits illustrate independent problems. Long before the welfare state, Article 21 of the French Declaration of Rights of Man and the Citizen (1793) stated: "Public assistance is a sacred duty. Society owes subsistence to unfortunate citizens, whether in finding work for them, or in assuring the means of survival of those incapable of working." More recently, Article 25 of the Universal Declaration of Human Rights claims each person has a right to "a standard of living adequate for the health and well being of himself and of his family, including food, clothing, housing, medical care, and necessary social services."

But rights entail obligations. It is common that rights are to *do* something (to believe or speak as one wishes, to own property, to vote, to bear arms), so that the corresponding obligation, applicable to everyone, is an obligation to not interfere. Rights against unlawful seizure or arrest entail an obligation of the police to refrain from certain actions. Rights to equal treatment under the law entail the obligation of judges and juries to be impartial. For a broad class of rights, it is clear what the obligation is and to whom it applies.

Rights to receive something (except for contractual rights, which specify who is obliged to provide the benefit) are more problematic. Who is obliged to provide the entitlement? If rights to receive entail societal obligations, are these obligations of every society? If we are talking about rights to economic goods, this is unreasonable, for there are impoverished societies incapable of providing material benefits. What distinguishes societies that are obliged to supply entitlements from those that are not? If a society is too poor to provide entitlements, does the obligation to provide them fall on the international community?

These considerations extend to other rights. Just as a government may be too poor to provide entitlements, it may be too poor to pay a police or fire-fighting force to protect private property.

Libertarians often argue that while it is appropriate for government to protect private property and insure the integrity of the free market, it is inappropriate to redistribute wealth by providing material entitlements. But the protection of private property is an entitlement that can cost as much money and redistribute as much wealth as entitlements to food or medical care. If the tax system is not steeply progressive — and ours is not — then government protection of private property redistributes wealth, but redistributes it upwards, from the middle class to the wealthiest, who benefit most from this protection. What is the difference between the entitlement to the protection of private property and entitlements to adequate shelter, medical care, and nutrition such that it is appropriate for government to provide the former, but not the latter?

If these questions about rights are difficult, this is because, contrary to the implicit libertarian message, the nature of rights is complex and subtle. It requires careful analysis.

Freedom, too, is a subtle notion. Most who have written about freedom — even committed anti-libertarians — mistakenly equate freedom with license. In *Slouching Towards Gomorrah*, Robert Bork criticizes the liberal tradition for seeking to maximize freedom, to remove all constraints on action. Kant, by contrast, saw that freedom requires self-discipline. An addict is a slave to his addiction and is hardly free, even if he has no external constraints. Similarly, a person who is manipulated into beliefs and actions is not free, even if he has no external constraints. Replacing external constraint by understanding and commitment to internal restraint, encouraging the autonomous obedience of moral laws just because they are moral, is a worthy program, necessary to freedom. (To the extent this is part of the liberal tradition, so much the better for liberalism.)

Basing a theory of government on the goodness of rights, freedom and liberty may sound appealing; but without careful analysis it is just empty sloganeering. Significantly, careful analysis does not support the libertarian position. "[R]ights should be associated not with a hands-off but with a liberal, as opposed to authoritarian, regulatory style." (Holmes and Sunstein, *The Cost of Rights*, p. 154.)

Rather than reflecting an understanding of the nature of liberty, freedom and rights, the libertarian position reflects a visceral reaction to the tension between liberties and rights, to the conflict caused by the fact that every right entails an obligation and so restricts liberty. Libertarianism values liberties, as opposed to rights. In the extreme, we would be in Hobbes's state of nature. If less government is automatically better, the government that governs best does not govern at all. We would have complete liberty do anything we wish, but no rights — since others would have the liberty to violate any such rights.

Despite, and because of, unconstrained liberty, a world of this sort would be an unpleasant and dangerous place. As Isaiah Berlin noted, freedom for the wolves means death for the sheep. Hobbes depicted the pre-government state of nature, characterized by unlimited liberty, as " ...that condition which is called war, and such a war, as is of every man against every man... [takes] no account of time; no arts; no letters; no society; and which is worst of all, continual fear, and danger of violent death; and the life of man, solitary, poor, nasty, brutish, and short." (*Leviathan*, chapter 13.)

That condition is so miserable that any government, even a despotic one, would be an improvement. For this reason, Hobbes concluded, "No Law can be Unjust." What a remarkable consequence of pure libertarianism!

Some libertarians admit that their position, taken to an extreme, is unacceptable. They concede there could be no society without the ability of government to deter violence and fraud, to force citizens to obey laws. They claim the principle of non-intervention is not intended to be taken to an extreme. There are necessary rights that government must protect, but government interference should be restricted to the protection of just those necessary rights.

This raises further questions. Are certain rights more important than others, so that government should protect only those essential rights? What makes those rights so important? Why, in general, should liberties be preferred to rights? In the face of such questions, it is doubtful an acceptable libertarian position could be articulated, much less justified.

Libertarians tend to be particularly sensitive to economic liberties. They agree that we have the rights to our own bodies and to the product of our labors, but insist that nothing should constrain our liberty to exchange our labor for various goods. Presumably, if we were sufficiently desperate, we could sell ourselves into slavery in a futures market for labor. This in itself raises questions. The most urgent of these has implications for the role of government. Having greater physical power does not give anyone the right to injure, or even threaten, others. It is appropriate for government to interfere to protect our right to be free from physical intimidation. Do similar considerations govern economic power?

Suppose Mr. Sluggo is in a position to fire Mr. Bill from a job he desperately needs. Is he entitled to extract anything at all from Mr. Bill in return for not firing him? After all, Mr. Bill does have the freedom to refuse the offer. And libertarians insist that economic interactions within the scope of the free market involve decisions made of one's own free will and are therefore unobjectionable.

But if Mr. Sluggo had pointed a gun at Mr. Bill's head, offering to not pull the trigger in return for anything at all, Mr. Bill would have the very same freedom to refuse the offer. In both cases, refusal may mean death. But there is still the "freedom" to refuse. Is there a relevant difference between the two situations, based just on the difference between economic and physical extortion?

If there is no relevant difference then it should be just as legitimate for government to protect Mr. Bill from economic extortion as from physical extortion. Yet many libertarians, even those who admit we have physical rights and that it is a legitimate function of government to protect us from physical extortion, adamantly deny there are corresponding economic rights. They deny it is a legitimate function of government to protect us from economic extortion.

(There is irony in this denial. Marx's most important error may have been his failure to appreciate the extent to which government intervention to limit economic extortion would increase standards of living for the proletariat, and even the capitalists. Intervention by European governments to implement radical suggestions Marx himself had made in *The Communist Manifesto* — to end child labor, to provide free education, to institute a progressive income tax — may be the primary reason Marx's prediction of necessarily increasing misery of the working class failed to materialize. This may explain why communist revolutions did not take place in advanced states, as Marx had predicted, but rather in peripheral peasant economies in which governments did not intervene on behalf of their citizens. So it is ironic that while Marx denied the possibility of independent political action, libertarians deny its propriety.)

Extortion is extortion. Why should it matter whether it is physical or economic? Libertarians insist that government must protect against physical extortion, but that it may not protect against economic extortion. Yet they fail to find a relevant difference between the two. As a result, libertarianism lacks coherence. Why, then, is this doctrine popular with many of our brightest minds? To answer this, it is necessary to address the tacit presuppositions underlying the characteristic non- or minimal-interference principle of libertarianism.

LIBERTARIANISM AND THE RELATIVITY OF VALUES

For most libertarians, the principle of non-interference is not just a matter of the incompetence of government. If it were, libertarianism could be countered by proposals designed to improve the quality of government. But even if such proposals were effective, they would not address the most important libertarian concerns. These concerns imply the absolute impropriety of unnecessary interference, even from the most enlightened government. They stem from basic libertarian values.

One precept held by many libertarians is the propriety of self-determination, that each person should arrive at his own values and that it is morally objectionable to impose values on others. A second is the Protagoran principle that man is the measure of all things, at least in the realm of values.

Values are ultimately subjective, matters of taste rather than fact. There is no objective right or wrong. It is just a matter of how we feel.

These two precepts are often run together, the subjectivity, or relativity, of values cited as the reason it is wrong to impose values on anyone. Libertarians then argue that government interference must be inappropriate because it represents the imposition of its own values.

Libertarians fail to appreciate that these two basic principles, rather than reinforcing each other, are mutually incompatible. That it is wrong to impose one's values on others is itself·a value. If all values are matters of subjective taste rather than objective fact, then the impropriety of imposing values must also be a matter of subjective taste. There cannot be anything objectively wrong with imposing values on anyone. It can only be a matter of how we feel.

The view that all values are subjective is unreasonable. Despite this, it has become fashionable, partly in reaction to generations of religious leaders claiming a monopoly on "absolute" moral truth. But religious leaders had earlier claimed a monopoly on "absolute" scientific truth, and their monopoly on moral truth was a fallback position. (The doctrine of papal infallibility when speaking *ex cathedra* on moral issues became Catholic dogma only in 1870, well after the church had lost the battle over science.) Despite claims of religious authorities to possess ultimate scientific authority and despite the fact that different people and different societies have held conflicting scientific beliefs, we don't claim that science is relative, just a matter of taste.

Scientific theories *are* true or false. That is the impetus driving scientific progress. Astronomers rejected the Ptolemaic geocentric picture of the solar system and replaced it with a heliocentric model and Kepler's laws, despite the unintuitive nature of the heliocentric model. (After all, the earth does not appear to be moving.) For Kepler's laws were simpler. These laws also provided new predictions, beyond the scope of Ptolemaic geometry, simply relating the periods of planetary orbits to their distances from the sun.

Kepler's laws in turn were replaced by Newton's theory of gravitation, of which Kepler's laws are a limiting case (in the limit that the ratio of the mass of the sun to that of the planets is infinite). Kepler was close but Newton was more accurate, and Newton explained both terrestrial and celestial motion within the same theory. Newton's theory of gravitation in turn was replaced by Einstein's theory of general relativity, of which Newton's theory is a limiting case (in the limit that the curvature of space is zero).

Each of these theories is an improvement, in a well-defined sense, over its predecessor. (Laszlo Tisza elegantly discusses this in *Generalized Thermodynamics*. In effect, the replacing theory contains new parameters — the speed of light, mass [or the ratio of masses], wavelength [or the change in wavelength over the distance of a wavelength], the number of degrees of freedom — such that for limiting values of those parameters, usually 0 or ∞, the equations of the replacing theory reduce to those of the replaced theory.)

Were science just a matter of taste, there could be no such thing as scientific progress. We would flit from one theory to another for no objective reason. This conception of science is absurd. Scientists emphatically and justly reject the notion that science reflects taste, rather than fact.

We have no problem acknowledging that scientists are justified in insisting on the objectivity of their disciplines, despite the facts that religious authorities have claimed absolute knowledge of scientific truth, that different people and different societies have held competing scientific beliefs, and that individual scientists may have their own subjective axes to grind. Why should values be different?

The most common response is that scientific theories, unlike moral beliefs, can be proved. This misunderstands science. Kepler's laws claim to hold for all planets and all time. Even if all measurements to date confirmed these laws, they could not prove them. It would always be possible that more accurate measurements might show planets to obey different laws, of which Kepler's are but an approximation. It is also possible that in the future planetary orbits will not follow Kepler's laws. No conceivable experimental evidence could prove Kepler's laws.

What about disproof? It has been claimed (notably by Popper in *The Logic of Scientific Discovery*) that purported scientific laws can be proved false by experiment or observation. Not so. Despite a logical structure that appears to allow for falsification, scientific theories have a deep structure that can deflect potential falsifications.

Examples go back centuries. The correspondence at the end of the seventeenth century between Isaac Newton and Flamsteed, the Royal Astronomer, shows that Newton was able to use theoretical considerations to correct the very observations Flamsteed had cited to falsify Newtonian theory.

When Niels Bohr was developing his quantum model of the hydrogen atom, combining the quantization of momentum and energy with the Rutherford solar system model of the atom, he was confronted by apparent experimental falsifications. He dealt with these by continuing to develop his solar system model. He considered elliptical, rather than circular, orbits, took into account the mass and finite dimensions of electrons, and showed that as the model became a more accurate model of the solar system, it increasingly conformed to experimental results.

When Einstein was asked about discrepancies between relativistic predictions of the gravitational deflection of light by the sun and experimental measurements, he replied: "For the expert, this thing is not particularly important, because the main significance of the theory does not lie in the verification of little effects, but rather in the great simplification of the theoretical basis of physics as a whole." (C. Seelig, *Albert Einstein*, p. 195.) (The ability of scientific theories to withstand apparent falsification is carefully discussed in the writings of Imre Lakatos — especially in "Criticism and the Methodology of Scientific Research Programmes" — in the context of an attractive account of the nature of scientific theories and scientific progress.)

Taking experimental falsification too seriously has led even great scientists in the wrong direction:

> I might tell you the story I heard from Schrödinger of how, when he first got the ideas for this (Schrödinger) equation, he immediately applied it to the behavior of the electron in the hydrogen atom, and then he got results that did not agree with experiment. The disagreement arose because at that time it was not known that the electron has a spin. That, of course, was a great disappointment to Schrödinger, and it caused him to abandon the work for some months. Then he noticed that if he applied the theory in a more approximate way, not taking into account the refinements required by relativity, to this rough approximation his work was in agreement with observation. He published his first paper with only this rough approximation, and in this Schrödinger's wave equation was presented to the world. Afterward, of course, when people found out how to take into account correctly the spin of the electron, this discrepancy between the results of applying Schrödinger's equation and the experiment was completely cleared up.
>
> I think there is a moral to this story, that it is more important to have beauty in one's equations than to have them fit experiment. If Schrödinger had been more confident of his work, he could have produced it some months earlier, and he could have published a more accurate equation. The equation is now known as the Klein-Gordon equation, although it was really discovered by Schrödinger before he discovered his nonrelativistic treatment of the hydrogen atom. (P.A.M. Dirac, "The Evolution of the Physicist's Picture of Nature," *Scientific American* (208) 1963, p.467.)

So scientific theories are not falsifiable by experimental facts. Theories have been rejected and replaced, but it has required a more successful competing theory, and not just recalcitrant experimental results, to discard an accepted theory.

This is why a number of historians of science have followed Thomas Kuhn (*The Structure of Scientific Revolutions*) in talking about scientific paradigms or worldviews rather than theories, and about anomalies rather than falsifications. Kuhn assimilates paradigm changes to *gestalt* shifts and likens the acceptance of a new paradigm to a religious conversion. Radical philosophers have taken this theme further and argued that there are no objective standards by which to choose among scientific theories. But few scientists take this seriously. Natural scientists, in particular, regard such analysis as bad comedy.

There are rational standards for scientific acceptability. These are subtle and involve considerations of not only experimental evidence but also theoretical simplicity and relation to other accepted scientific theories. (I tried to elucidate these in *Predictive Simplicity*.) Still, there is no question but that science itself is objective. Yet it remains fashionable to claim moral standards are subjective, just a matter of taste.

Perhaps a different tack might be tried to justify the view that value judgments, unlike scientific theories, are subjective. After all, scientific beliefs are functional or dysfunctional. If you build a bridge without taking into account the mechanics governing stresses and strains, it will collapse. If you treat a person for disease on the basis of medieval medicine, he probably will die.

But values, too, can be functional or dysfunctional. The cargo cults of South Pacific islanders, dissuading people from sustaining themselves, encouraging them instead to wait for the return of cargo planes laden with all their needs, were dysfunctional. It is arguable that religions teaching that the causes of sufferings and salvation lie outside ourselves are dysfunctional for just the same reason: they dissuade people from assuming responsibility for their lives. The Soviet system, based on state planning, the discouragement of individual enterprise and responsibility, the elimination of meaningful feedback, and the intolerance of substantive criticism, was dysfunctional. The abrogation of individual moral responsibility associated with religious cults, exemplified by Jim Jones in Guyana and David Koresh in Waco, Texas, is dysfunctional.

Considerations of this sort are not limited to fringe groups or the social and political systems of other countries, but penetrate deep into the fabric of our own society. We celebrate rock stars. Many of these culture heroes use drugs and sing about them. Naturally, this leads to greater drug use. Mass media target adolescents with visceral pleasures and pervert the development of youth. Advertising routinely degrades women as sex objects, leading society to become more accepting of such stereotypes. The entertainment industry portrays casual sex and violence as normal, helping us overcome inhibitions.

These cultural artifacts lie close to home and they are dysfunctional. Our society overwhelmingly acknowledges such dysfunction but is unable to do anything about it. That, too, is dysfunctional.

Many believe their happiness depends on their external environment. If only they had a better job, more money, a more understanding spouse, less rebellious children, better health... This neglects our ability — rarely exercised — to develop an internal state of profound happiness that is more than a mere effect of external circumstance. (The importance of one's internal state of life may extend to physiology. Pathogens live in even healthy bodies. So why do some individuals remain healthy while others get sick? How do we explain the relation between a person's spiritual health and positive outlook on life and his resistance to disease?)

Such an internal state, which can exert a powerful influence on one's environment, lies at the heart of Buddhist thought and practice. A lesson to be learned from Buddhism, which is less a religion in the Western sense and more a practice aimed at leading a fulfilling life, is that we misplace the fulcrum of our lives, locating it outside, rather than inside, ourselves. The evanescence of externally-based happiness, the brevity of life, and the importance of focus on lasting value are issues central to Buddhism.

> How long does a lifetime last? If one stops to consider, it is like a single night's lodging at a wayside inn. Should one forget that fact and seek some measure of worldly fame and profit? Though you may gain them, they will be mere prosperity in a dream, a delight scarcely to be prized. You would do better simply to leave such matters to the karma formed in your previous existences.
>
> Once you awaken to the uncertainty and transience of this world, you will find endless examples confronting your eyes and filling your ears. Vanished like clouds or rain, the people of past ages have left nothing but their names. Fading away like dew, drifting far off like smoke, our friends of today too disappear from sight.... The spring blossoms depart with the wind; the maple leaves turn red in the autumn showers. All are proof that no living being can stay for long in this world. (*The Major Writings of Nichiren Daishonin*, v. 5.]

In opposition to this insight, contemporary "developed" societies encourage an addiction to external fulfillment. For many, even if they achieve their immediate desires, new unfulfilled desires surface, leaving a new hunger in place of the old. The fulfillment of their desires does not change either the nature or the long-term intensity of their hunger. Meaningful and sustainable change for both individuals and society requires that people address their internal lives. In neglecting such a dimension, views deeply embedded in modern society are dysfunctional.

Similarly, the belief that if each person works for just his own immediate economic ends, then the invisible hand of the free market will guarantee maximum benefit to society, is patently dysfunctional. For it implies there is no value in long-term planning, integrity, social concern, or democratic responsibility. This is partly responsible for our decline in government, education and values.

Value beliefs matter, and matter as deeply as scientific beliefs. Just as false scientific beliefs can be dysfunctional, misguided value beliefs can be dysfunctional. There is no valid reason to believe there is so great a difference between scientific judgments and value judgments that the former are true or false, but the latter are only matters of subjective belief.

Still, it is inappropriate to impose values on others, and for just the same reasons that it is inappropriate to impose scientific beliefs. It is not just that autonomy and tolerance are objective moral virtues. Freedom of inquiry, intellectual integrity, and the willingness to tolerate different views are necessary to discover the truth — but are hardly necessary if there is no truth to discover. If values or scientific theories were merely matters of taste, there would be no truth to discover and nothing to be gained from tolerance. So a belief in the subjectivity of either values or science actually impedes the spirit of tolerance.

It is worse. The doctrine that all values are subjective is not only false, but dangerous. If there are no objective values, it cannot be a matter of discovering what values are appropriate. It can only be a matter of positing values, arbitrarily selecting certain values and committing yourself to them. It is not reason that counts, but commitment.

In fact, this marks a classic line of demarcation, one of the most important in the history of philosophy. There is a powerful tradition that lauds positing values and commitment, independent of reason. This tradition characterizes a broad and, at times, dominant current of European thought, from Rousseau to Nietzsche to Weber to Heidegger. It has influenced disciplines ranging from philosophy to politics, from psychology to literary criticism (deconstructionism).

The popularity of such a tradition is understandable. A world of pure reason leaves no room for creativity, for the will, for the heroic. The sterility of a life of pure reason is the basis of Nietzsche's criticism of Socrates. There may be value in this Nietzschean theme: the autonomy presupposed in positing values and in acting on the basis of those values. One does not reason and discover. One chooses. One acts. One is authentic. No wonder this philosophy was so closely associated with the Romantic Movement.

Despite its popularity, this tradition has a dark side of terrible potency, which has been associated with the worst atrocities in history. It may seem odd, but the problem with this dark side stems from its value relativism. If there are no objective values, it cannot matter what values are posited, those of Hitler or those of Gandhi. All that matters is the charisma of the value-positor. Perversely, the most charismatic figure of the twentieth century was Hitler. And leading advocates of positing — as opposed to discovering — values, true to their tradition, were enthusiastic supporters of the Third Reich.

Even today, relativism underlies the fashionable claim that social scientists, historians, literary critics and others necessarily bring their own biases to their research, biases that make objectivity impossible. At a deeper level, according to this line of reasoning, any observation must be filtered through language, experience and beliefs. All data we process must pass through the filter of our consciousness. So all we can ever have is different interpretations of different perceptions. There can be no independently accessible objective reality against which to measure their accuracy.

Because there can be no independently accessible objective reality, there can be no objective legitimacy. We can never say one view or theory is better, a more accurate representation of reality, than any other. As a result, we cannot argue against those who claim slavery was a beneficial institution or those who deny the holocaust. For these are just different interpretations of different perceptions.

The intellectual poverty of such an approach can be highlighted by extending it to the natural sciences. Natural scientists are humans. They, too, filter everything through their language, experience and beliefs. They have their own biases, which — presumably — distort their research, just as biases distort the research of social scientists, historians, etc.

So consider the flat earth hypothesis. There is a Flat Earth Society whose members either ignore or explain away the evidence that our planet is spherical. The same arguments used to claim that a historian's version of an event is just his interpretation of his perception can be applied equally to the Flat Earth Society. Only their interpretation of their perception — including their perception of the scientific evidence — is that the earth is flat.

Despite these arguments, we refuse to take their "science" seriously, even though they have no ulterior motives — it is just that there is so much physical evidence against their claims. Yet even where there is overwhelming sociological or historical evidence, many still treat crackpot — and often racist and neo-fascist — sociological and historical claims as just different interpretations of different perceptions, to be automatically accorded their own legitimacy. (Even in science, ulterior religious agendas have led some to insist that Creationism has the same status as evolution theories.)

To the extent that libertarianism is based on the relativity of values, its foundation is dangerously flawed. It has no ability to distinguish between tolerating potentially valuable new insights and tolerating anything, even intolerance. This provides no sustenance to either tolerance or other traditional values.

DEMOCRACY

DO WE (SHOULD WE) HAVE A DEMOCRACY?

Do We?

Libertarians find fault with interventionist government. Contrary to their views, interventionism is not the problem. Our real problem lies deeper, in the very nature of our government. Its consistent failure to be responsive to the needs of citizens, but to be solicitous, instead, of special interest groups, is symptomatic of a structural flaw. Politics has been reduced to an arena in which rich and powerful interests vie for greater riches and power.

This is due to a loss of individual influence in the political process, a loss that stems from size. The public feels no sense of participation in or responsibility for legislative decisions. This encourages governments to adopt short-term palliatives rather than deep-seated solutions that might cause temporary pain. For the public will turn on politicians only if it is suffering.

Special interests, called "factions" by our founding fathers, breed in the widening gap between representative and voter. Elected officials cater to these special interests and disregard their constituents with impunity, for if people are economically sated, they care little about the political arena and will passively re-elect incumbents running smooth well-funded campaigns.

This problem must be faced by any large democracy, and it calls into question the viability of this form of government for large heterogeneous countries. The prototypes of successful democracies, classical Athens, Germanic

185

tribes in the days of the Roman Empire, the early U.S., and even the short-lived eighteenth century democracies in Corsica and Haiti, had small, homogeneous, self-sufficient populations. Citizens could identify with each other. It was easier to preserve a sense of community and an interest in the common good.

Early nineteenth century New England town meetings, paragons of democracy, were held in small communities in which citizens had similar backgrounds, outlooks and interests. Broad political participation was common. The lack of socio-economic status did not discourage anyone from having political opinions and expressing them. "American mechanics, it was said, 'are not untaught operatives, but an enlightened, reflective people, who not only know how to use their hands, but are familiar with principles.'" (Lasch, *The Revolt of the Elites and the Betrayal of Democracy*, p. 60.)

But as our society has grown larger and more heterogeneous, it has become more difficult to conduct meaningful dialogue, to obtain informed consensus on issues, and to deal with the conflicting interests. People have become less inclined to transcend their private interests in favor of needs of the community. Attitudes have increasingly diverged from those regarded by the classical Athenians as integral and necessary to democracy. This calls attention to one of Tocqueville's chief concerns: Can participatory democracy be viable on a large scale?

That remains a critical question today, more than 150 years later. Of course, the politically correct answer is that the U.S. is even now a perfect example of a viable democracy.

But do we really have a democracy? In the wake of the growth of mega-corporations, which have replaced small proprietorships and farms over the last century and a half, participatory democracy has declined. Our practice of democracy, broad-based public participation in the political process, has been subtly transformed. While we have retained the forms of democracy, we have auctioned off its substance and its spirit.

We are not unique in this. "Romans liked to congratulate themselves for following what they called *mos maiorum* — 'the ways of our ancestors'. They were fond of old traditions and liked to keep alive old ways of doing things... Even when doing something new, the Romans liked to wrap it up in antique packaging. The names and forms of many republican institutions — and the delusion that the state was a republic and not a monarchy — endured long after they ceased to be appropriate." (Roberts, *A History of Europe*, p. 50.)

A millennium later, in a different culture: "When a ruler assumed the throne, there was a ceremony of investiture (bay'a), a vestige of the early Islamic convention that the ruler was chosen by the people." (Hourani, *A History of the Arab Peoples*, p.136.)

Public faith in the sanctity of our own *mos maiorum* has led us to close our eyes to developments that subvert the spirit of democracy, for we are uncomfortable with the politically incorrect. Yet inexorable forces have gradually pushed us in this direction.

Nearly 200 years ago Nicholas Biddle, a staunch adversary of Andrew Jackson, counseled William Henry Harrison's campaign: "Let him say not one single word about his principles, or his creed — let him say nothing — promise nothing. Let no committee, no convention — no town meeting ever extract from him a single word about what he thinks now, or what he will do hereafter..." (Muller, *Freedom in the Modern World*, p. 87.)

Biddle's advice was ahead of its time. As our country has grown and prospered, the increased sophistication of marketing, the tools and techniques available to well-funded campaigns, and the size of political spoils have changed the very nature of the political process. Stakes have grown too high to leave politics to chance. Market research, product selection and advertising now drive the process. Not only the tools of advertising and marketing, but also the vehicles, the mass media, have come to play a dominant role. Politics has become an industry driven by free market principles and in free market vehicles.

The cost of these vehicles has imposed a new structure on politics. Politicians at all levels understand it is the best packaging and most effective marketing that win elections. Marketing the candidate, reaching people with a short simple message that provides name recognition and a warm feeling, requires expensive media ads and drives up the cost of running for office. The high cost of campaigns, which must be borne by the candidate and his supporters, reduces the electoral process to an auction and perverts the spirit of democracy.

In the spirit of this perversion, special interest groups are delighted to serve as underwriters. They contribute to candidates and parties in return for influence on legislation. These groups spend billions of dollars in the political arena to increase their income by tens of billions through tax benefits, trade legislation, or the structure of government programs. They profit handsomely from the privatization of government.

Little pretense is made that the aim is to benefit the American people. If it were, special interests would not have to spend billions of dollars on lobbying. We would not need 100,000 registered lobbyists. Nor does anyone pretend campaign contributions are an expression of political ideology or confidence in a candidate — for large organizations contribute heavily to both political parties at the same time, and to anyone likely to win.

These contributions are investments, money spent to exact favors from whoever wins. They are good investments. If they were not, if they failed to generate significant incremental contributions to bottom lines (at our expense, for they create no new wealth), organizations would have stopped making such contributions long ago.

It is only natural that these investors, the campaign donors who are responsible for who gets elected, ultimately wield the power. "Decision making in the city [Washington D.C.] has increasingly come to be a polling of affected campaign donors and interest groups, rather than of the people..." (Kevin Philips, *Arrogant Capital*, p. 36.) These donors use their economic power to purchase political influence to protect and increase their economic power.

Philip Morris is one of the largest investors in the lobbying industry. Its contributions have been directed to maximizing political leverage to advance its economic interests. *The Economist* (August 31 — September 6, 1996) reports that in California it contributed $125,000 to a Republican candidate who barely won against an anti-tobacco candidate and became the majority whip. This contribution and others, to the Democratic ex-speaker of the house and the Republican attorney general, insured California's refusal to join other states in suing the tobacco companies.

Some states could be bought more cheaply.

> Gov. Bill Owens appoints a tobacco lobbyist to head a Colorado health care agency. She helps him craft a plan to aid uninsured breast and cervical cancer patients. The governor puts the plan on this week's special session agenda — but says lawmakers must pay for cancer treatments solely from programs designed to reduce tobacco use. Some public health advocates say that adds up to a deliberate raid on programs proven to save lives. "It's difficult to conclude anything but he's going after tobacco prevention," said Bob Doyle of the American Lung Association....
>
> State election records show Owens received a $5,000 campaign contribution from cigarette maker Philip Morris three weeks before announcing his plan. They also show that Karen Reinertson, a state official who helped developed the plan, lobbied for tobacco interests for seven years before Owens

appointed her to head his Department of Health Care Policy and Financing. (*The Denver Post*, September 19, 2001, p. B1.)

This is only the tip of the iceberg. Spending at the state level is small potatoes. Given the enormous spoils at the national level, huge amounts have been invested to sway public opinion and lawmakers' votes. "In 1993-1994, during the height of a national debate over health care reform, interest spending on outside lobbying alone totaled an estimated $790 million." (Schier, *By Invitation Only: The Rise of Exclusive Politics in the United States*, p. 171.)

In a similar vein, "The telecommunications fight pitted competing economic interests...as they fought over the spoils. The interest that was hardly heard in the struggle was the public's." (Drew, *The Corruption of American Politics*, p. 80.)

In some cases the *quid pro quo* is blatant. "When Amway founder Richard M. DeVos and his wife Helen each gave $500,000 to the GOP in April 1997, the payback came from the two most powerful people in Congress. In July, Senate Majority Leader Trent Lott and House Speaker Newt Gingrich slipped a last-minute provision into the hotly contested compromise tax bill that granted the DeVos family's company, Amway, a tax break on the Asian branches, saving it $19 million.... 'I know a little something about soft money, as my family is the largest single contributor of soft money to the national Republican Party,' Betsy DeVos wrote in an op-ed for the Capitol Hill newspaper Roll Call. 'I have decided, however, to stop taking offense at the suggestion that we are buying influence. Now I simply concede the point. They are right. We do expect some things in return.'" (*Mother Jones*, November-December 1998, p. 56.)

This sort of investment may skirt the legal definition of "bribery." But it fully captures the essence of the term. It explains why people resort to bribery, and why we have made it a crime. Isn't it ironic that bribery is a felony while pseudo-bribery in the context of political campaigns is the effective basis of our political power? Is this compatible with democracy? And people wonder why we have lost confidence in the system!

Even initiatives, long hoped by reformers to restore a measure of direct democracy, have become a tool of narrow moneyed interests. It requires capital to hire consultants to couch the initiative in the most appealing terms. It costs up to $5 per signature to get the initiative onto the ballot. It is expensive to air the necessary advertising. "The single most important finding in this study concerns the crucial role of money in campaigns on ballot questions... Time after time I have noted the initially favorable attitudes of voters shift to negativism, in large part as a result of advertising that is at best simplistic...and at its worst deceptive." (Zisk, *Money Media and the Grass Roots: State Ballot Issues and the Electoral Process*, p. 245, 264.)

The practice of investing in the political process to maximize influence, in addition to forging an alliance among capital, issues and candidates, has changed our notion of the ideal campaign and the ideal candidate. In campaigns it has replaced the focus on broad themes geared to the general electorate with niche marketing, for this is the most efficient use of capital.

> In recent decades, parties, interests, and campaigns have discovered what has become the most efficient way to succeed in elections and policy making.... The cost and risk of reaching out to all citizens is increasingly irrational for these elites. Providing exclusive invitations is the rational way to political success.... It is now possible for candidates, parties, and interests to rule without serious regard to majority preferences.... These strategies don't aim at the improvement of the commons as a primary goal...but instead serve to further narrow group or campaign goals. (Schier, *By Invitation Only*, p. 1-22.)

Candidates have been similarly transformed. It is less their understanding of the issues, their commitment to a well-conceived platform, or even their character and record in public service. It is more their ability to play the role designed by the professional political team.

Perversely, this has made the selection procedure for the best candidates incompatible with a selection procedure for the best elected officials. "The new technology has fundamentally altered the way in which the modern political candidate perceives his role. The great statesmen of the past saw themselves as heroes who took on the burden of their societies' painful journey from the familiar to the as yet unknown. The modern politician is less interested in being a hero than a superstar. Heroes walk alone; stars derive their status from approbation. Heroes are defined by inner values, stars by consensus. When a candidate's views are forged in focus groups and ratified by television anchor-persons, insecurity and superficiality become congenital.... Glibness rather than profundity, adeptness rather than analytical skill constitute their dominant traits." (Kissinger, *Years of Renewal*, p. 29, 1066.)

Our government sounds disturbingly like Plato's cynical caricature of democracy in *The Republic*. "[W]ith a magnificent indifference to the sort of life a man has led before he enters politics, it would promote to honor anyone who merely calls himself the people's friend.... Accordingly, we can now go back to describe how the democratic type develops from the oligarchical. I imagine it usually happens in this way. When a young man, bred, as we were saying, in a stingy and uncultivated home, has once tasted the honey of the drones and keeps company with these dangerous and cunning creatures, who know how to purvey pleasures in all their multitudinous variety, then the oligarchical constitution of his soul begins to turn into a democracy."

Plato's insights notwithstanding, we have evolved in just the opposite direction. As our government has become less responsive to citizens and more solicitous of groups that fund campaigns, we have moved away from democracy and toward oligarchy or plutocracy.

Reflecting the distance between the reality of our political power structure and democracy, John Ralston Saul (*Voltaire's Bastards*) characterizes our government as corporatist, rather than democratic. Corporatism deals with organizations — corporations, unions, lobbies — rather than individuals. It was preached by nineteenth century political philosophers and reached its zenith in the fascist regime of Mussolini. Our present alignment of government with such interests constitutes the central element of corporatism. Even the trappings, including the use of symbolism as a substitute for substantive political debate, are characteristic of corporatism.

(It might be objected that the comparison with Mussolini's fascism is overly harsh; for in fascist Italy, the government controlled the corporations and told them what to do. By contrast, in our political-economic structure, corporations are autonomous. Such an objection is overstated. In Mussolini's Italy the largest and most powerful corporations had *Il Duce*'s ear and were able to influence government policy. Many made their own decisions as much as contemporary corporations do. And Mussolini effectively guaranteed huge profits to cooperative corporations. What more could one want?)

Many political and social scientists defend a clone of corporatism. They are faced with the politically uncomfortable reality that all important public decisions are made by a privileged elite, the top echelon of powerful organizations. So they have argued — unconvincingly — that our elitism is pluralist and that this pluralism makes it compatible with traditional democratic ideals. Even if our elitism were pluralist, it would still be incompatible with traditional democratic values. A pluralist elite would only broaden the oligarchy.

This attempt to justify pluralist corporatism blurs the distinction between democracy and corporatism. It is already too easy to slide from the former to the latter. This makes it even easier. It exacerbates a most worrisome aspect of our drift toward corporatism — that it has occurred so gradually and so naturally that we are unaware of the extent to which the nature of our government has changed. It is not that large corporations stealthily executed a *coup d'état*. This change did not require subversion or anything sinister. Our government, under subtle but constant pressure, has gradually metamorphosed. One can trace this development, in an oversimplified way, through remarks from past presidents:

"There was a time when corporations played a very minor part in our business affairs, but now they play the chief part, and most men are the servants of corporations." (Woodrow Wilson)

"The chief business of the American people is business." (Warren Harding)

"This administration is not sympathetic to corporations, it is indentured to corporations." (Richard Nixon)

This transition illustrates the enormous power exerted over time by corporations acting rationally in their economic self-interest. It is in their economic interest to have a favorable public image, independent of their actual business practices. Thanks to the power of mass media, the image they have been able to fabricate is totally benign. Whatever the reality, we are unable to penetrate this self-serving facade.

As but one measure of the power of corporate advertising to confound our perception, The Bureau of National Affairs estimates that the monetary value of corporate crime is 10 times greater than that of individual crime. "One study of seventy of the nation's largest manufacturing, mining, and mercantile corporations revealed that 60 percent had been convicted of criminal charges on an average of four times each." (Spence, *With Justice for None*, p.284.) But despite our concern with crime, we are blind to this. For large corporations, through their advertising muscle, control the media and determine how we view them. They influence even news reporting and blur the difference between objective news and self-serving infomercials.

Just as it is in the interest of corporations to shape a benign image, it is in their interest to bend government policies to their favor. The exercise of such influence has increased gradually over decades, and at all levels of government. Corporate officers can now argue that since other corporations and special interest groups are procuring government policies favorable to them, it would be irresponsible to their shareholders if they neglected to do the same. It is hardly surprising that it has become common and accepted corporate practice to influence government policies in areas of concern.

As one result of this practice, in the 1980s interest deductions — not granted to individuals — enabled corporations to significantly reduce their tax bill. The ability to purchase net operating losses to generate tax deductions further reduced corporate income taxes. In 1950, corporate taxes produced four times as much revenue as payroll taxes. Now, reflecting the political clout of corporations and the lack of political clout of payroll workers, payroll taxes generate three times the revenue of corporate taxes. In the past two decades the corporate share of federal income taxes has declined from one-third to one-tenth. In 1998, more than half of our 250 largest corporations paid effective federal income tax rates of less than 10%.

Enron, one of the largest contributors to political campaigns, and cited by some authors as the model modern energy corporation, paid no federal taxes at all from 1996 through 1999, despite financial statements showing a net income of $2.3 billion. "Enron documents suggest General Electric, Microsoft, Merck and other giants were involved in similar dealings. Additionally — as illustrated by the recent debacle at Sprint Corp. — corporate executives have been using complex shelters to avoid paying income taxes on their massive stock options profits." (Al Lewis, *The Denver Post*, February 16, 2003.)

As corporations have become more successful in these efforts, our political system has moved further from its origins as a democracy. What remains of our democracy is its symbolism. We have our *mos maiorum* in quadrennial presidential election dramas, presented by the media as a political Super Bowl. Even biennial congressional elections are presented with all the drama and passion of a televised high school football game. But if you consider where the political power really lies, it is with large corporations, unions and special interest groups.

It is not that corporatism is necessarily a bad form of government, despite representing a concentration of political and economic power antithetic to the vision of our founding fathers. South and East Asian countries have practiced it and have generated high levels of economic growth, much of it benefiting ordinary citizens. (One reason we have done poorly is that we are mediocre corporatists, preoccupied with the short term.)

Our problem is that we have failed to examine the merits and pitfalls of corporatism, much less the culture necessary to make corporatism effective. Rather, we have pursued corporatist policies blindly, unaware of our self-deception. We have pretended to have a democracy, while autonomous economic interests wield the real power.

Should We?

We have deceived ourselves by reducing "democracy" to a label. We "know" we have a democracy. Most of us find offensive any suggestion that our government is not a democracy. And we "know" democracy is good, the best possible form of government. But we are careful not to look too closely. We deliberately avoid those aspects that suggest dysfunction, and many bridle at the unpatriotic notion that democracy might be less than perfect. But despite our faith in this form of government, democracy can give rise to serious problems.

Democracies are prone to corruption. In an absolute monarchy, the wealth of the state belongs to the monarch, to whom the ministers must answer. In a democracy, the wealth of the state belongs to that amorphous entity, the people. One does not have to answer to anyone in particular, especially if one controls the government. The risk in siphoning off wealth is diminished, and the temptation to divert some into one's own pocket increases.

Democracies are also prone to jingoism and ultra-nationalism. If an absolute monarch decides to go to war, he can conscript his citizens and order them to fight. In a democracy, by contrast, it is necessary to "persuade" citizens that their opponents are evil and that the war is good and just. This requires a campaign to generate animosity toward some group designated as the "enemy." Jingoism can be an attractive platform for gaining political power.

Even internally, democracy maximizes both the incentive and the opportunity to incite hatred and pander to prejudice. In an absolute monarchy, a demagogue has little to gain from fanning flames of prejudice. If he does, the monarch can warn him against endangering his subjects and can also take more emphatic, punitive, action should he choose. There is no counterpart to this in a democracy.

It is generally easy to incite people, and democracies have provided many examples of parlaying prejudice into political power. The Nazis, playing on the harsh terms imposed by the Allied powers at the end of World War I and on widespread anti-Semitism, won power in free democratic elections. The governments of those Balkan states that carried out "ethnic cleansing" were democratically elected. Our own democratic institutions did nothing to mitigate our shameful treatment of African-Americans and Native Americans. In our recent history, consider both the intent of the Willie Horton campaign ad and its effect on the 1988 presidential election.

In countries in which there is no strong commitment to the whole, democracy begets factionalism. If one faction gains power, it often represses others. Minority factions with little chance to share power may resort to violence. The exclusivity of religious factionalism caused electoral and economic discrimination against Catholics in Northern Ireland and spawned violence throughout the United Kingdom. Algeria has been plagued by violence ever since it became a democracy. Tribal allegiances in African democracies led to civil wars and to genocide.

Modern democracies are particularly susceptible to an insidious form of factionalism. Mancur Olson (*The Logic of Collective Action, The Rise and Decline of Nations*) has called attention to a critical asymmetry. It is easy (and can be highly profitable) to form a special interest group seeking to redistribute national wealth in its own favor. By contrast, it is nearly impossible to dissolve such a group once it has been formed. As a result of this asymmetry, special interest groups, seeking to gain at the expense of others, proliferate. These groups employ lobbyists and spend heavily to influence legislation and, if necessary, public opinion to their advantage. Such spending often produces greater profits for these groups than any other investment, even though it produces no new wealth for the economy as a whole.

(Such an alliance between the political and the economic is not limited to democracy. It characterized European mercantilism well into the Industrial Revolution and was partly responsible for the inefficiency of that political/ economic system. Mercantilism, characterized by government regulations designed to protect politically powerful groups or industries, is presently the political system of most Third World countries. It impedes their economic development, just as it had impeded the economic development of Europe centuries ago. But despite its well-known drawbacks, the ability of large economic institutions to purchase political power and use that power to enhance their economic interests creates dangerous pressure to introduce mercantilism to the U.S. by the back door.)

It is estimated that more than 5% of our GNP is invested in lobbying. Beneficiaries of government programs fight fiercely to retain what they have. Programs and subsidies live on and on, no matter how useless they may be to society as a whole. By competing for capital and reducing investment in instruments that would create additional wealth, competition for government largesse diverts wealth creation into wealth distribution without producing collateral benefit.

As a result, public resources become increasingly devoted to the obsolescent with established lobbies, placing innovation at a disadvantage. The country's competitive position deteriorates. This politically-engineered diversion of capital also creates rifts between the few who benefit from the redistribution and others who find such collusion unfair.

It may sound odd, perhaps unpleasant, but unless certain preconditions are satisfied, democracy may not be the best form of government, even for the ordinary citizen.

Singapore provides an instructive example. When it gained independence from Malaysia in 1965, there was little assurance that it would survive. It is a small island, less than 250 square miles, with little arable land. It has a multi-ethnic (Chinese, Malay, Indian), multi-racial, multi-religious (Buddhist, Muslim, Christian, Hindu, Sikh, Taoist, Confucian), multi-lingual (Chinese, Malay, Tamil, English) population. It had a history of civil strife and labor disputes. To make matters worse, on gaining its independence the country had to face rising barriers to trade with neighboring Malaysia.

Lee Kuan Yew, the country's prime minister, established a one-party state, not a democracy. The state controlled the media and suppressed political dissent. Even today, Singapore has only one real party, the People's Action Party, holding 80 of the 83 seats in the legislature.

Despite its autocratic form of government, the country's achievements have been admirable: a mixing of ethnic groups by integrating schools and building multi-ethnic public housing, high-quality public education that has achieved a 90+% literacy rate and helped establish a sense of national identity, the development of industrial estates to attract foreign investment, effective government investment in private enterprise (government-linked corporations, which account for 60% of Singapore's GNP). These measures have led to impressive growth benefiting all strata of society. Singapore has surpassed the U.S. in GNP per capita and also in average life expectancy.

It is unlikely that this could have been achieved under a democratic regime. It may seem paradoxical, but it is plausible that Singapore is nearer to functional democracy than it would have been had its government of the past 35 years been democratic.

Had Singapore been a democracy from the start, groups opposed to government policy would have formed coalitions to maintain their influence at the expense of the whole. Unions would have insisted on their prerogatives to control workflow and would have killed the legislation that increased working hours. Threats of labor unrest would have diminished the attractiveness of Singapore to potential investors. Landowners would have blocked the establishment of industrial estates. The rich would have objected to the heavy social spending on the middle and lower classes. Ethnic groups would have resisted the forced integration. Many from all walks of life would have fought the mandatory savings imposed by the government.

The integration, the high levels of educational proficiency, and the sense of nationhood would have come grudgingly, if at all. The notions would not have arisen that primary allegiance is due to the country as a whole and that the whole country could prosper if special interest groups would take a back seat — or if government would force them to do so. These are preconditions to functional democratic government anywhere, even in the U.S. (Still, a severe global economic contraction would provide a sharp test of Singapore's young society, as it would for all democracies.)

It is deceptively easy to overstate the significance of these problems for democracy. These problems do not show democracy to be an inferior form of government. They do not justify replacing democratic institutions with non-democratic ones. They only show that certain conditions involving the attitudes, priorities and understanding of citizens are necessary for democracy to function effectively.

Ironically, the major challenge to democracy in the U.S. does not come as a frontal assault by some foreign totalitarian state. Rather, it comes by stealth from an emanation of our own economic philosophy. Our political and economic infrastructure has incubated Public Choice Theory, the political correlate to *laissez faire*. This theory is a potent deterrent to democratic action. It claims that ideally, politics should be modeled after the free market, in which people's spending reveals their true preferences. Unfortunately, the political arena bears little resemblance to the financial arena of the free market. Unlike the financial markets, in which fully informed people vote freely with their dollars to maximize their expected benefit, the world of politics distorts information and is inherently opaque, inefficient and biased. Individuals may vote for their own interests, but the very structure of politics thwarts the desires of voters — who rationally should not expend the effort to vote at all.

The acceptance of such a theory would leave the free market secure in its revealed preferences. It would guarantee the victory of large voting blocs of money: "one dollar, one vote," over the public "one person, one vote." Because these large blocs of money consistently vote for their own interest, to become even larger blocs, the immediate effect would be to transfer wealth from the lower and middle classes, which have few dollars of influence, to the wealthy. In the longer term it would increase economic disparity and would destabilize society to everyone's detriment.

Appropriately, it was political action taken after *laissez faire* last discredited itself, in 1932, that remedied the most egregious excesses of the free market. This provided an example of democracy in action, an example fittingly contrary to the central assumptions of Public Choice Theory.

This example, in its very success, calls into question the assumptions of Public Choice Theory. These assumptions, particularly about the financial markets, are implausible — if not ludicrous. It is painfully clear that investors and purchasers are hardly ever fully, or even adequately, informed. Who would have bought or driven a Ford Pinto, secure in the knowledge that its gas tank might explode? Who would have bought stocks on the basis of recommendations by Merrill Lynch analysts, knowing that these analysts privately referred to their recommended stocks as garbage? What investor would have bought stock on the basis of any broker-dealer recommendations, knowing that the tenor of such recommendations was often dictated by prospects of lucrative investment banking contracts rather than the prospects of the company itself?

Not only are investors and purchasers inadequately informed, but many studies show that their decisions are often not rational. Efficient pricing exists only in the minds of some economists. Economic playing fields are hardly ever level, and players with the most money often tilt the field in their own favor.

The very fact that politics has taken over the tools, techniques and personnel of the advertising industry shows that the alleged contrast between the pristine economic and the corrupt political is grossly exaggerated by Public Choice Theory. Indeed, it is unlikely that this theory would ever have been taken seriously if we had not so shamelessly enslaved ourselves to theological *laissez faire*.

This should call attention to the disingenuousness of much of the criticism of government intervention, intervention often geared to protect the public, workers, and the environment from the rapacity of corporations. It is not easy being a shepherd when you are constantly told that your dogs are too expensive, that in their arrogance they keep the sheep from the best pasture, and that even in principle the sheep would be better off without dogs or shepherds. But it is a bit easier when you learn that it is wolves who are telling you this.

DEMOCRACY VS. LAISSEZ FAIRE

It is not democracy, but corporatism, that dovetails with *laissez faire* and libertarianism. Where enormous power is concentrated in the hands of a few mega-corporations, government is the only counterweight that can provide protection from economic aggression. Where government will not intervene, because it has been "bought" by powerful economic interests and because an influential group is philosophically opposed to government interference under any circumstances, the power of the free market — including the power of economic intimidation — is complete.

It is here that the difference between the democratic agenda and the *laissez faire*-libertarian agenda is critical. It is here that the libertarian approach is most dysfunctional.

Consider the insistence by our founding fathers on the importance of vigilance in the defense of democracy. For democracy, "That which your fathers have bequeathed to you, earn it anew if you would possess it." (Goethe, *Faust.*) Since Pericles, democratic thought has appreciated the need for citizens to transcend personal interest in favor of the common good. This stands in stark contrast to an economic theory that tells us the common good is best served if everyone pursues only his own personal interests.

The vast difference between the democratic conception of man and the *laissez faire* conception of man as an apolitical animal exclusively concerned with his own immediate economic gain is reflected in etymology. Our word "idiot" derives from a Greek word that referred, not to persons of limited intellectual capacity, but to individuals unconcerned with the state and needs of the community.

Such an idiot fits perfectly into *laissez faire*, where the invisible hand of the free market maximizes benefit for the entire society if each person just looks out for his own ends. The doctrine of the invisible hand, omnipotent and beneficent, implies there is nothing to be gained by fostering a community of disinterested public-spirited citizens. (Adam Smith himself held a jaundiced view of idiocy. "Some men turn every quality or art into a means of making money; this they conceive to be the end, and to the promotion of the end all things must contribute." [*The Wealth of Nations*, Book I.])

Like *laissez faire*, corporatism both encourages and feeds off a lack of public interest — a citizenry of *idiots*. So it is not coincidence that the increasingly corporatist nature of our government since the Civil War has paralleled our irregularly increasing proclivity to accept a radical free market approach to politics and economics. It is only natural that this has been accompanied by a decrease in citizens' commitment to the common good.

This illustrates the extent to which the self-serving claim of free market apologists, that *laissez faire* and democracy go hand in hand, is profoundly misleading. It is not just the ease of combining free market capitalism with totalitarian government. Nor is it the absence of financial markets in early democracies. It is not even the lack of traces of democracy in mediaeval empires that had flourishing financial markets and large banking establishments. It is primarily that the ideal democrat is so vastly different from the free market *homo economicus*. This explains why the growth of democracy has been unrelated to the growth of free markets.

It is true that democracies are found in economically advanced states, which are capitalist. But this does *not* entail that capitalism is the magic ingredient that creates democracy. It is far more plausible that a broad dispersion of wealth is necessary for democratic society. If many are desperately trying to survive amidst the conspicuous affluence of a privileged few, they have little reason to place the common good ahead of their own needs. A most important prerequisite to democracy is missing.

This fits the pre-capitalist democracy of ancient Athens and democracies in "primitive" societies in which poverty was not institutionalized. It explains the rejection of democracy by capitalist economies during periods of severe economic stress and extreme poverty (Weimar Germany), and also the failure of democracies in ex-colonies, even ones with capitalist economic structures. (India, a rare democratic success, has always been skeptical of the pure free market.)

It is also true that those states at the economic and political hub of European civilization — Venice in the fifteenth century, Holland in the seventeenth, England in the nineteenth — were driven by commercial interests and also were less despotic than the peripheral states. But the explanation for this, too, has little to do with democracy. Despotism discourages wealth building. Why build wealth if the ruler can arbitrarily confiscate it? The incentive to engage in industry or commerce requires the stability and lawfulness to guarantee you will be able to reap the fruits of your labor.

But such stability does not require anything like democracy. Even in the fifteenth century, the doge and the Medici understood that respect for law and freedom from caprice were necessary to the continued success of their commercial empires. They equally understood that civil liberties and broad participation in the political process were not necessary.

This pattern — free markets plus a measure of freedom, even privilege, for the wealthy scions of commerce, juxtaposed with authoritarian political power — is common throughout history.

Free markets with sophisticated financial instruments facilitating the building of personal fortunes flourished in ancient civilizations in which there were no traces of democracy. "[A]s witness ancient Babylon, which had bankers, merchants engaged in distant trade, and all the instruments of credit, such as bills of exchange, promissory notes, cheques..." (Braudel, *The History of Civilizations*, p. 386.)

Two millennia later, free market institutions thrived in Middle Eastern empires — absolute autocracies. "Chance has preserved letters from the Jewish merchants in Cairo at the time of the First Crusade (1095-9). They show knowledge of every method of credit and payment, and every form of trade association.... Huge fortunes were made under a capitalistic trading system, well ahead of its time, that extended as far as China and India, the Persian Gulf, Ethiopia, the Red Sea, Ifriqya and Andalusia. 'Capitalist' is not too anachronistic a word. From one end of Islam's world connection to the other, speculators unstintingly gambled on trade.... In Basra, settlements between merchants were made by what we should now call a clearing system...." (*Ibid.*, p. 63-4, 71.) In mediaeval Russia the *gosti*, the top echelon of merchants, were granted far-reaching privileges and accumulated massive wealth. But they remained absolute vassals of the tsar.

Even in European history free markets flourished long before the *philosophes* of the Enlightenment constructed the philosophical foundations of modern democracy. The notion, proffered by *laissez faire* apologists, that free markets first emerged in nineteenth century Europe, at the same time as modern democracy, is simply false.

The Amsterdam stock exchange dates back to 1530. And Amsterdam was a relatively new financial center. Money-changers, merchants and notaries conducted business near St. Martin's Church in Lucca in 1111. As early as the twelfth century, fairs throughout Europe had a sophisticated financial component as well as a commodity component. Private merchant banks, founded in the twelfth century to finance trading establishments, flourished in the thirteenth century, loaning money to kings and financing military campaigns. State-owned banks were established in the thirteenth century. Checks and holding companies as well as double-entry bookkeeping were common in thirteenth century Florence. The Bourse in Bruges, the center of a flourishing money market, was built in 1309. Stocks were traded in the Leipziger Messe in the 1300s. The Lonja in Barcelona was completed in 1393. Similar financial exchanges appeared in Antwerp in 1460 and Lyons in 1462. The central bank of Venice, a lender of last resort, was established in 1585.

This early capitalism was not limited to the financial markets. Fourteenth century Genoa and Venice were colonial powers — and colonialism is supposedly a hallmark of advanced capitalism. Marx maintained that the mediaeval Italian city-states were the first to engage in capitalist means of production. In the sixteenth century the Fuggers were involved in both commercial and industrial capitalism. *What has this got to do with democracy?*

Even today, the institutional agents of the market, as typified by the Federal Reserve and the World Trade Organization, are not elected by any democratic constituency. They are, in effect, agents of the large banks and financial establishments. These agents act to advance the interests of their constituents, independent of democratic will and independent of the effects of their actions on ordinary people.

Laissez faire capitalism is not a straightforward counterpart to democracy. While it may be compatible with the forms and rituals of democracy, it can easily become incompatible with the substance of democracy. Where a concentration of economic power can purchase political power and thereby eliminate the only counterweight to the unbridled exercise of that economic power, where that generates a government that may be of the people but is certainly not for the people, a *laissez faire*-libertarian approach only makes matters worse. It supports the natural affiliation of a free market economy with corporatism.

Is Local Government the Answer?

Because corporatism is a natural correspondent to *laissez faire*, efforts to restore substantive democracy face a formidable challenge. Due to the impossibility of countering big money at the national level, many have given up on national politics. Where political interest remains, it is at the local level, reflecting the hope that citizens still retain a measure of input in their communities. This supports the call to decentralize government.

Politicians have exploited this in their drive to allocate government policies and services to increasingly local levels. They have told us that the advantages of relegating policy making to state and local communities would include greater public influence on decisions as well as a more effective guarantee of individual rights. Wrong!

Contrary to the notion of community government as a panacea, the community has not been a reliable guardian of either civil liberties or democracy. Ironically, it was federal intervention in the South to protect the civil liberties of African-Americans from flagrant violations by states and communities that rekindled interest in States' Rights and the move to smaller government. For many, the appeal of the move to smaller government had little to do with any desire to protect civil liberties.

There is no reason to expect the move to smaller government to enhance civil liberties. Prejudice tends to be more uniform and more intense at local levels where the population is often homogeneous. The lack of meaningful political competition in many communities diminishes respect for civil liberties, an effect often associated with one-party rule. Discrimination is easier.

The push to smaller government has not even aided citizens' efforts to secure greater control over their own communities. At state and local levels it is easier for corporations to "purchase" opportunities to prey directly on citizens. *Consumer Reports* (July 1998) reports: "A lobbyist and former speaker in the Florida House reportedly helped draft that state's 1995 title-lending law, which allows annual interest rates of 264 per cent. Since then, the industry, mainly Title Loans of America, has given more than $94,000 to Florida legislators in both parties. For two years, lawmakers have refused to pass reform legislation, even after their own task force recommended repealing the 1995 law."

The smaller the community, the less leverage it has in bargaining with large corporations seeking profit-maximizing concessions. Nike, having claimed an interest in building a facility in Golden, Colorado, withdrew because Colorado's offers were not in the ballpark with offers from other states — a 10-year waiver of corporate income tax and a $10 million interest-free forgivable loan. Kentucky had earlier provided $325 million in incentives to induce Toyota to build an assembly plant in that state. For the country as a whole, the corporate share of property taxes has declined from 45% to 16% in the last 40 years. But there is no free lunch. The decreased tax burden borne by corporations has necessitated an increase in property taxes on private individuals.

Consider, too, the ability of a company that emits toxic pollution to hold an auction, offering to locate in the community that treats polluters most favorably. It would provide jobs and tax revenues in return for the license to pollute. Communities would compete with each other to offer the most attractive packages, minimizing taxes and maximizing allowable pollution. The company would choose the package that maximizes profits.

Such an auction — states or local communities bidding to attract industry by providing an environment most favorable to maximizing profits, even at the expense of residents — is not fantasy. A similar phenomenon has occurred with states that have passed right-to-work laws. These laws reduce economic pressure to belong to a union by giving non-union members the same major benefits without their having to pay union dues. As one would expect, right-to-work laws reduce union membership.

Having to deal with unions lessens management control and often decreases profitability. By discouraging unions, right-to-work laws provide an incentive for corporations to locate in right-to-work states. In keeping with this incentive, corporations have pressured states to adopt such legislation, arguing that a pro-business anti-union attitude leads to increased corporate investment, higher employment and greater wealth. But while there is clear evidence that such auctions — in effect, volunteering labor at lower cost — have lured corporations to right-to-work states, it is less clear that they have benefited the residents of those states.

None of the 10 richest states are right-to-work states. But 15 of the 20 poorest states have been right-to-work states for generations. The great majority of right-to-work states have a lower output per resident and a lower per capita income than the average for union states. (*New York Times 2000 Almanac*, p. 336.) The correlation coefficient between per capita income and being a right-to-work state is -.45. So decentralizing by having states adopt their own labor laws has not benefited citizens. Instead, it has further increased the power of large corporations.

There are a number of reasons why right-to-work laws have not benefited states or communities, but have instead padded the bottom lines of large corporations. One is that unions can have a positive impact, fostering increases in productivity. Unions have also forced companies to compete based on innovation, productivity and service, rather than cutting labor costs. Independently it is primarily the poorer states that passed right-to-work legislation. These states were unable to fund critical aspects of their infrastructures, from education to transportation to medical care. As a result, they were unable to attract capital or profitable industries. Poverty breeds poverty even at the state level.

Still, it does not appear that right-to-work legislation has helped these states raise their standards of living. Decentralizing by having states adopt their own labor laws has not benefited citizens. Instead, it has further increased the profitability and power of large corporations.

(This is not to deny advantages to community control, or at least community input. But there is also the need to protect the individual against the community and the community against institutions that have greater economic power. Such protection cannot be secured at the local level.)

The response that most corporations are publicly owned is disingenuous. Half of all stocks and bonds are owned by the wealthiest 1% of the population, whose economic interests are served by corporatism. Many of these individuals comprise America's elite aristocracy. They belong to the same clubs. They send their children to the same private schools. They have the same doubts about democracy, parallel to doubts of many of our founding fathers. Can the masses be entrusted with the responsibility of government?

Historically, this issue has marked a primary fault line in American politics. The delegates to the 1787 Constitutional Convention had serious misgivings about broad-based political participation. They supported property qualifications not only for holding office, but even for voting. The Constitution does not contain such anti-democratic measures only because the committee responsible for proposing specific guidelines was unable to resolve differences between landowners and merchants over what sort of property should count — so the delegates left the matter to the individual states, which were equally wary of democratic populism, as was reflected in their own property requirements for voting.

These requirements excluded not only minorities and women, but even most white men, from voting. John Jay, the first Chief Justice of the Supreme

Court, defended this plank of the Federalist platform: "Those who own the country ought to govern it." While Federalism was opposed by Jefferson and ultimately succumbed to Jackson's populism, this sentiment resurfaced in the Whig tradition. We have always had powerful factions for whom this is a core belief, though it is now couched in more politically acceptable language.

PREREQUISITIES TO FUNCTIONAL DEMOCRACY

MASSES VS. ELITES

Many who have written skeptically about democracy have sought to link its appeal to a utopian belief in the perfectability of mankind. Skeptics have contended that a more realistic appraisal of our species would facilitate a more realistic view of government. As Plato insisted, the great unwashed masses are inherently incapable of governing, and there is little reason to be so optimistic as to believe that education would enlighten them to the point that they could be entrusted with political power. Even they would be better off if qualified experts ran society. Our founding fathers echoed this sentiment.

But the rationale for democracy does not depend on universal enlightenment. Neither does the notion of government of, by and for the people imply that each person should be capable of running a government. The notion of the wisdom of ordinary people is not simple-minded. It is a belief in character, more than education or cleverness. Typified by Lincoln's remark, "But you can't fool all of the people all of the time," it is reflected in our language, "common sense" and "common decency."

It may sound strange, but democratic sentiment reflects grounding in practical reality, as opposed to abstract theory. In the last 2,500 years no one has surpassed the characterization of democracy given by Pericles.

> Our constitution...favors the many instead of the few; this is why it is called a democracy. If we look to the laws, they afford equal justice to all in their private differences; if to social standing, advancement in public life falls to

207

reputation for capacity, class considerations not being allowed to interfere with merit; nor again does poverty bar the way, if a man is able to serve the state, he is not hindered by the obscurity of his condition. The freedom which we enjoy in our government extends also to our ordinary life.... But all this ease in our private relations does not make us lawless as citizens. Against this fear is our chief safeguard, teaching us to obey the magistrates and the laws...

Our public men have, besides politics, their private affairs to attend to, and our ordinary citizens, though occupied with the pursuits of industry, are still fair judges of public matters; for...we regard the citizen who takes no part in these duties not as unambitious but as useless, and we are able to judge proposals even if we cannot originate them; instead of looking on discussion as a stumbling block in the way of action, we think it an indispensable preliminary to any wise action at all. (*The Landmark Thucydides*, p. 112-3.)

Pericles was not an academic theoretician, but governed Athens when it was engaged in the Persian War, and later the Peloponnesian War, multi-decades life and death struggles that engulfed the entire Greek world. He was a tough practitioner of *Realpolitik*. He knew from experience the value of expertise and recommended that meritorious individuals be recognized for their contributions. An astute strategist, diplomat and political leader, he was not deceived about the enlightened wisdom of ordinary people. He understood that not just anyone could formulate satisfactory policy, especially in complex and dangerous times. Yet he remained a democrat, keenly aware of the advantages of an open society in which ordinary citizens could discuss, debate and vote on policy proposals.

It may seem odd that Pericles was so staunch a democrat, for elitist theory sounds impressive. After all, shouldn't those who have the requisite capacity and who are specially trained be the ones who would best govern? Not necessarily. What sounds impressive often fails. Reality often differs from high-sounding theory. As an antidote to dwelling excessively on the lack of capability of ordinary people, it may be useful to consider the track records of elites. The best and the brightest have regularly produced not just disappointments, but disasters.

History is replete with elitist policies characterized by two dangerously misguided themes. One is that the ends justify the means, that even massive suffering in the near term is a small price to pay for the better world that is sure to be attained by the policies in question. Too often have elites caused horrendous suffering in the name of wonderful ends, sacrificing common decency as though it were an inferior standard that the powerful and enlightened could transcend on behalf of their cause.

Chateaubriand expressed this with sardonic elegance:

> The members of the Convention prided themselves on being the most benevolent of men. Good fathers, good sons, good husbands, they took their children out walking; they acted as nannies, they wept with tenderness at the sight of their children's simple games; they would lift those little lambs gently in their arms, to show them the horses pulling the tumbrels that were taking the victims to execution. They sang of nature, peace, piety, charity, innocence, the domestic virtues. These bigots of philanthropy had their neighbors' heads cut off with extreme sensitivity, so that the happiness of the human race might be ever greater. (*Mémoirs d'outre-tombe*, v. 1, p. 292.)

How similar this is to the "Long Telegram" of George F. Kennan, which did much to influence our view of the U.S.S.R. "In this dogma, with its basic altruism of purpose, they found justification for their instinctive fear of the outside world, for the dictatorship without which they did not know how to rule, for cruelties they did not dare not to inflict, for sacrifices they felt bound to demand."

Even the Grand Inquisitor was there to save souls.

The other theme, also focused narrowly on ends, is the disregard of practical ramifications, of what could go wrong. Some of our own most foolhardy policies illustrate this pattern. "These dilemmas deepened when, in 1962, Secretary of Defense Robert McNamara adopted the strategy of "assured destruction," which based deterrence on the calculation of civilian devastation that would be theoretically unacceptable to the Soviet Union. This essentially academic concept presupposed unlimited willingness to threaten civilian casualties; minimum estimates involved tens of millions. This professorial strategy calculated everything except the willingness to resort to it. Inevitably it created a huge gap between our awesome military capacity and the moral convictions of almost any foreseeable American leader." (Kissinger, *Years of Renewal*, p. 116-7.)

More recently, the diversion of water from the two rivers that feed the Aral Sea in Kazakhstan, while it reflected the benign intent to irrigate 18 million acres of land and increase agricultural production, failed to consider environmental consequences. "Predictably this major diversion of water caused the Aral Sea to shrink rapidly. By the late 1980s two thirds of it had dried up, exposing the seabed across an area of over 12,000 square miles. Major climatic changes resulted — temperatures rose and rainfall fell. The effects locally were devastating. Nearly all the species of fish in the sea became extinct, the fishing industry collapsed and large numbers of villages were abandoned. The salinity of the Aral tripled; salt-dust storms swept the area; the water table fell, causing the sewerage system to collapse, with the result that typhoid rates rose thirty-fold, and nine out of ten children were diagnosed as being permanently ill." (Ponting, *The Twentieth Century*, p. 73.)

Good intentions are not sufficient, even for the morality of an act. It is not enough to mean well. One must also try to anticipate consequences. When it is known that some people have an allergy, potentially fatal, to penicillin, it may be immoral for even a well-meaning doctor to treat a patient with penicillin before checking to see if he is allergic to it.

Despite many avoidable disasters, one might still try to construct a favorable case for elites where society has attempted to institutionalize a meritocracy: Confucian China, with its rigorous examinations for those wishing to enter government service; and nineteenth century England, with Eton and Harrow grooming a select portion of the upper class for Oxford and Cambridge, which then prepared them for government or the foreign service. Did these elites have better track records? Even though elitism does not by itself guarantee competence, it is plausible that providing a carefully selected elite with rigorous training might insure sensible far-sighted decisions.

However, as if to fly in the face of such theoretical plausibility, carefully selected and well trained elites have displayed egregious incompetence for generations, without affecting their elite status. Despite the rigorous training of the Chinese mandarins, their inflexibility at critical times was damaging to China.

At the beginning of the fifteenth century, the Chinese were poised to become the dominant civilization on our planet. They had a large population base and an impressively ordered central government. They were the technology leader in shipping, having invented the compass and astrolabe and having built ships of a size that dwarfed European efforts. Cheng Ho had led naval expeditions as far as Africa.

The carefully selected and diligently trained mandarins squandered this impressive head start. "By the mid 1430s, the Confucians had not definitively won the factional struggles. But their values were well on the way to a near-conclusive triumph. The abrogation of overseas expansion, the demotion of commercial values and the renunciation of shipbuilding became such important badges for the scholar-elite that bureaucrats destroyed all Cheng Ho's records in an attempt to obliterate his memory. The examination system and the gradual attenuation of other forms of recruitment for public service meant that China would increasingly be governed by a code of scholars, with their contempt for barbarism, and of gentlemen, with their indifference to trade." (F. Fernandez-Armesto, *Millennium*, p. 133.)

Nearly five centuries later this scholarly elite sided with the Dowager Empress in opposing the reform and modernization of Chinese society. Serious reform would have changed the future of China. It might have prevented, or at least changed the character of, Mao's revolution.

We have our own elite mandarins. For more than two centuries, elite military staff officers have been specially trained to run armies in much the same way MBAs are now trained to run corporations. They have a horrid track record, typically mounting unimaginative strategies based on little more than amassing an overwhelming advantage in firepower (Saul, *Voltaire's Bastards*). These strategies, including the bombing of population centers, have maximized civilian casualties and economic devastation while minimizing strategic military gain.

In addition, military elites have resolutely resisted nearly every imaginative — and ultimately successful — effort to change the existing paradigm: from air power (Billy Mitchell, Claire Chenault) to tank strategy (Percy Hobart, Heinz Guderian); from small, highly mobile, specially trained units (Charles de Gaulle, Erich von Manstein) to nuclear submarines (Hyman Rickover) to guerrilla tactics (Orde Wingate).

That the proponents of such unconventional — at the time — approaches to warfare were individualists who did not fit into an established old-boy network may have buttressed the stubborn resolve of General Staffs to sabotage any recommended changes. But such a picture of an elite General Staff hardly fits with competence, much less the ingenuity to lead armies.

It is important to understand why elitist policies have failed so often. These failures are not coincidence but stem from endemic defects of institutionalized expertise. Sapin and Snyder's description of the military mind-set: "Rigidity in thought and problem analysis — the rejection of new ideas and reliance on tradition rather than the lessons learned from recent experience..." ("The Role of Military Institutions and Agencies in American Foreign Policy" in Snyder and Furniss [eds.] *American Foreign Policy*), applies to other elites as well.

General Staffs, like mandarins and other elites, resemble scientific communities in their preoccupation with applying existing paradigms to a delimited range of well-defined problems. Comfortable with their traditional understanding of the world, they resist paradigm changes, radical original thought, just as scientific communities resist major theoretical change.

This may explain why radical progress often occurs in areas far from cultural or economic centers. The development of nation states in the fifteenth and sixteenth centuries occurred in England, France, Spain, Eastern Europe and Scandinavia. These were backward areas in contrast to northern Italy, Germany of the Danube and the Rhine, and Holland. The more economically advanced areas, dominated by city-states, were slow to develop national identities. They were comfortable with their political paradigm and reluctant to change. They were surpassed by the newer states.

Centuries later, the industrial revolution started in Manchester, Liverpool, Sheffield, Birmingham and Leeds, far from London, England's center of nearly everything. Even now, a disproportionate number of major advances in technology are made by smaller companies with a fraction of the research budgets of the giants. In the spiritual realm as well, each of the three major Western religions was born on the fringes of civilization, far from centers of culture and power. Shakyamuni, the founder of Buddhism, was born to a minor clan far from the mainstream of Indian civilization.

A common theme underlies these examples. Where a conservative elite, resistant to paradigm change, is in a position of power, understanding ossifies along lines of pre-established doctrine and the potential for progress atrophies.

Given the propensity of elites to insist on their established paradigms and to summarily reject radically new perspectives, given their chronic insensitivity to consequences of their actions, and given their track records, it may be appropriate to insist on reality checks on their recommendations.

In government the notion of widespread competence and interest characteristic of participatory democracy may provide proper restraint. It is reasonable that while the conception and proposal of major new policies be relegated to elites, those policies should not be implemented until the common people have been legitimately convinced of their propriety. There may be wisdom in taking this Periclean principle seriously. "At the root of this [Athenian] constitution lay distrust of expertise and entrenched authority and confidence in collective common sense." (J. Roberts, *The Penguin History of the World*, p. 189.)

Despite this, we have seen a gradual devolution of power away from ordinary citizens to a variety of specialized elites. This is most evident in our judicial system. The power of juries has eroded, and judges have inordinate influence on court decisions. Even in the face of unanimous juries, judges can overturn the verdict or call for a new trial.

Judges, an elite group of elite lawyers, are different in education, income, race and political inclinations from the average citizen. Until 1953, the American Bar Association did not admit African-Americans. Until 1967, the American Bar Association's Standing Committee on the Federal Judiciary was all white, all male. Despite minor (token?) changes in the composition of this committee, little else has changed. The Judicature Society, assessing this committee's evaluation of candidates for federal judge, concluded: "[T]he strongest possible relationship which emerged in our analysis was that between the American Bar Association rating and the candidates' white male status." (Elliott E. Slotnick, "The American Bar Association's Standing Committee on Federal Judiciary, A Contemporary Assessment," *Judicature*, 66, p. 383.)

Does this produce a higher caliber of justice? It has been argued forcefully that it does not, that juries of peers are fairer than elite judges, who tend to systematic bias. "More often than not, our cases on appeal are decided by a jury of judges composed of persons most lawyers would have challenged summarily from any jury panel. An attorney for a party injured in an automobile collision might be guilty of malpractice were he to accept a juror who had spent his life working for a liability insurance company. But, on appeal, his case will often be decided by judges who, before they rose to the bench, spent their lives and amassed modest fortunes defending insurance companies in similar cases." (Spence, *With Justice for None*, p. 93.)

This reinforces an old judicial pattern:

Through tattered clothes small vices do appear;
Robes and furred gowns hide all. Plate sin with gold,
And the strong lance of justice hurtless breaks;
Arm it in rags, a pygmy's straw does pierce it. (Shakespear, *King Lear.*)

Despite compromising our ideal of equal justice, judicial power, like political power, serves large corporations. This, too, fits corporatism rather than democracy. As in the political arena, corporate influence in the judicial arena does not reflect a premeditated power grab. Aided by our tendency to associate (confuse) wealth with respectability, the corporatist transfer of judicial power has been inexorable, but gradual, imperceptible. We have failed to notice the change.

The ease of transition from democracy to corporatism in both the political and judicial arenas underlines the importance — and difficulty — of vigilance in defense of democracy. But because most of us are leading comfortable lives, we barely notice what has happened to our government. Our corporatist system has not been working, but its failure has been covered by a rising economic tide. The relative decline in the economic status of the middle class has produced only stagnation in its absolute purchasing power. We are comfortably numb.

Social mores exacerbate the situation by stressing that we have earned our leisure and richly deserve it. Modern culture has all but deified the freedom to do what we want while creating a bevy of diversions that our grandparents would neither understand nor value. We have become addicted to these diversions, to the honey of Plato's drones. Even aside from the problems created by the *laissez faire* mindset, commitment to democracy and the effort it requires is overshadowed by personal agendas. We just don't have the time. So why change?

It may take a protracted economic decline — which is likely, given our record levels of debt, the potential for massive losses in the equity market, and the adverse economic impact of the negative wealth effect — to cut through our complacency and sharpen our perception of the unfairness of the system. But such a catalyst would be fraught with danger.

In so far as poverty and a decline in standards of living breed fear and violence, an extended economic downturn could revive latent xenophobic tendencies, known to surface even in good times. Because we have a tradition in which fomenting hatred directed at powerless minorities has been used to political advantage, there is precedent to redirect economic frustration and pain into sociopathy. To the extent that populism generated by widespread economic hardship panders to scapegoating, it would endanger the fabric of society.

The most viable alternative to seeing our problems as the work of "bad guys" may be seeing them as reflecting systemic flaws. For generations we have been tweaking our institutions in response to perceived short-term inadequacies. Only in the last decade have advances in computer modeling enabled us to gain insight into the longer-term behavior of systems. Sophisticated models show that systems — even economies — designed for optimal short-term performance often perform poorly in the long run. Sprinters don't win marathons. It will be important to consider a number of our institutions in this light.

Our democracy may be the most important of these. Short-term pain jeopardizes incumbents, even if that pain is necessary to avoid more serious consequences later. That makes the primary political rationale — to get elected or re-elected — incompatible with a long-term approach. By the time a problem grows to the point that band-aids no longer work, it will be someone else's problem. So there is little incentive to pursue anything more than short-term palliatives, even at the expense of the long-term health of society.

At least in today's world, natural selection does *not* favor democracy. The success and even the survival of this form of government requires a conscious effort to develop a citizenry that is both aware of and committed to its obligations as citizens. Otherwise, citizens may abrogate those obligations and the democracy may quietly slip into an oligarchy with democratic trappings, as it has done in the U.S.

The need for a citizenry that understands long-term societal needs and is willing to place those ahead of private desires is why a realistic commitment to democracy requires a commitment to a broad education based on the traditional, classical view. It underscores the wisdom in H.G. Wells' remark (*The Outline of History*) that history is a race between education and catastrophe. For it is doubtful that a democracy of *idiots* can survive in the modern world.

THE CRITICAL ROLE OF EDUCATION

ULTIMATE R&D: EDUCATION

If we are to avoid a citizenry of *idiots*, education will have to play a decisive role. But we seem confused as to what that role should be. At one end of the spectrum, the focus of education can be the individual's development of those foundational skills and attitudes that will enable him to realize his potential (Rousseau, Pestalozzi, Dewey, Piaget). At the other end, it can be the specific skills that are currently prized by society and can best contribute to the collective (Plato, Locke, Fichte).

Not only are we unclear as to what is the role of education, but at times we seem unsure whether it has any value at all. On the positive side of the ledger, formal education has made important contributions. It has provided the foundation in culture, skills and values that enables individuals to live within and contribute to society. In addition, "The ability to learn faster than your competitors may be the only sustainable competitive advantage." (Arie De Geus, in Senge, *The Fifth Discipline.*)

But on the negative side, the short-term economic contribution of education to the individual is negative, and the long-term contribution can be measured only indirectly, as in the expected incremental earnings associated with a high school diploma or an advanced degree. Moreover, even on such a measure the net present value of education is minimal (*The New York Times Almanac 2000*, p. 352). So it is not surprising that education, our most important R&D, should be shortchanged by *laissez faire*.

217

Cultural factors exacerbate our tendency to undervalue education. Since our colonial days, from Ichabod Crane on, we have held teachers in low esteem, unlike the near reverence in which they are held in Europe and democratic Asia. The saying "Those who can, do. Those who cannot, teach," reflects a uniquely American attitude that while honoring the practical, rejects the philosophical associated with our European forebears. This is a far cry from Benjamin Franklin and Thomas Jefferson, who understood the need for the theoretical, even the philosophical, and who sought to marry theory and practicality.

A marriage of the philosophical and the practical lies at the heart of classical education. In the golden age of Greece, education was viewed as the development of the complete person, mentally, physically, spiritually. It addressed character as well as knowledge. *Paideia*, the classical Greek notion of education, encompassed art, poetry, philosophy, science, and civic responsibility. Its aim was the development of the ideal person (*humanitas*): spiritual, cultured, capable, with a broad foundation of skills and interests.

For Socrates, education was primarily moral in scope and was designed to start by awakening people to how little they really know. The ends of education were the stimulation of the desire to learn, the nurturing of courage to question and examine, and the development of an open, yet critical, mind.

Cicero, influenced by Greek thought, claimed that all creatures other than humans have a final cause, a pre-ordained end or essential nature, into which they naturally develop. In humans the final cause is left incomplete. It is up to education to provide direction.

Contemporary scientists express the same idea in different language. "Virtually no serious natural scientist speaks about genes and environment any longer as if they were opposed. Indeed, every serious investigator accepts the importance of both biological and cultural factors and the need to understand their interactions. Genes regulate all human behavior, but no form of behavior will emerge without the appropriate environmental triggers or supports. Learning alters the way in which genes are expressed." (Howard Gardner, "Cracking Open the IQ Box," *The American Prospect*, Winter, 1994.)

Widely different cultures have prized education for its role in providing direction. The Chinese ideograph for "education" combines "question" and "study." Respected Chinese scholars, like the classical Greeks, saw education as an ongoing process of questioning and studying, continually refining one's direction. This differs from the prevailing contemporary view of education as formal training that in itself transforms one into an educated person, an end.

The traditional view sees education as integral to human development, enabling people to change themselves in important ways, as opposed to an adjunct focused on marketable skills. It embraces the Socratic dictum: "Education is the kindling of a flame, not the filling of a vessel." This contrasts to our present focus, stuffing information into the crevices of a mind.

There is a thread of the classical view in our own tradition. John Dewey saw education as an ongoing process, a means to enable people to realize their latent potential. But it is rare to see such a view put into practice because a conflicting view developed at the same time as Dewey's, one more preoccupied with the bottom line.

In the early twentieth century a new vision of education became fashionable, influenced by the success of assembly line manufacturing. Its methods were to be the newly discovered methods of industry that had dramatically increased efficiency. The extension of assembly line concepts to education embodied a view of education as training to be accomplished at minimal cost. Teachers were the assembly line workers in the education factory, and students were the product to be turned out as rapidly, cheaply and efficiently as possible. (The application to education of the dubious wisdom of Frederick Taylor — those areas to which his methodology best applies are just those areas in which people could be most easily replaced by machines — is critically discussed in Raymond Callahan's *Education and the Cult of Efficiency*.)

A contemporary variation on this theme is on-line education (e-ducation), presently focused on higher education, but readily extended to lower grades. Led by the "buzz" words "technology," "efficiency" and "profitability," the driving force behind this movement is the prospect of leveraging eminent professors' lecture material, offering it over the Internet to students who could download it at their leisure.

In this manner a single professor could reach many thousands of students. Assignments would be graded by low-paid instructors, and the enterprise, saving on bricks and mortar and on salaries, could be highly profitable. A 1998 Coopers and Lybrand report claims technology can replace not only college campuses, but faculty. This mass production paradigm could change the very nature of education.

On-line education resembles the correspondence courses that proliferated more than a century ago. These courses fostered profitable correspondence schools, and in the late 1800s they were thought to be the future of education.

But contrary to expectations, they did little to either improve quality of education or extend education to a significantly wider audience.

The purported advantages of e-ducation are just the same as those of correspondence education: the convenience of the students, the ability to leverage lectures of a few super-star professors, the freedom from expensive college campuses and tenured faculty, and the resulting profits.

So are the disadvantages. A University of Illinois study noted that the time needed to respond to queries by e-mail would make e-ducation — if it were to be handled responsibly — more labor intensive than conventional education. More important, the lack of interaction with faculty and other students would deprive e-students of the environment and practice necessary to build a foundation in essential skills of dialogue and critical thinking. (It is possible, but far from certain, that forums, chat rooms and teleconferences could remedy this.)

If we are not overawed by the technology, we can see that e-ducation is virtually identical to the old correspondence courses. The only difference between them is that the material is delivered via the Internet as opposed to the postal system. The factors that had discredited correspondence education should equally discredit e-ducation; but because of our infatuation with technology and the potential for profits, we have ignored them.

One of the issues implicit in e-ducation is the distinction between teaching and training. Advocates of on-line education typically envision courses designed to prepare students for careers by training them in requisite skills and certifying that they have mastered those skills. (Note that a well-crafted text supplemented with paradigmatic problems carefully worked out could train as effectively. All the on-line program could add would be the certification. And how much should we pay for that, when we could certify delimited technical competence by standardized tests?)

To the extent that our sole interest is technical competence, an on-line approach might suffice. But historically, at least, the role of education has been broader and deeper. To put it bluntly, in *The Odyssey* Circe, the sorceress, changed Odysseus's crew into pigs. Suppose those pigs were happy. Suppose they possessed important "professional" skills, perhaps truffle hunting, that insured they would be well treated and even pampered. Is that all there is to life?

Not even the most sophisticated career training deals with this. Nor is it plausible, despite the attention philosophers, novelists and poets have given to this and related matters, that it could be handled effectively without the personal interaction characteristic of the traditional college environment. These issues, an important part of education, if not training, require a more traditional approach.

Classical education sought to encourage students to wrestle with questions designed to force them to examine their lives and their values. In this way it aspired to enable students to recognize and adopt positive values, to develop wisdom, and to live more meaningful lives. Unfortunately, the bottom line profit center approach to education is incompatible with these traditional ideals.

Allan Bloom (*The Closing of the American Mind*) argues passionately that even the traditional colleges have turned their backs on these ideals. They have lost sight of the purposes and priorities of higher education. They value information more than knowledge. They value knowledge more than wisdom. Without a rudder, they have drifted toward a simple accommodation of career goals, training students to master skills presently prized by future employers.

In doing so they have set themselves up for on-line education. Elevating the efficiency of vocational training over the more painstaking exploration of values has left universities open to the promise of an even more efficient training — in this case one that bypasses the university.

Despite its purported efficiency, this paradigm falls short. It is not just that the factory floor view of education as the efficient training of a workforce is far removed from classical ideals. This approach to maximizing efficiency can be short sighted in providing adequate vocational training; for even good training may require a sound foundation.

A mid-century incident bears this out. In the 1950s, the MIT approach to electrical engineering was regarded by industry with a jaundiced eye. Rather than providing hands-on experience with vacuum tubes, MIT concentrated on theoretical issues concerning the generation of wave patterns. Graduates were relatively unfamiliar with the electronic devices of the day and could not contribute immediately to the top or bottom lines of their employers. In the short term, they were an economic drag.

It was the transistor revolution that turned things upside down. Within a few years vacuum tubes nearly disappeared, transistors taking their place. It was soon apparent that the traditional curriculum did little to help graduates understand transistors. Even conventional industrial-training advocates realized there might be some point in approaching technology education from a more generalized, foundational perspective. Within a few years, most electrical engineering programs in the country were patterning themselves on the MIT approach.

This lesson favors a classical approach to education. So does the development of modern information technology. As it becomes easier and cheaper to access information through computer databases, understanding and creativity become more important than mere factual knowledge.

In cultivating competent individuals, it is less important to fill them full of information. It is more important to refine their skills in locating and defining problems, posing penetrating questions, expressing ideas clearly. In teaching them to address real problems it is valuable to hone their abilities to consider less obvious paradigms and perceive interrelationships among apparently disparate phenomena. In helping them fulfill their potential, it is necessary to kindle a flame, to inspire them to find what they love and to be creative. In building a foundation for them to function as citizens, it is essential to develop a commitment to society and the quality of life of those even beyond immediate family and friends.

These are mutually interrelated skills, propensities and attitudes, rather than bits of information. As such, they are difficult to measure and more difficult to teach. They require a more patient assessment and a greater investment of time and effort. Yet we have barely moved in this direction. At all levels our education is focused on training. Even after an undergraduate education plus a graduate degree, few Americans are literate in both arts and sciences. Rarely does understanding extend past one art or one science. We miss a lot.

Much of graduate education focuses on applying the tools of one's field to those types of problems that can be readily solved. A doctoral dissertation is typically an attempt to utilize a range of standard techniques and problem-solving skills in defining and solving a delimited problem. Nor is this confined to the sciences. In Biblical studies one may apply archaeology, regional history, comparative linguistics, and the decay of radioactive isotopes to date and interpret an ancient text.

The development of sophisticated problem-solving skills is valuable, not only in the context of the discipline in which they are learned but also because these skills can be transferred across disciplines. This is important because it is often difficult to be creative in one's original field of study. Training involves learning what sorts of problems can be solved as well as how to set them up and solve them in terms of the traditional paradigms. This makes it difficult to consider problems from alternative perspectives and develop new paradigms.

Transferring problem-solving skills into a new discipline, in which one has to figure out what are the problems and to which one may be able to transfer paradigms from a previous discipline, encourages greater originality.

It is no coincidence that many contributors to intellectual progress initially specialized in fields different from the ones in which they made their major contributions. Nor is it coincidence that the most vibrant fields of study lie at the interstices of previously well-defined disciplines: art and music therapy, artificial intelligence, biochemistry, biophysics, forensic pathology, geochemistry, geophysics, genetic engineering, information technology, molecular biology, psychopharmacology, social network analysis.

By sacrificing breadth to training, we have retarded the growth of interstitial disciplines and the development of new insight they provide. Have we been compensated for such a sacrifice by the development of a cadre of competent technicians, be they in art, history or engineering? Have we at least built a foundation that will enable students to grow into capable musicians, scientists or teachers? Not at the primary or secondary level.

Despite the importance of technology, we have lagged even in this arena. For many it was Sputnik and the fear of being leapfrogged in critical military applications that first illuminated the flaws in the training provided by our system. But despite a brief well-publicized flurry to improve the quality of science and mathematics in our primary and secondary schools, progress has been minimal. The echoes of the Sputnik reveille faded quickly.

While our educational achievement was stagnating, other countries perceived the vital importance of this basic R&D, despite its failure to contribute immediately to the bottom line. They invested heavily in this sector and set high standards. As a result of their progress, they have surpassed us. We have declined relatively, if not absolutely.

Our decline in educational standards may be only relative, but it has disturbing implications. We have been surpassed not only by our trading partners but also by our societal needs. Our technology-based economy requires higher levels of linguistic and mathematical literacy than those of just a few generations ago, when the work force was predominantly blue collar. Recently, New York Telephone had to test 57,000 applicants to find just 2,100 people qualified to fill entry-level jobs.

We cannot afford this. In a trans-national economy, where multinational corporations can purchase skilled labor anywhere in the world at the lowest costs, our educational institutions may be the most important long-term investment we can make. But because there is no immediate economic impact and because it is difficult to measure the longer-term economic benefit, our commitment to this area has been neither massive nor focused.

Consider the competition. Those countries that have surpassed us in education have all adopted policies of strict central control, high national standards, and relatively high pay and prestige for teachers. Decision-making rests with the central government and teachers, as opposed to parents and communities. Such an approach is typical for important crash programs in any society. It is how we structured our space program.

But we have not done this in education. Having been surpassed by our trading partners, we have sought to catch up by running in the opposite direction. How odd! Imagine the efficacy of our space program had we designed it along comparable lines — belittling scientists and calling for community control. Yet this is what we have done in education.

Influenced by *laissez faire*, politicians and some business leaders have argued that alternatives based on the discipline imposed by the free market must be an improvement over our faltering public schools. They claim that a network of competing private schools, partly supported by government vouchers but chosen by independent "consumers" of education, would provide a better education for our children. Competition would force the poorer schools out of business, for no one would send their children to those schools. The most successful schools would be those that provide the best education. Quality would be reflected in the bottom line.

Such a conclusion is strange. For one thing, it is generally easier to compete on the basis of price than on the basis of quality. Especially in service industries, from day care to HMOs, from nursing homes to airline transportation to municipal water management, competition has done little to improve quality. Rather, it has fostered cost cutting even at the expense of quality. What reason is there to believe education would be different? Why not minimize expenses in the name of maximizing efficiency and profitability?

Independently, perceptions of quality, which can be influenced by advertising, are more important than actual quality. It is often less expensive and more effective to mount an advertising campaign than to improve quality. Quality itself does not serve the bottom line. So why should we expect the primacy of the bottom line to serve quality?

In addition, there is no reason to expect education to be immune to the trend of other industries toward oligopoly. In other sectors oligopolies restrain competition and limit innovation. Why should education be different?

Finally, television programming makes clear the priority of anything that sells — often sex or violence — over quality, taste, or propriety. This priority provides for better economic returns. Why should education be different? Why should substantive quality prevail over the lowest common denominator?

In fact, the conclusion that education should be privatized may be unrelated to considerations of quality of education. Michael Lind [*Up From Conservativism*, p. 161 f.] argues that advocates of privatization are driven by an ulterior motive — the avoidance of court-ordered integration. Aside from Lind's contention, the annual tuition in most non-religious private schools exceeds $10,000. Even with the small stipend ($2,500 or less) proposed in privatization programs, these schools would remain out of the economic reach of most middle class families, especially those with more than one child. Disproportionately, it would be the wealthy families, many of whom are already sending their children to private schools, who would use the vouchers to defray the cost of such schools. It is the wealthy who would benefit from the vouchers provided in the context of privatization. Privatizing education would redistribute income from the poor and middle class to the rich.

Contrary to the free market agenda, there is little reason to believe that concentration on the bottom line is the answer to mediocrity in education. Nor has modeling education on free market principles improved quality of education. Rather, our economic paradigm has led to the replacement of traditional curricula by alternatives based on student appeal. In the spirit of *laissez faire*, we regard students as consumers of education. We market education to provide them with the product they want. Unfortunately, we give less thought to what they need.

What is the "take" on student preferences? That students want courses that lead to high-paying employment — hence the proliferation of business administration programs. That students do not want to work too hard at their courses but want a feeling of accomplishment — hence the dumbing-down of courses and grade inflation. That students want to celebrate the importance of their own sub-culture — hence the proliferation of degree programs in popular sub-cultures. That alumni as well as students want to be proud of their school in terms easily understandable to others — hence the significance attached to sports, especially football.

This is most serious at the college level, where there are many electives and an often-undisguised economic competition among academic departments, and also colleges, for students. A department's funding is determined by the number of students in its courses. If its courses are too hard or its grades too low, fewer students take those courses. The department then loses funding and faculty positions; so the courses are made easier and the grades higher.

None of this improves quality of education. Yet critics motivated by the free market paradigm still insist that our problem with education is a lack of attention to the bottom line. How would we test this claim? Profitability is easy to measure. But how can we measure quality of education, taking into account the diversity of students' backgrounds and aptitudes and also the limitations of machine-graded tests? Especially at the primary and secondary levels, it is implausible that the bottom line would reflect quality of education, as opposed to the socio-economic status of the community.

In fact, standardized tests show a strong correlation between scholastic performance and socio-economic status. Even students from poor families perform better in schools that are predominantly upper-middle class. Moreover, excessive reliance on such tests can compromise quality of education. Attaching economic incentives to performance on such tests encourages "teaching to the test" at the expense of more important educational objectives.

There are other problems with education driven by bottom line considerations. Consider the hypothetical Ayatollah Khomeini School, teaching that authors like Salman Rushdie should be exterminated, or the Klan School, teaching that African-Americans are a genetically inferior race whose breeding should be strictly controlled and limited.

Such schools are likely to find devoted clients, independent of academic standards. They could become the most profitable schools in the country despite — and because of — their promulgation of doctrines that are offensive and dangerous. Do free market considerations apply to such schools? Why not?

(One area in which the bottom line has entered public education is the propensity of even wealthy school districts to solicit funds from industry. These funds typically come at a price. There is no free lunch, not even free Coke. "A top official in District 11 [Colorado Springs] has sent administrators a letter urging them to boost Coca Cola sales in their schools.... Bushey's letter instructed principals to allow students virtually unlimited access to Coke machines and to move them to 'where they are accessible to the students all day'.... Bushey also recommended that teachers consider allowing students to drink Coke products while in the classrooms...." (*The Denver Post*, November 22, 1998.) All across the country, in-school television bombards impressionable students with sophisticated advertising for junk. It is amazing what one can buy for 30 pieces of silver.)

In view of these considerations it is unlikely that privatizing education will provide an acceptable solution to our chronic mediocrity, that it will enable us to gain ground against those education systems — all public — that have surpassed us.

Independently, our education system has been charged with helping maintain the social mobility associated with the meritocracy we claim to have. Bright and motivated, if poor, students who do well in secondary school can gain scholarships to colleges and can then find good jobs. This has been an important function of public education.

Even our most right-wing spokesmen profess an allegiance to equality of opportunity, in part because it justifies any degree of economic inequality. If you haven't made it to the top, you have only yourself to blame, because you had the same opportunity as anyone else.

Equality of opportunity sounds pretty. But what does it mean? If it means only that we all have the same opportunity to be born into rich and powerful families, even the most rigid class-bound society provides equality of opportunity. Equality of opportunity, to be meaningful, must insure that those born into poor uneducated families have opportunity to succeed comparable to the opportunity of those born into rich families. Public education has played a vital role in this.

Privatized education could too easily magnify inequalities, restricting social mobility. Excessive differences between the quality of education received in well-funded primary and secondary schools and that received in poorly-funded schools would overwhelm motivation and native intelligence. With our economic, political and judicial systems increasingly reflecting the views and priorities of an elite minority, our society has a natural tendency to create a large hereditary underclass. An education system that affords roughly the same opportunity to all is one of our most important defenses against such a danger. Privatization would undermine this defense.

This is not intended to minimize the endemic flaws in our present system of education. Some of these stem from our low regard for the field. Our teachers are undereducated, underpaid and undervalued. After all, they teach because they cannot do. As a result, there is little incentive to go into teaching. Too many potentially gifted teachers choose other occupations, leaving teaching mostly to those who are less likely to succeed in other areas and who are willing to settle for low pay and prestige. We exacerbate the problem by treating teachers as civil servants, demanding hours of meaningless paperwork to assure compliance with specific techniques and substance and to minimize creativity and flexibility.

Mediocrity intensifies beyond the classroom. It is remarkable how often students planning to enter education administration have achieved the very lowest scores on the Graduate Record Examinations. Coupling marginal competence with a desire to wield power has hardly been a boon to the education establishment.

Unfortunately, we are ill equipped to deal with such problems. Our propensity to focus on the short term conditions us to look for the quick fix. It is unlikely, however, after generations of mediocrity, that a quick fix of our chronic debility in education is possible. It will require greater investment to attract outstanding teachers necessary to upgrade the perceived quality of public education. But in order to make such an investment, we will need to convince the public that improving public education is important and also feasible. Yet without highly competent and motivated teachers, it will be hard to satisfy a skeptical public. We are caught in a vicious circle.

Even if we do succeed in attracting outstanding talent, our present system has developed both the hierarchical seniority structure and the "by the book" mentality of civil service. It has amassed a numbing inertia over decades. Powerful vested interests, ranging from unions to teachers' colleges, are well positioned to thwart reform. It will be difficult to effect meaningful change without the support of entrenched faculties and administrations, who are likely to feel threatened — justifiably — by such change.

As critics of public education justly complain, public schools have long been a protected monopoly prone to the defects characteristic of monopolies: inefficiency, rigidity, mediocrity, lack of concern. Our challenge is to break the monopoly and encourage meaningful competition and experimentation while retaining broad control over substance and standards and limiting inequality between education for the rich and education for the poor.

However difficult this challenge, it will be necessary to try different approaches to break our present educational stalemate if we hope to thrive economically and survive as a democracy. There is no guarantee that functional democracy can survive in the modern world — or, for that matter, that it has survived.

EDUCATION AND THE FOUNDATIONS OF DEMOCRACY

The most serious shortcoming of our education system may be its failure to develop a foundation for democratic values. It does not address the attitudes, understandings or skills that are essential to democracy, especially in the contemporary world.

We live in a consumer society. The purpose of the advertising industry is to arouse a desire for the advertised products and manipulate potential consumers into purchasing particular brand names. The sophistication, subtlety and success of this industry are impressive. (We spend more on advertising than we do on education.)

Politics has adopted the mindset and techniques of this industry, cunningly manipulating voters to support particular candidates and platforms. Without the skills and habits of critical thinking, which can be developed in the course of education, we are vulnerable to subtle indoctrination.

In societies of previous centuries, the opposition of competing interests, church versus state, monarch versus noble versus commoner, resulted in a balance of powers. It was often possible to find an interest both inclined and able to provide refuge for advocates of unpopular views. The elimination of these independent power centers has not been entirely positive. For where there is only one power, even if it is democratic, there is little protection for advocates of the politically incorrect. As Tocqueville warned, democracy threatens to impose a tyranny of public opinion.

While tyranny of public opinion occasionally drove the Athenian democracy to violent excess and was responsible for the death of Socrates, both the nature and the problems of modern democracy are more complex. On the positive side, modern societies are heterogeneous. At least in theory, this offers refuge to advocates of unpopular views, provided some segment of the population finds those views attractive. But on the negative side, contemporary society provides the opportunity for subliminal indoctrination. We may fail to notice that we have been manipulated into our views, surreptitiously conscripted to fight the battle against the politically incorrect.

Our preoccupation with private affairs and our lack of interest in society, which increase our vulnerability to such manipulation, would have been surprising to the classical Athenians. They assumed that citizens are naturally concerned with the health of their city-state and that they regard the vitality of their community as essential to their own well-being. There is reason to take this classical view seriously as a foundation for modern democracy.

Yet our present understanding of democracy differs sharply from the classical view. In contrast to the ancient Greeks, modern democracy does not assume that citizens will, should, or need be interested in the common good. The British Empiricist foundation of democracy regards the matter from a different perspective.

Locke started from a utilitarian view, assuming that people naturally seek to maximize pleasure and minimize pain. But a pre-government state of nature, free from constraints except for the moral obligation to preserve the peace and refrain from injuring others, is ill suited to a utilitarian enterprise. That is because some individuals may seek personal gain by violating the natural rights of others. A social contract in which people in the state of nature voluntarily transfer their natural rights to a government, able to prevent violations of rights, provides an environment more conducive to maximizing utility. This social contract does not require any commitment of citizens to the whole. Rather, these individuals seek only to increase their own utility. Still, according to Locke, this social contract is the basis of government. Because this social contract is among equally free people, ultimate sovereignty must lie with the people.

Even though we regard this philosophy as the foundation for our own democracy, it is a fragile foundation, equally compatible with monarchy. Locke himself regarded a constitutional monarchy as the ideal form of government, with the executive and judicial powers in the hands of the monarch and the legislative power in the hands of an elected assembly.

In general, justifying any form of government in terms of a state of nature and intrinsic human nature is suspect. How would Locke respond to Hobbes, who sees the state of nature as the universal war of every person against every other person? How would Hobbes or Locke respond to Rousseau? Rousseau paints a more benign picture of the state of nature and a more complex portrait of human nature. He maintains that our suffering and our artifice are caused by our alienation from the state of nature, supposedly the very state of nature from which Hobbes and Locke are trying to escape.

How would Hobbes, Locke or Rousseau respond to Freud? Freud's vision of a libidinous id rebelling against a repressive superego is equally incompatible with all their views. From a different culture, the Chinese ideograph for "person" shows two persons leaning on and supporting each other. This calls attention to yet a different aspect of ourselves, one more akin to the Greek perception of human nature than to those of Hobbes, Locke, Rousseau or Freud.

Such radically different portraits of human nature suggest it may depend on our environment. A *laissez faire* environment in which resources are scarce might fit a Hobbesian view of the state of nature as universal war. Any government, no matter how tyrannical, would be an improvement. But in an environment in which the economic survival of the individual is not constantly challenged, Aristotle's view that man is essentially a political animal might provide a more viable foundation for political systems.

Because modern industrial democracies provide social safety nets, our obsession with economic survival has diminished; so the Greek understanding of democracy may be more appropriate to modern society than either Hobbes's view that any alternative is preferable to chaos or Locke's more calculating social contract.

Unfortunately, something has got in the way. Our obsession with survival has been replaced, not by an Aristotelian interest in the good of the community, but by the frenetic pursuit of small pleasures. This self-indulgence is the product of a culture that values — and teaches the value of — consumption over anything else. Is this an advance over classical Greece?

The Greeks would not have thought so. They characterized a slave as a person concerned only with filling his belly. Our values have reduced us to the status of slaves — rich slaves, perhaps, but slaves nonetheless. It is not just food that is the item of concern, but our material possessions that increasingly define our lives. (They may define our lives, but they do not make us happier. Studies have shown that beyond a minimum threshold, wealth is irrelevant to happiness. Perversely, the pursuit of wealth often detracts from enterprises that would add more value and happiness to our lives.)

In contrast to modern democracy, classical Athens was characterized by a culture that valued community and instilled a sense of responsibility to others. Citizens understood that public service creates value, even if it does not pay well. It is both an obligation and an honor. They also understood, to paraphrase Pericles, that a person unconcerned with the state of society around him is useless — no matter how much wealth he may amass.

Such a culture reflected a view of community as extended family. It was easy to identify your own interest — and fate — with the community, and not just your family, clan or faction. That is why the early democracies were found in relatively small homogeneous communities.

This sentiment may be necessary for the long-term survival of democracy, even — and especially — in the contemporary world. In its absence a democracy can too easily degenerate into a plutocracy or a corporatist state.

But this sentiment is hardly to be found today. In modern industrial democracies there is a failure to value even immediate community. This failure that may be symptomatic of a deeper insularity, a spiritual malaise wrought, ironically, by the benefits of modern society. "The civilized being of the immense cities returns to the wild state — that is, to a state of isolation — because the social mechanism allows him to forget the need for community and to lose his feelings of connection to other people, which were once kept alive by his wants. Every improvement in the social mechanism renders useless certain acts, certain ways of feeling, certain attitudes toward communal life." (Max Stirner, quoted in Roberto Calasso, *The Ruin of Kasch*, p. 263.)

When our ties to family, friends and community had survival value, they were stronger. They also had spiritual value. Now that their survival value has disappeared, the ties themselves have weakened. While we have mastered techniques of socialization, these are superficial. We have become spiritually solitary beings. This isolation has impoverished us, even if our poverty is not reflected in monetary measures.

While these issues have been addressed by religion, they are too often addressed within a narrow context. Religious communities are comprised solely of co-religionists and encourage the view that those outside the community are less deserving. This creates competing sub-communities and weakens the whole. The resulting factionalism can destroy democracies. That is why diversity, in religion or in other areas, presents such a challenge to democracy. It is why Rousseau advocated a single unifying civil religion to which all citizens must belong.

How can we teach the value of heterogeneous community? How can we teach this without creating an opposition between those inside and those outside the community? How can we create a culture that prizes democratic values but is sensitive to the potential shortcomings of democracy? How can we create it without the indoctrination recommended by Plato (*The Laws*) and without the imposition of artificial homogeneities? This is not to belittle the warmth of the nuclear or extended family. It is rather to encourage extending these sentiments more widely, as Einstein had recommended.

The notion that we are all mutually interrelated suggests an attitude that takes a step beyond Kant's categorical imperative. At a societal level this attitude embodies the concept underlying Gandhi's *satyagraha*, Reinhold

Niebuhr's nonviolent coercion, Martin Luther King's militant nonviolence, and Daisaku Ikeda's soft power. This attitude can generate a reasonable foundation for the resolution of intra- and international conflict, as well as a basis for peaceful, but concerted, opposition to real or perceived injustice. It can also deepen our commitment, presently a shallow one, to democracy.

Because we are the oldest modern democracy and because we are a powerful country, it is easy to flatter ourselves. We pretend to have a vibrant democracy in which our citizens both understand and are committed to democratic values. It may be pretty to think so. But we do not merit such flattery. Studies show that most of our citizens, while they may pay lip service to democratic ideals, have little tolerance for the politically incorrect.

It is here that education can play a vital role. Even though our present curriculum gives minimal attention to democratic values, work by social scientists (Lipset's *Political Man*, among others) have identified a person's level of education as the variable having the greatest positive impact on his commitment to democratic values. Imagine what could be accomplished with a better-focused higher-quality education.

This underlines the importance of education in the classical sense, and not mere training. We need more than mere lip service to democracy and democratic ideals. We need, in addition to a citizenry that truly values democratic government, an overriding morality that values all people, including future generations, as ends in themselves. We also need the skills and attitudes necessary to independent thought, the acceptance of diversity, the appreciation of community, and the autonomous commitment to value.

These skills and attitudes are best taught within public education. Privatization driven by free market considerations would not satisfactorily address issues related to democracy, for these have no immediate economic impact. According to our economic paradigm, those values necessary to democracy are not values at all.

If we aspire to bring up individuals concerned with more than feeding their bellies, we will have to transcend the *laissez faire* paradigm. If we are to transcend this paradigm, the quality and priorities of our education will be critical issues. It is not training that speaks to these issues, for training may be conducive to a slave mentality. Rather, it is those aspects that go beyond training, that teach critical reasoning, the value inherent in all people, the ability to make a difference.

It is unfortunate, perilous, that we have given these matters so little attention.

FINALITY?

DENOUEMENT

THE FREE MARKET VS. THE ENVIRONMENT

The inadequacies of the *laissez faire*—libertarian paradigm are not just theoretical. Bad theory can lead to devastating consequences. It may be that the environment, where effects are typically long term and potentially severe, will produce the most serious ones.

We can defile the environment for a long time before we see the results. We may even become convinced that no matter how much pollution we discharge, the environment is large enough to absorb it and remain unaffected. Removing just one rivet at a time, we may be surprised, and pleased, at how well the structure appears to be holding together. Perhaps it doesn't need rivets at all. By the time we see and recognize the first effects of our pollution, the damage we have caused may be irreversible. The structure may fall apart.

Nonlinear processes play a role in this. Our pollution gradually and imperceptibly takes some environmental system away from a locally stable equilibrium. Nothing seems out of the ordinary and the process is reversible. Everything appears fine — until we cross some bifurcation point to an area of instability. Then, without any additional pollution, positive feedback takes over and carries the system further from equilibrium. The process, now irreversible, can lead to environmental disaster. The minor, barely noticeable, cause of crossing the bifurcation point translates into a major unpleasant effect.

Unfortunately, it is not natural for an economy driven by *laissez faire* to sacrifice immediate profits to the cause of preserving the environment. The only institution with the consistent concern for and power to protect the environment is government. While government has been aided in this effort by groups of scientists and environmental activists, industry has generally chafed at environmental regulation and has been able to use its political power to blunt regulatory efforts. Attempts to forestall even serious environmental damage have faced uphill battles, and even the small successes have been hard-won.

Still, some successes have had important long-term ramifications, justifying the environmentalists' persistence. One of the most meaningful contributions of an alliance between science and environmental concerns is a ban on the use of chlorofluorocarbons (CFCs). The significance of this issue stretches well beyond CFCs. It has led to the realization that human pollution can affect the entire planet, a realization that has since been extended to other pollutants. It has also provided an object lesson in the economically motivated reaction of industry to such concerns.

CFCs are the primary cause of the destruction of stratospheric ozone, which plays a vital role in absorbing harmful ultra-violet radiation. Scientists had suspected such destruction before 1960, and as early as 1970 it was suggested that some uncommon chemical in the stratosphere might act as a catalyst, facilitating the decomposition of tri-atomic ozone into di-atomic oxygen without being consumed in the reaction. In this way a single molecule might account for the destruction of many ozone molecules. In 1974, Mario Molina and F. Sherwood Rowland published a paper in *Nature*, theorizing that CFCs, used primarily as refrigerants, industrial solvents, and aerosol sprays might be the culprit and suggesting the mechanism by which the ozone destruction occurs.

Many scientists reacted by advocating a ban on CFCs. They stressed that the damage caused by the destruction of the ozone layer was not worth the modest benefits provided by CFCs. A higher incidence of skin cancer due to the increase in ultraviolet radiation, previously absorbed by the ozone, was not their only worry. More important was the possibility that this radiation might fry both the phytoplankton that lie at the base of the marine food chain and the microorganisms that lie at the base of the land food chain. The ultimate risk, according to the pessimists, was the destruction of all life on this planet.

Industry reacted sharply, calling environmentalists' concerns premature and arguing that it was inappropriate to take concrete measures until the connection between CFCs and ozone depletion had been proved. (This was a remarkable argument, considering the relative magnitudes of risk and reward in continuing to use CFCs.)

At first, Du Pont, the largest producer of CFCs, claimed there was no experimental evidence supporting the Molina-Rowland hypothesis and noted that some studies had even shown an increase in stratospheric ozone. "One CEO told an industry trade magazine that their [Molina's and Rowland's] notions, so disruptive to capitalism, only made sense if the pair were KGB agents." (Horton, "Strong Weather," *Rolling Stone*, March 20, 1997.) Even when evidence of Antarctic ozone depletion became undeniable, Du Pont insisted that it did not matter since it was evident only in the Antarctic and only during the Antarctic spring, ozone levels returning to normal within a few months.

Fortunately, in the 1970s large industrial interests had less influence on Federal regulatory agencies. These agencies banned the non-essential use of CFCs as a propellant in aerosol sprays, an action followed by other countries over the next five years. As a result of work by the U.N. Environmental Program, the Vienna Convention for the Protection of the Ozone Layer persuaded 20 countries to sign an agreement proposing the phase-out of CFCs. But little of additional substance was accomplished for a decade.

Then, in the Antarctic spring of 1985, a British Antarctic survey team noticed a sharp 40% reduction in the ozone layer, much larger than anyone had expected. (Ironically, satellite surveys had collected comparable data for years, but scientists rejected the data as spurious because the ozone losses recorded were so much larger than expectations.) At that time, however, there was little domestic political support for environmental issues. Also, since the 1977 domestic ban, the European Community had taken the lead in CFC manufacture and export. England and France were intransigently opposed to any ban on CFCs.

It was the rotation of the EEC presidency from England to Belgium, a country less pressured by industrial lobbies, that enabled the passage in 1987 of the Montreal Protocol, calling for a reduction in the manufacture and use of CFCs. (It also helped that the major CFC producers had developed HFCs, hydrofluorocarbons, environmentally friendlier replacements for CFCs.) Still, as late as March 1988, Du Pont argued there was no need to reduce CFC emissions.

Now there is widespread agreement, even within the chemical industry, that a ban on CFCs is appropriate. Can we really trust the invisible hand and considerations of short-term profitability to make wise judgments affecting the survival of the species?

Neither can we abrogate our responsibility to the professional environmentalists, who have become politicized, specializing in dramatic slogans and doomsday predictions to raise money for their organizations. These have become large, rich and powerful. They have economic, as well as environmental, agendas. The annual budgets of the largest environmental organizations add up to more than $500 million and call attention to the extent that environmentalism itself is an industry. Senior executives of these corporations, many of them accomplished spin-doctors who are paid handsome salaries, are motivated by economic considerations. Environmental organizations, despite the importance of their concerns, are like other large special interest groups.

If environmentalism were no more than a response to environmental needs, if it were not an industry requiring a healthy economy, a solid upper-middle class, and government tolerance, Russia and China would be swarming with environmentalists. They are not. Even in the U.S., economic declines have periodically elevated worries about jobs above environmental concerns.

It may seem distasteful to pure-minded worshippers of Gaia, the Greek goddess of the earth, but environmentalism has much in common with *laissez faire*. Darwin, whose work did so much to make us aware of the role of nature in determining the forms of life, was clearly influenced by Adam Smith. "The theory of natural selection lifts this entire explanatory structure [of Adam Smith's *laissez faire*] *virgo intacta*, and then applies the same causal scheme to nature..." (Gould, *The Structure of Evolutionary Theory*, p. 123.)

Both environmentalism, at least in its radical forms, and *laissez faire* imply it is wrong to interfere in any way with nature. Just as mining perturbs the natural functioning of the environment and so is wrong according to many environmentalists, government intervention perturbs the natural functioning of an economic system and so is wrong according to free market economists.

Such a view, which forgets that humans and their activities are themselves a part of nature, is based on the appeal of "natural." Just as "liberal" evokes negative emotions, "natural" evokes a favorable emotional response. Even bottled water advertises itself as "natural." (What is "non-natural" water?)

Such a philosophy — don't mess with Mother Nature — may sound good, but it does not stand up. Forces of nature are not necessarily benign. Droughts, major climatic changes, earthquakes, plagues, some of the most potent toxins and carcinogens, are natural. Nearly all animals die prematurely, neither peacefully nor painlessly. The "J" curve, in which a population grows geometrically and then collapses to near zero, does not describe a benign process. (Unless we stem the exponential growth of our own population growth, there is little reason to believe *homo sapiens* will escape this fate.)

Within Western history, the harshest and most inhumane prescriptions as to how we should treat our fellow humans stem from Social Darwinism. This philosophy seeks to model our behavior after the natural, in which the less fit do not, and so presumably should not, survive. This dovetails with *laissez faire*. If government does not interfere to protect the poor, then it will be the fittest — at least within the economic environment we have created — who survive. Natural selection (within our artificial environment) will prevail. That is why Social Darwinists like Herbert Spencer were stout defenders of *laissez faire* and government non-intervention. Millennia before Social Darwinism, Aristotle had used similar arguments to defend slavery as natural, and therefore appropriate.

The sanctification of raw nature, though it may have a superficial appeal, leaves much to be desired: culture, scientific understanding, morality, even the leisure to be concerned about the environment. Only by advancing beyond raw nature do we become more than just another animal. Neither Gaia nor Mammon should be worshipped blindly.

Yet neither the occasional misbehavior of environmentalists nor their misplaced faith in nature should obscure the significance of environmental issues. We presently face a problem similar to the destruction of stratospheric ozone in the greenhouse effect and global warming.

Venus is the hottest planet in the solar system, some $100°C$ hotter than Mercury, despite Mercury being much nearer the sun. This is due entirely to the greenhouse effect. We see the greenhouse effect in the temperature of a car that has had its windows closed on a sunny day. Glass is transparent to sunlight, which enters the car and is absorbed by the interior fabric. The fabric re-radiates longer-wavelength infrared radiation. Glass is opaque to this infrared radiation and reflects much of it back to the interior of the car. So, initially, less energy is radiated from the car than is absorbed by it. The amount of energy inside the car increases. This raises the temperature to the point that the amount of energy re-radiated by the car equals the amount of energy that is absorbed.

The greenhouse effect is useful for passive solar heating, and it raises the temperature of the Earth by $30°C$ over what it would be if we had no atmosphere. The planet Venus appears to carry it a bit far. The dense Venusian atmosphere is 97% carbon dioxide, which like the windows of a closed car, is transparent to sunlight but opaque to the longer-wavelength radiation re-radiated by the ground.

Our atmosphere, by contrast, is composed primarily of nitrogen and oxygen, neither of which is a greenhouse gas. They are transparent to the re-radiated infrared energy and allow it to pass through to space without heating up the atmosphere. But our burning of fossil fuels: coal, oil and natural gas, gives off carbon dioxide, 7 billion tons per year. An additional 2 billion tons of carbon dioxide are produced from forest clearing. Our level of atmospheric carbon dioxide has reached 0.036%, still minuscule in contrast to Venus, but 25% above our highest levels of the past 400,000 years. Methane, an even more powerful greenhouse gas, has risen to twice its highest levels of the past 400,000 years.

Most scientists agree that our climate has warmed by 1°C over the past century. Many believe this warming has been caused by the greenhouse effect. Several believe we face a serious danger of a runaway greenhouse, elevating ambient temperatures to a point that human life could not be sustained.

The debate over the greenhouse effect highlights a peculiarity characteristic of environmental issues, one that makes rational argument difficult. The most important environmental matters are characterized by three cross currents: (i) We are rolling dice. (ii) They are heavily weighted in our favor. (iii) The consequences of losing are terrible.

First, we are rolling dice. Our long-range predictive powers are minimal, in part because so many mutually interacting mechanisms are involved. Our pollutants include CFCs, carbon dioxide, dioxins, herbicides, methane, nitrogen and sulfur oxides, PCBs, particulates, pesticides, volatile organic compounds, and many others. Even traces of antibiotics have been found in many of our streams and rivers. We have no idea how these pollutants interact with each other and how their combinations react with our climate or with living organisms (particularly microbes). We have no clue as to where the fine lines lie between processes that are reversible and those that are irreversible, or as to the damage that could be inflicted by positive feedback in irreversible processes.

Second, the dice are loaded in our favor. The likelihood of our causing a global environmental disaster that would wipe out all life is remote. Our planet has already been through many cataclysms. Intense vulcanism and strikes by comets or asteroids have generated acid rain on a scale we could not possibly match. They have caused sudden and prolonged ice ages. Intense bombardment by cosmic ray storms has imperiled the micro-organisms that lie at the base of food chains. Such catastrophes have occurred — and are likely to recur —

during the lifetime of species that are still around. These species have survived conditions worse than anything we might produce.

In addition, nature has recovered from environmental disasters, ranging from oil spill of the Exxon Valdez in Prudhoe Bay to the eruption of Mount Saint Helens. It has recovered more quickly than even optimists had hoped. So we might be making a climactic mountain out of a climatic molehill. The George C. Marshall Institute insists that the greenhouse effect — if it exists at all — is greatly exaggerated by scientists who argue for public policy to reduce greenhouse gas emissions.

Third, even though it may be unlikely, it is nevertheless possible that the consequences of crossing a bifurcation point from an area of stability to one of instability could be dire. Positive feedback could trigger the extinction of many species, including our own. They could enact the prophecy of Chief Seathl: "Continue to contaminate your bed, and you will one night suffocate in your own waste." While the probability of this may be low, the magnitude of a potential disaster is enormous, so that the risk may be unacceptably high.

Such disparate considerations provide ample material for both pessimists and optimists. Pessimists grimly fixate on the last of these considerations, the potential for catastrophe. Optimists point to the second, the low probability of disaster, and note that so far, at least, environmentalist prophecies of doom have failed to materialize.

The issue of global warming provides an arena for both sides. On the pessimistic side, computer models predict an acceleration of global warming, with the average temperature of the earth rising by an additional 1.5°C to 6°C over the next century. Some glaciologists have warned that such a rise in temperature could melt the Antarctic ice sheet and raise sea levels by as much as 75 meters. This claim is controversial, but there is little controversy in the claim that even small increases in average temperatures would cause large changes in precipitation patterns. Computer models agree with geological evidence in predicting a decline in precipitation in the breadbasket of the Great Plains, which could endanger our food supply.

Lower precipitation in the Midwest would be balanced by more precipitation in the North Atlantic. Surprisingly, this effect of global warming could cause a new ice age. A theory of the Younger Dryas, our most recent ice age that occurred only 12,000 years ago, claims it was caused by a decrease in salinity in the surface waters of the North Atlantic. Relatively fresh water, less dense and with a higher freezing point, remained near the surface. This caused the North

Atlantic to ice over in winters, blocking the escape of heat from the ocean and increasing the albedo, the amount of solar energy reflected by the Earth. (Ice reflects more light than water.) Some climatologists have suggested the transition from a "normal" climate to an ice age took as little as 20 years. Our generation of greenhouse gases could bring about a sudden return of an ice age that would be disastrous to humanity.

Even more worrisome to the pessimists than a new ice age would be the potential for a runaway greenhouse effect. There are positive feedback mechanisms that could magnify the effect of global warming. There are meteorologists who claim that a warmer climate would be accompanied by reduced cloud cover. That would decrease the albedo of the earth, leading to even warmer temperatures. These warmer temperatures would melt the polar ice caps, further decreasing the albedo and leading to still warmer temperatures.

Other feedback mechanisms could further increase global warming. More carbon is stored in dead organic matter than is contained in the atmosphere. This carbon is gradually converted into carbon dioxide and methane by soil micro-organisms. An increase of only a few degrees in soil temperature would increase the rate at which conversion occurs and would also change the relative amounts of carbon dioxide and methane (which is more than 20 times as powerful a greenhouse gas as carbon dioxide). We have little knowledge about feedback mechanisms governing this process and no way to estimate the potential for a positive feedback loop (higher methane levels → increased global warming and higher temperatures → still higher methane levels → even higher temperatures) and a runaway greenhouse effect.

Finally, water vapor is a greenhouse gas and presently accounts for most of our global warming. At higher temperatures the atmosphere can hold more water vapor, which would further increase temperatures, which would further increase the amount of water vapor in the atmosphere... Positive feedback could trigger a truly vicious circle, for we do not need to get as hot as Venus to feel uncomfortable. We boil near 100°C.

These arguments have fed an environmental panic, propagated and amplified, if not created, by the media (as news of impending disaster is always more exciting and produces higher ratings than news that things are not so bad). But this is only one side of the greenhouse gas debate. Optimists, even those who admit the reality of warmer temperatures over the past century, have their own story to tell, one that calls attention to the improbability of environmental disaster.

First, they point to the fact that there have been times (100 million years ago) when our planet was 20°C warmer than it is now. Those times did not trigger a runaway greenhouse effect. Why should our present round of moderate global warming trigger a runaway greenhouse effect?

Optimists also call attention to the sensitivity of pessimists' computer models to parameters whose values can only be vaguely estimated. How important are CFCs, sulfur dioxide, and other pollutants in global warming? To what extent does the ocean, which contains far more heat than the atmosphere, moderate warming? To what extent does solar activity affect the temperature of the Earth? They emphasize the fact that tiny changes in answers to these questions lead to large changes in predictions. They argue, with reason, that computer models are too unreliable to serve as the basis for sensible policy.

They also point to natural buffering effects. Each year plankton remove 100 billion tons of carbon dioxide from the atmosphere. It is plausible that global warming would lead to higher ocean temperatures, increasing the plankton population and increasing their uptake of carbon dioxide. Trees and other land-based plants, which also remove 100 billion tons of carbon dioxide from the atmosphere, should also thrive in a warmer environment, taking in more carbon dioxide. So the global warming caused by our production of carbon dioxide would set in motion natural forces to absorb the carbon dioxide we produce.

Finally, they suggest that long-term temperature cycles suggest that our planet should now be cooling toward a new ice age. They argue that global warming, in balancing this natural cooling, could be a positive, averting or at least postponing a new ice age.

Despite the potential for devastating effects, the scientific debate surrounding it has been plagued by research sponsors making it understood, at least implicitly, that ongoing funding is contingent on getting the "right" results to support some pre-existing position. This calls into question the disinterest of the science. Because intelligent and resourceful scientists can develop or interpret data to support any conclusion, a lack of objectivity taints the results of any scientific inquiry.

As Einstein glumly noted: "1. Almost all scientists are economically completely dependent. 2. The number of scientists who possess a sense of social responsibility is so small..." (Nathan and Norden, *Einstein on Peace*, p. 456.) Norbert Wiener put it more caustically, saying that "The degradation of the position of the scientist as independent worker and thinker to that of a morally irresponsible stooge in a science factory has proceeded even more rapidly and devastatingly than I had expected." (*Bulletin of the Atomic Scientists.*)

The environment, because of the diversity of mutually interacting mechanisms and the difficulty of long-range prediction, provides a fertile field for scientific prostitution. This is dangerous. The reduction of scientific inquiry to an auction for the most immediately profitable — or politically correct — answers can be disastrous when the ultimate truth dwarfs the immediate economic impact.

While the potential for an environmental calamity should not paralyze us, it should at the very least suggest the propriety of values other than immediate profits. Looking at the environment from a broader perspective, as long-term residents of the planet, may help us evaluate the alternative solutions that will be proposed to assess and, if appropriate, remediate the greenhouse effect. It may facilitate dismissing the solution, eagerly proffered by true believers in *laissez faire*, of simply relegating the matter to the invisible hand of the free market. The invisible hand cannot get even economic matters right. One could hardly expect it to do better in matters related to the long-term survival of the species.

Unfortunately, despite the failure of *laissez faire* even in its own field, the combination of libertarianism and free market economics has become a near religious item for a powerful contingent within the American political establishment. In October 1997, the House of Representatives, in a politically charged atmosphere, voted to eliminate EPA funding for global warming research. Arguments were more appropriate to a mediaeval religious council than a scientific colloquium, and the vote was strongly influenced by industry lobbying, especially the coal lobby, which stands to lose heavily if permitted levels of greenhouse emissions are reduced.

In the same spirit, the *Rocky Mountain News* reported: "Conservative groups are demanding the White House withdraw a recent report to the United Nations detailing the likely impact of global warming on the United States. The Competitive Enterprise Institute, an industry-oriented think tank, is circulating a letter directed to President Bush among conservative activists criticizing the document produced by the Environmental Protection Agency. The letter urges that federal employees involved with the report's preparation be punished..." (June 6, 2002, p. 42.)

It is common that even intelligent and well-meaning true believers are uncritical when it comes to assessing fundamental aspects of their faith. People who were otherwise rational, even brilliant, and who gained fame in the arts as well as the sciences, were orthodox Marxists, even Stalinists. We all compartmentalize, so that in certain fields we may be extraordinarily perceptive while in others we cannot see the obvious. Just as orthodox communists were blind to the flaws of Stalinism, orthodox free marketers are blind to the flaws of *laissez faire.*

Unfortunately, while there are times that selective blindness can do little damage, the present is not one of them. We face a critical period for the development of our country, for the quality of life of our children and grandchildren, and, perhaps, for the survival of our species.

> Fate succumbs
> many a species: one alone
> jeopardizes itself.
> > (W.H. Auden)

In this context, our environment may provide the most important illustrations of the failure of the free market, for this is the arena in which maximizing short-term profits can produce the most devastating long-term consequences.

In our single-minded haste to score, we have forgotten something: *Nature bats last.*

La commedia è finita.

REFERENCES

Aristotle (1957) *Aristoteles Politica.* (W. David Ross, editor) Oxford University Press, New York

Arrighi, Giovanni and Silver, Beverly (1999) *Chaos and Governance in the Modern World System.* University of Minnesota, Minneapolis

Barton, Bruce (1999) *The Man Nobody Knows.* Buccaneer Books, Cutchogue, N.Y.

Batra, Ravi (1987) *The Great Depression of 1990.* Simon & Schuster, New York

Bloom, Allan (1987) *The Closing of the American Mind.* Simon & Schuster, New York

Bloom, Harold (1995) *The Western Canon: The Books and Schools of the Ages.* Riverhead Books, New York

Bork, Robert (1996) *Slouching Towards Gomorrah: Modern Liberalism and American Decline.* Regan, New York

Braudel, Fernand (1981) *The Structure of Everyday Life: The Limits of the Possible.* Harper & Row, New York

Braudel, Fernand (1992) *The Wheels of Commerce.* University of California, Berkeley

Braudel, Fernand (1992) *The Perspective of the World.* University of California, Berkeley

Braudel, Fernand 1995) *A History of Civilizations.* Penguin U.S.A., New York

Callahan, Raymond (1964) *Education and the Cult of Efficiency.* University of Chicago, Chicago

Cannon, Geoffrey (1995) *Superbug: Nature's Revenge.* Virgin Publishing, London

Chateaubriand, (1989) *Memoirs d'Outre Tombe.* Livres de Poche, Paris

Davies, Norman (1998) *Europe: A History.* Harper, New York

Dewey, Edward and Dakin (1964) *Cycles: The Science of Prediction.* Foundation for the Study of Cycles, Wayne, Pennsylvania

Dobzhansky, Theodosius (1962) *Mankind Evolving: The Evolution of the Human Species.* Yale University Press, New Haven

Douthwaite, Richard (1999) *The Growth Illusion.* New Society Publishers, Gabriola Island, B.C., Canada

Drew, Elizabeth (2000) *The Corruption of American Politics.* The Overlook Press, New York

Duchin, Faye and Lange, Glenn-Marie (1990) *Trading Away Jobs: The Effect of the U.S. Merchandise Trade Deficit on Employment.* M.E. Sharpe, Armonk, N.Y.

Einstein, Albert and Seelig, Carl (1988) *Ideas and Opinions.* Bonanza Books, New York

Fernandez-Armesto, Felipe (1996) *Millennium: A History of Our Last Thousand Years.* Doubleday Canada, Toronto

Figgie, Harry and Swanson, Gerald (1993) *Bankruptcy 1995: The Coming Collapse of America and How to Stop It.* Little Brown, New York

Fischer, David H. (1996) *The Great Wave: Price Revolutions and the Rhythm of History.* Oxford University Press, New York

Fosback, Norman (1983) *Stock Market Logic.* The Institute for Econometric Research, Fort Lauderdale, Florida

Friedman, Kenneth (1990) *Predictive Simplicity: Induction Exhum'd.* Pergamon, Oxford

Garraty, John and Gay, Peter (eds.) (1972) *The Columbia History of the World.* Harper & Row, New York

Gassett, Jose Ortega y (1994) *The Revolt of the Masses.* W.W. Norton, New York

Gleick, James (1998) *Chaos: Making a New Science.* Penguin U.S.A., New York

Gould, Stephen Jay (2002) *The Structure of Evolutionary Theory.* Harvard University Press, Cambridge, Massachusetts

Hamilton, Alexander, Madison, James and Jay, John (eds.) (1961) *The Federalist Papers.* New American Library, New York

Heer, Friedrich (1998) *The Medieval World: Europe 1100-1350.* Welcome Rain, New York

Henry, William III (1995) *In Defense of Elitism.* Anchor, New York

Herrnstein, Richard and Murray, Charles (1999) *The Bell Curve: Intelligence and Class Structure in American Life.* Free Press, New York

Hilts, Philip (1996) *Smoke Screen: The Truth Behind the Tobacco Industry Cover-Up.* Addison Wesley, Boston

Hobbes (1982) *Leviathan.* Viking Press, New York

Holmes, Stephen and Sunstein, Cass (2000) *The Cost of Rights: Why Liberty Depends on Taxes.* W.W. Norton, New York

Homer (1998) *The Odyssey.* Noonday Press, New York

Hourani, Albert (1991) *A History of the Arab Peoples.* MJF Books, New York

Howard, Philip (1996) *The Death of Common Sense.* Warner Books, New York

Jaeger, Werner (1962) *Paideia: The Ideals of Greek Culture.* Oxford University Press, New York

Kairys, David (1993) *With Liberty and Justice for Some: A Critique of the Conservative Supreme Court.* The New Press, New York

Kennedy, Paul (1992) *The Rise and Fall of the Great Powers.* Random House, New York

Kissinger, Henry (1999) *Years of Renewal.* Simon & Schuster, New York

Kuhn, Thomas (1996) *The Structure of Scientific Revolutions.* University of Chicago, Chicago

Kuttner, Robert (1997) *Everything for Sale: The Virtues and Limits of Markets.* Knopf, New York

Lakatos, Imre and Musgrave, Alan (1970) *Inductive Logic.* North Holland, Amsterdam

Lasch, Christopher (1996) *The Revolt of the Elites and the Betrayal of Democracy.* W.W. Norton, New York

Lind, Michael (1998) *Up From Conservativism: Why the Right is Wrong for America.* Free Press, New York

Lipset, Seymour (1960) *Political Man: The Social Basis of Politics.* Doubleday, New York

Marx, Karl and Engels, Friedrich (1998) *The Communist Manifesto.* Verso, New York

Mattera, Philip (1990) *Prosperity Lost.* Addison Wesley, Boston

Meredith, Hugh Owen (1958) *The Economic History of England.* Pitman, London

Millman, Gregory (1999) *The Day Traders: The Untold Story of the Extreme Investors and How They Changed Wall Street Forever.* Times Books, New York

Mitchell, W.C. (1972) *Business Cycles and Their Causes.* University of California Press, Berkeley

Muller, Herbert (1965) *Freedom in the Modern World.* University of Chicago, Chicago

Nathan, Otto and Norden, Heinz (eds.) (1981) *Einstein on Peace.* Avenel, New York

Nichiren (1984) *The Major Writings of Nichiren Daishonin.* NSIC Press, Tokyo

Norske, Ragnar (1962) *Problems of Capital Formation in Underdeveloped Countries.* Oxford University Press, Oxford

Olson, Mancur (1971) *The Logic of Collective Action: Public Goods and the Theory of Groups.* Harvard University Press, Cambridge, Massachusetts

Olson, Mancur (1984) *The Rise and Decline of Nations: Economic Growth, Stagflation, and Social Rigidities.* Yale University Press, New Haven

Ormond, Paul (2001) *Butterfly Economics: A New General Theory of Social and Economic Behavior.* Basic Books, New York

Philips, Kevin (1995) *Arrogant Capital: Washington, Wall Street, and the Frustration of American Politics.* Little Brown (1995)

Pirenne, Henri (1958) *A History of Europe.* Anchor, New York

Plato (1991) *The Republic of Plato.* (Allan Bloom, editor) Basic Books, New York

Plato (1988) *The Laws.* (Thomas L. Pangle, translator) University of Chicago Press, Chicago

Ponting, Clive (1999) *The Twentieth Century.* Henry Holt, New York

Popper, Karl R. (1959) *The Logic of Scientific Discovery.* Hutchison, London

Popper, Karl R. (1966) *The Open Society and Its Enemies.* Princeton University, Princeton

Prigogine, Ilya (1981) *From Being to Becoming: Time and Complexity in the Physical Sciences.* W.H.Freeman, New York

Roberts, J.M. (1995) *The Penguin History of the World.* Penguin U.S.A., New York

Roberts, J.M. (1997) *A History of Europe.* Allen Lane, New York

Santayana, George (1981) *The Life of Reason.* Macmillan, New York

Saul, John Ralston (1992) *Voltaire's Bastards: The Dictatorship of Reason in the World.* Free Press, New York

Schier, Steven (2000) *By Invitation Only: The Rise of Exclusive Politics in the U.S.* University of Pittsburgh Press, Pittsburgh

Senge, Peter M. (1994) *The Fifth Discipline.* Doubleday, New York

Smith, Adam (2000) *The Theory of Moral Sentiments.* Prometheus, Amherst, N.Y.

Smith, Adam (1994) *The Wealth of Nations: An Inquiry into the Nature and Causes.* Modern Library, New York

Smith, Adam (1988) *The Roaring '80s.* Summit Books, New York

Snyder, Jack and Furniss, Edgar (eds.) (1954) *American Foreign Policy.* Rinehart & Co., New York

Soto, Hernando de (1989) *The Other Path.* Harper Collins, New York

Soto, Hernando de (1992) *The Mystery of Capital: Why Capitalism Works in the West and Fails Everywhere Else.* Basic Books, New York

Stone, Charles and Sawhill, Isabel (1986) *Labor Market Implications of the Growing Internationalization of the U.S. Economy.* National Commission for Employment Policy, Washington, D.C.

Spence, Gerry (1990) *With Justice for None: Destroying an American Myth.* Penguin U.S.A., New York

Strauss, William and Howe, Neil (1998) *The Fourth Turning.* Broadway Books, New York

Thucydides (1998) *The Landmark Thucydides.* Touchstone, New York

Thurow, Lester (1980) *The Zero Sum Society: Distribution and the Possibilities for Economic Change.* Basic Books, New York

Thurow, Lester (1983) *Dangerous Currents: The State of the Economy.* Random House, New York

Thurow, Lester (1997) *The Future of Capitalism: How Today's Economic Forces Shape Tomorrow's World.* Penguin U.S.A., New York

Tisza, Laszlo (1966) *Generalized Thermodynamics.* M.I.T. Press, Cambridge, Massachusetts

Tocqueville, Alexis de (1998) *The Old Regime and the French Revolution.* University of Chicago Press, Chicago

Twain, Mark (1990) *A Connecticut Yankee in King Arthur's Court.* New American Library, New York

Wells, H.G. (1920) *Outline of History.* Reprint Services Corp., St. Paul, Minnesota

Wolman, William and Colamosca, Anne (1997) *The Judas Economy: The Triumph of Capital and the Betrayal of Work.* Perseus, Cambridge, Massachusetts

Wright, John W. (ed.) (1999) *The New York Times 2000 Almanac.* Penguin Putnam, New York

Zisk, Betty (1988) *Money, Media and the Grass Roots: State Ballot Issues and the Electoral Process.* SAGE Publications, Thousand Oaks, California

INDEX OF NAMES

INDEX OF TERMS

Index of US Corporations

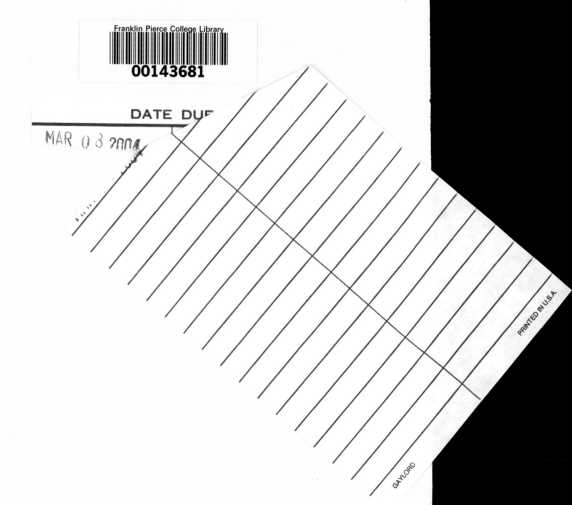

DATE DUE

MAR 0 3 2004

PRINTED IN U.S.A.

GAYLORD

Printed in the United States
1028000002B/1-15

9 780875 862231